(continued from front flap)

asking price? Did you know that some manufacturers deliberately turn out cheap merchandise to provide discounters with hidden markups and phony high list prices?

The results of all these practices reach far beyond the individual consumer. Some discounters boast that within fifteen years they will take over almost all U.S. retailing. Frequent refusal to stock needed but slower-moving merchandise is destroying effective retail service in much of the country. This assault upon the marketplace is forcing many manufacturers to compromise their own standards. In the end, where will the customer be able to find real value? A generation from now, will he even know it exists?

In his thoroughly documented survey, based on years of Congressional hearings and many other sources, Mr. Nelson shakes the reader out of his complacent attitude toward discounting. He shows how the stranglehold huge discount chains are tending to establish over manufacturing and purchasing may threaten new-product development, cut the ground from under independent retailers and manufacturers, and lead to an ever increasing concentration of wealth
The results to the cons
tragic. History has nev
nevolent monopoly.

THE
GREAT DISCOUNT
DELUSION

Books by Walter Henry Nelson

SMALL WONDER
The Amazing Story of the Volkswagen

THE GREAT DISCOUNT DELUSION

THE
GREAT DISCOUNT
DELUSION

Walter Henry Nelson

DAVID McKAY COMPANY, INC.

New York, N.Y.

THE GREAT DISCOUNT DELUSION

COPYRIGHT © 1965 BY WALTER HENRY NELSON

LIBRARY OF CONGRESS CATALOG CARD NUMBER: 65-14963

MANUFACTURED IN THE UNITED STATES OF AMERICA

VAN REES PRESS   •   NEW YORK

Acknowledgments

Material quoted from *The New York Times* is taken from the following issues: (July 21, 1963; October 18, 1963; January 26, 1964; August 5, 1964). Copyright 1963, 1964 by The New York Times Company. Reprinted by permission.

Material quoted from E. B. Weiss's study, "Marketing's Stake in the Low-Margin Retailing Revolution," is reprinted with permission of Doyle Dane Bernbach, Inc. Copyright 1961.

Material quoting *Home Furnishings Daily* is reprinted by permission of HOME FURNISHINGS DAILY (April 3, 1958; October 2, 1959; September 14, 1960; January 11, 1961; March 9, 1961; April 4, 1961; April 17, 1961; February 13, 1962; February 14, 1962; April 18, 1962; April 11, 1963; November 8, 1963; December 4, 1963; December 23, 1963; December 26, 1963; December 31, 1963; January 3, 1964; January 7, 1964; January 15, 1964; February 11, 1964; June 19, 1964). Copyright 1958, 1959, 1960, 1961, 1962, 1963, 1964; Fairchild Publications, Inc.

Material quoted from *The Discount Merchandiser* is reprinted with permission from THE DISCOUNT MERCHANDISER (December, 1961; January, 1963; April, 1963; October, 1963; December, 1963; January, 1964.) Copyright 1961, 1963, 1964.

For Roger, Gregory, and Victoria:

You cannot make a cheap palace

Emerson

Introductory Note

A BOOK about an industry, such as this one, deals in broad terms by its very nature. Consequently, exceptions to such generalizations of course exist. References to discounters in general and to industry practices should not be taken to include all discount houses, but rather as references to practices commonly engaged in by some discounters. It is also obvious that discounters who engage in certain of these practices do not necessarily engage in others.

Discounting, however, is based on price-cutting and, in the mind of this writer, the pernicious effects of this practice are as far-reaching as they are unrecognized by the bargain-hungry public. To my way of thinking, Justice Louis D. Brandeis was right when he warned that price-cutting leads almost inevitably to monopoly and to the ultimate exploitation of the consumer. Thus even the most ethical and most respected discounter erodes the marketplace and, in my opinion, is destructive of the interests of consumers, manufacturers, retailers, and the nation as a whole. How this erosion takes place, how consumers are being hurt daily, and how the practices prove corrosive throughout, is the subject of this book. In reading it, readers may also wish to refer to the Addenda in the back of this book. Keyed to the individual chapters, they provide further data and comment, elucidating the material in the chapters themselves.

I am indebted to a number of persons in writing this book, particularly to the Senators and Representatives who, in exploring the subject of discount houses and retailing in general for several years, provided much of the data available through transcripts of their hearings. Their names and their comments may be found throughout this book. I am also indebted to the many retailers, manufacturers, economists, marketing and merchandising consultants, and others who have testified on this subject and whose names and comments are also prominent in these pages. I am grateful to Earl Lifshey, columnist for and former managing editor of *Home Furnishings Daily*, whose courageous and outspoken columns did much to focus my attention on the subject of discount houses. Mr. Lifshey was generous also in his suggestions concerning the book and in commenting on portions of the manuscript, especially in its early planning stages. My gratitude also goes to Kennett L. Rawson, for his editorial guidance and his keen understanding of the importance of the issues being discussed; to Phyllis E. Grann, for her invaluable editorial assistance, and to Ada Brinton, for help with the preparation of the manuscript itself.

For their criticism, encouragement, and suggestions, I am indebted also to John Dodds, Morton H. Kaplan, Konrad Kellen, David S. G. Lewiston, Mavis McIntosh, Maurice Mermey, Eleanor Rawson, Harold N. Schott, Jr., Mary Ann and James Wright, and to my wife Rita. For their interest and assistance, I am also indebted to Al Seidman, of the United States Federal Trade Commission; to Assistant District Attorney Joseph Stone of New York County, N.Y.; to New York City Markets Commissioner Albert S. Pacetta; to Assistant Attorney General Barnett Levy, who heads the Bureau of Consumer Frauds and Protection, Department of Law, New York State; and to Stephen E. Mindell, also an Assistant Attorney General of Mr. Levy's bureau. It goes without saying that my acknowledgment of my debt to all the aforementioned does not necessarily imply their full agreement with me on all matters here discussed.

Finally, my gratitude goes to my wife for yet another reason, and to my children—Roger, Gregory, and Victoria—as well: for somehow arranging their daily lives to accommodate this book, and for making allowances.

Table of Contents

THE
GREAT DISCOUNT
DELUSION

1

Where There's Smoke...

Those who cut prices on branded merchandise do
not do so from purely altruistic reasons.

—HERBERT KOSHETZ, *The New York Times*, July
21, 1963

GOOD things for less: that's the promise of those who cut
prices. Brand name products sold "below list": that's
the nearly irresistible lure that brings millions of us into
discount houses, "cut-rate stores," and those "mass merchandisers" who seem to specialize in the Big Bargain.

It's a lure that seems to work anywhere. And why shouldn't
it? Today's shopper is more price-conscious than ever, suspicious
of manufacturers' "list prices" and anxious to save money by
buying "at discount." He has been led to believe that discounters can operate on lower margins and markups, and consistently pass on their savings to the consumer. He has been told
that discounters are today accepted and well-regarded members
of the retail trade, and that those who buy at list and not at discount are, all too often, "suckers."

There's no question about it: when the bargain offer is genuine, we save money. Sometimes, however, it isn't our shopping
dollar we've stretched; it's only our imaginations. Sometimes,
the savings can be illusory. And such illusory savings raise questions about the very nature of discounting itself.

1

Let's see how the system worked in one case a few years back.

The scene was Washington, D.C. The retailer in question was Giant Food, Inc., a big chain operating in the Washington area and elsewhere. It sold not only food and food products, and those non-food items that we expect to find in many large chain groceries; in its "Super Giant" stores, it also sold appliances, clothes, drugs, housewares. The "Super Giant" stores were, in effect, combinations of large supermarkets and department stores.

How did Giant Food manage to offer the bargains it advertised? One of its ads put it this way: "Giant's employment of self-service supermarket techniques enables it usually to sell below suggested list prices." The device, in other words, was much the same as that claimed by other "mass merchandisers": especially efficient methods of operation. In the terms we employ in this book, Giant Food was a "discounter," that is, a retailer offering "discounts" below suggested list price. Let's have a look at some of the discounts it offered.

"Proctor Steam & Dry Iron #10010
Reg. Price $15.95. Adv. Price $8.47."

"Regina Twin Brush Waxer #400
Reg. Price $66.00. Adv. Price $35.47."

"Sunbeam Mixmaster $24.88—
Manufacturer List Price $37.95."

Big savings? Big discounts? Were customers who bought these products at Giant Food really saving $7.48 . . . $30.53 . . . $13.07? *Not so.* The Federal Trade Commission found that the ads were false and deceptive, and these conclusions were later upheld by the United States Court of Appeals, District of Columbia Circuit [322 F. 2d 977 (1963)].

Here's what the FTC found: The high price shown in Giant Food's advertisements was not the customary retail price in the area. It was deceptive, in that Washingtonians were falsely led to believe that they would have to pay this high "regular" or "manufacturer's list" price elsewhere if they wanted to buy these products.

At the hearings, a Giant employee admitted his company's stores had never sold the items at the so-called "regular" price; the FTC found that this "regular" price was completely false. As for the "manufacturer's list" and variations thereof, the FTC found that the price shown by Giant was "substantially in excess of" the usual and customary retail price.

Where were the savings? Where were the discounts? Those who bought the waxers, the irons, or the kitchen appliances, and congratulated themselves on savings up to $30.53 had simply been fooled by an old technique that many discounters continue to use: "discounting" against what is merely an artificial and inflated list price.

Where do those list prices come from? In this particular case, an answer can be found in an FTC case against Regina Corporation [322 F. 2d 765 (1963)]. There the FTC concluded that Regina knew or had reason to know that its suggested list prices weren't being adhered to by retailers, but that it nevertheless spread such list prices around and even contributed to the cost of retail advertisements that published these meaningless figures. What's wrong with that? The U.S. Court of Appeals, Third Circuit, in upholding the FTC's findings, put it this way:

"The vice inherent in the representations is the inability of the 'gullible' price-conscious consumer to control his urge to make what he erroneously may believe is a good buy.... It is now settled that deception may be accomplished by innuendo rather than by outright false statements."

A Discount Tour of the Nation

How many "gullible, price-conscious" consumers were taken in by Giant Food's misleading high list prices and false and deceptive ads? How many expected the big savings the ads promised, only to be disappointed? How many congratulated themselves on having been smart shoppers and told their friends and neighbors to buy only "at discount" or "off list"?

All this, it seems to me, raises fundamental questions about just how discount stores operate and just what kind of a deal we may get there. It makes us wonder what safeguards we have as consumers, and how we may exercise them. Finally, it makes us begin to query the very nature of discounting itself.

This book is not about Giant Food or any one particular chain. The story of what happened in Washington, D.C., is told only to illustrate one facet of what seems to be going on in the retail market. What follows shows some other facets of the same story. These facets consist of individual instances from all over the country, and there is no intent to suggest that Giant has ever engaged in other practices that some stores go in for, or, for that matter, continues to engage in the practices found false and deceptive by the FTC.

Item: In testimony before a subcommittee of the U.S. House of Representatives, a trade association director reported that, in Chicago, there exists a centrally operated chain of cut-price men's clothing stores, running its shops under several different names. They advertise both top-quality brands and off-brands. He says they offer what they call $99.50 suits for $63—but upon inquiry the manufacturer of these suits reveals that they are worth exactly $38.95 at wholesale. The $99.50 price is phony, and the $63 price is no discount. The same cut-price operator's advertisements feature top-brand names, leading the more gullible shoppers to believe that the "discount" prices listed underneath refer to these brands. Those who go in to buy find it just isn't so. There's no connection between the brand names and the prices, and the salesmen aren't pinned down in any way.

Item: In New York City, a Youth House officer of the Juvenile Court tried to buy his wife a Hoover vacuum cleaner he had seen advertised in a discount-store window. "They showed me a scuffed-up old Hoover which they said was a floor sample and the only one they had in the store," he recalls. "I told him I'd take it, but the salesman almost turned cartwheels to stop me from buying. Finally he called the manager and the two of them tried their best to get me to buy some other brand in the store. They just would not sell me the Hoover they had advertised, so I finally left in disgust without buying anything."

Item: One of the nation's largest discount department store chains entered a Midwestern city in 1963, with several stores, advertising fantastic bargains in its "Opening Day" ads. Within 60 days, under pressure from the local Better Business Bureau, it was forced to place a "correction ad" in a local newspaper, admitting to a battery of "inaccuracies." Among them:

Bargain sleeping bags, golf sets, golf bags, and movie cameras advertised as being of a famous make or by a famous maker proved to be something else. The sleeping bag turned out to be not full-size as advertised, but junior size, and none of the items were of a famous make. A bicycle offered at less than $20 turned out to be an American-made tubular bike, although the illustration shown in the ad featured an English Lightweight 3-speed bicycle. The bicycle illustrated actually was $32.88. The "Opening Day" ads showed TV sets for $74.88 and listed top-brand names such as Zenith, RCA Victor, Admiral, Philco, Westinghouse, and Sony. Actually, none of the famous brands listed were available for the $74.88 price. The chain stated it regretted the inaccuracies and invited dissatisfied customers to return the merchandise for refund. We do not know how many purchased the items that were "erroneously advertised" or how many came in to get their money back.

Item: On one Sunday in February, 1963, a major Midwest drug discounter opened more than a dozen stores in one city and simultaneously announced plans to open two more each month for the rest of the year. According to *The Discount Merchandiser*, trade journal and bible of the discount-store industry, the chain "burst on the scene by an advertising blast which emphasized... [its] low-low prices." Protests were soon heard. *The Discount Merchandiser* reports: "As a result of the drug ruckus," the chain "agreed to eliminate some of the more objectionable phrases in its ads...."

Item: Barnett Levy, Assistant Attorney General of the State of New York, reports that the Bureau of Consumer Frauds and Protection, which he heads, has received "hundreds of complaints and inquiries" about *just one* of the major discount department store chains in New York State, covering a variety of merchandise categories. Many of these have been settled amicably after the Bureau's intervention, for New York State is a pace-setter in the consumer protection field. Levy's bureau is unique in that it has a staff of 16, including nine attorneys, and a big budget. Founded by Attorney General Louis J. Lefkowitz in 1957, it saved consumers more than a million dollars through mediation and court action in 1964, responding to complaints and inquiries from 11,800 persons. A sizeable number of these complaints concerned merchandise purchased from the state's discount stores. Asked whether the "hundreds" of complaints received about the one major chain constituted an unusual volume, Levy said his Bureau had indeed received more concerning this chain than others of like size. Indeed, the majority of complaints the Bureau received dealt with discounters, cut-price merchants, and others specializing in the Big Bargain.

Item: In summer, 1963, a New York automobile salesman and his wife shopped in a Manhattan discount store and bought a window fan for $24.95. "There was a big-name-brand sign above the shelf or counter," the salesman remembers, "and the tag indicated a $10 discount. I didn't take a close look at it, I admit, but I thought that, after all, I was dealing with reputable people. When I got it home, I saw I'd bought a piece of junk. The only brand-name thing about it was its motor, but even that was an old model which I have to oil by hand. The fan itself carries a brand name I never heard of. It doesn't even reverse automatically." He says the final blow came when a friend of his bought a fully automatic, top-quality fan at a conventional store and paid the same low price. "I figure my fan's worth about $10," the salesman concludes dismally.

Item: A subcommittee of the U.S. Senate heard testimony concerning a Philadelphia discounter. The witness reported that this discounter advertised "Botany 500" suits at cut-rate prices. Once inside the store, the shoppers found these suits just about unobtainable. Salesmen steered them away from the 150 "Botany 500" suits and urged them to buy one of 700 cheaply made suits bearing a completely unknown label. The store had even removed the quality tags from the Botany suits and sewn them into the cheap suits. One group of comparison shoppers were told the cheap suits were actually made by Botany but were a better buy, while another group of shoppers were told a different story: that the unknown-brand suits were better than the Botany suits.

Item: In New York City, there's a discounter who, says Markets Commissioner Pacetta, slips lower-priced Bulova watches into high-priced Bulova boxes. The practice is not, apparently, unusual. A witness testified before a U.S. Senate subcommittee that cut-price operators often remove Hamilton Watch Company's factory-applied price tags and substitute higher ones. There are discounters who throw away a $45 Hamilton price tag, for example, slip in a tag reading $75 or $80, and then "discount" the watch to $50, plus Federal tax.

Item: Senator A. S. Mike Monroney of Oklahoma told a Senate subcommittee that off-brand mattresses in one New York City discount store are tagged at $20 more than they're worth and are sold to families who have been lured in by ads for Beautyrest mattresses at discount prices. The Beautyrest mattresses, however, are not for sale. In the language of the discounter, they're "nailed to the floor."

Item: Another witness told the Senate subcommittee that one Manhattan discounter made a name for himself in the trade by advertising a suite of Drexel furniture at deeply discounted prices —and never selling it. As a matter of fact, that suite of Drexel furniture was the *only* one in his store! He used it to attract the bargain hunters. Once they were in, his salesmen took over.

Item: In upstate New York, another witness charged before the Senate subcommittee, there's a discount store known to the trade for the cheap hats, shoes, coats, and suits it sells at "discount" prices. It gets its trade by luring families with a well-known line of copper-bottom kitchen utensils, offered as bait at cut prices. The store loses money on these, but makes its profits on the junk clothing. Apparently enough shoppers believe that these too are like the pots and pans—real discounts.

Item: According to testimony before a House subcommittee, a Connecticut discounter regularly advertises Florsheim shoes at $8.20 less than local shoe stores charge. Actually, he carries only *one* pair of Florsheims among 200 to 300 pairs of cheaply made foreign shoes on which he earns a handsome profit. This same discounter also claims to sell nationally advertised brands of children's shoes at $4 off. On examination, all of these turn out to be shopworn merchandise—although his ads of course do not mention that fact.

A Pattern of Deceit?

What's going on? Are these isolated instances? Are just a few local, even larcenous, discounters involved? Were just a few cities unlucky? Or are the practices of America's more than 10,000 discount stores pretty much the same everywhere? Are these instances *part of a pattern?* Is there, in short, something about discounting we don't understand?

When I first put these questions to myself, I encountered a few more. How is it, for example, that profits are often reported to be higher in discounting than in any other type of retail operation? How is it that discounting is so foolproof that a chain can "burst on the scene" with more than a dozen stores in one city on one day, when any storeowner can tell you how tough it is to make one shop succeed before you branch out and open another? Is there a "gimmick" to discounting that permits such growth?

The success of discounting has been phenomenal. There's no question about it: discounting is the biggest thing to hit the U.S. retail marketplace in decades. The discounter is no longer the underdog of retailing, the "little guy" trying to give the consumer a break, merely a marginal phenomenon representing a small proportion of the total retail market. Its profits, apparently, are whopping. According to marketing expert E.B. Weiss's study (*Marketing's Stake in the Low-Margin Retailing Revolution*), the percentage return on investment "is from 100% to 1,000%, larger than that of most traditional department stores and most traditional chains"; in more conservative language, an article that appeared in New York University's *Journal of Retailing*, as cited by the April, 1963, issue of *The Discount Merchandiser*, says "The discount firm realizes a return on investment that is above average." "Today," says Interstate Department Stores' Sol W. Cantor in the April 22, 1963, issue of *Barron's*, "we are seeing the formation of chains in the discount industry which tomorrow will be the giants of retailing." Discounting is big business today, and it is bigger than most. It influences us consumers more than we suspect. The discounting revolution has changed the policies of department stores and of small, independent merchants. It has had an effect on American manufacture, on the type and quality of the goods we buy, not just at discount stores, but everywhere. And it has a *direct* effect on our wallets and pocketbooks every time we shop.

None of the material in these pages is new—except to the consumer. A lot of people know the facts about discounting, and those facts have been published, but not where the consumer is likely to encounter them. The discounting trade press is filled with data. The retailing trade press has published the same. Congress has been holding hearings on the subject for some years, but the public has heard hardly a word about these proceedings. The general press has largely ignored the matter. The truth about discounting in America today has been kept a secret as carefully as though the nation's security were involved.

Now that discounting has grown up, it merits a full-scale examination. This book is the first attempt at providing just that.

Why the silence? Why the secrecy? If the nation's security is not really involved, at least its peace of mind is. We have not wanted to disturb that peace of mind. We have not wanted to dissect the discounter, to find out how he operates, to ask what kind of a deal we consumers often get at his hands.

What kind of a deal will that really be? That, of course, is likely to vary from store to store and, in any one store, often from day to day. This book dissects many of the techniques of discounting and, while all exist throughout the U.S.A., all do not exist together, in any one store's "manual of operations." Nor will a store that employs them do so consistently.

It should also be noted at the very outset that many of the techniques described are not exclusively the discounter's. There are conventional stores that engage in them as well. Some of the techniques, however, are part of a pattern the center of which is the Big Bargain. All tend to exploit the bargain hunter's peculiar psychology. And nowhere is that psychology more in evidence than among the customers of discount houses, so many of them true believers in the cathedrals of the cut price.

It is my belief that these facts, however disquieting, must be faced. They must be placed on the public record, though they are often not pretty, and they must be heeded by consumers, though what they say about us is not always flattering.

There are those who say that we get what we ask for. They say that the American consumer's gullibility and naive wish for something-for-nothing is at fault. They say that we, as shoppers, have often begged to be fleeced and have no right to complain. I do not put much stock in this argument. There is no doubt that each day consumers are played for suckers by those whose mercantile morals are venal and predatory. I believe, however, that what has led us to be so often hoodwinked and cheated, what has made us both targets and victims, is not our own greed, but our lack of information. We have not known the facts, nor how to get them. It is my hope, and, indeed, contention, that the American consumer will no longer play the patsy, once he knows these facts. This book aims at presenting them.

2

Borax in Pigeonville

> People who sell goods at prices lower than anyone
> else can meet are now considered benefactors, but
> the day will come when they will be looked upon
> as criminals.
>
> —MATTHEW WOLL, American labor leader [1]

"GENTLEMEN," Stephen Masters boasted before a subcommittee of the United States Senate, "there is a revolution in retailing spreading like wildfire throughout
this country." [2] He was, of course, referring to the rise of the discount store, a rise in which he pioneered. That rise has been
impressive. "Discounting," according to market authority E. B.
Weiss, "is on the march—and it is marching not merely double
time, but *triple* time." [3] [Weiss, who writes a weekly column for
Advertising Age magazine, is vice president and director of the
special merchandising service of Doyle Dane Bernbach, Inc., a
New York City advertising agency, and has written extensively
on marketing and merchandising.]

How has the discounting industry managed to move so fast?
To understand that, let us visit an allegorical American community and watch a discounter in action. We'll call this town
Pigeonville, U.S.A. Pigeonville may have a fictitious name, but it
is no less real than other American cities. The techniques of discounting that we will watch in Pigeonville are in use right now,
from New York to California.

11

In Pigeonville, the news that a discounter was coming to town had folks at a fever pitch and talking for weeks. Those who were considered in the know (like the local newspaper publisher) said that the lives of everybody would be changed for the better. The little fellow was finally going to get a price break! From the moment Harry Borax bought that property outside of town, at the junction of Route 45 and the new U.S. highway, tension kept mounting. Overnight, it seemed, the empty lot out there was transformed into a spanking new white concrete one-story building without windows, sporting a great big neon sign reading *Big B Bargains, The Family Discount Center*. There was a parking lot for 5,000 cars, and Harry Borax clearly expected traffic from the entire area.

Silas Dicker, editor and publisher of the local *Advertiser*,* couldn't have been more pleased with himself, with Borax, or with the Big B. Borax had come into his office one afternoon, carrying a package of advertising mats, and signed a contract for two or three pages of advertisements a week for six months. That was more than any other local merchant could afford, and Dicker decided then and there that Big B Bargains was a substantial member of the business community and would not only get the *Advertiser*'s frequency discount, but plenty of editorial support as well. From that day on until the Grand Opening, Dicker helped whip up the excitement. Editorials in the *Advertiser* hailed the advent of modern mass merchandising. "Some real competition is coming to town," Dicker chortled. "Folks will get a price break, the community will get a shot in the arm, and local store-owners will have to take another look at their prices if they want to stay in business. Maybe markups have been too high for years!"

The local merchants in Pigeonville held their breath and argued that shopping habits would be hard for Borax to break, that customers they'd known for a lifetime would continue to buy locally. None of these merchants was rich, and few were

* In this allegory of Pigeonville, the names of Harry Borax, Silas Dicker, the Advertiser, and of Big B Bargains are, of course, fictitious, just as is the town itself.

sharpies; they took what they regarded as a fair profit, gave as much service as customers demanded, and believed sincerely that this would be enough to assure them the continued patronage of their community.

How wrong they were! They had overlooked a large portion of the local population, those who slavered for bargains and were not of a critical or questioning nature. They'd overlooked the something-for-nothing syndrome of H. L. Mencken's *boobus Americanus*. Harry Borax had not overlooked it.

On Opening Day, the Big B offered in its ads General Electric dishwashers at dollars less than local dealers sold them for. RCA television sets were tagged lower than anywhere else in town. Brand-name radios, blankets, shirts, mattresses, toys, and cameras seemed drastically reduced in price. No one had any idea how Harry Borax managed to offer such savings. No one cared. No one questioned the matter. Opening Day saw the store jammed. The car lot was filled. The discount house did more business that day than all the other area merchants combined did in a week. Next day it was the same. And so it continued. Each week, the discount store's advertisements offered new, fantastic bargains, and each week the local paper grew more ecstatic in the praise it heaped on the Big B.

Within less than a year, Harry Borax had completely changed local shopping habits. Some of the older residents, perhaps out of a perverse loyalty, continued buying from independent Main Street merchants, but young couples with growing families bought almost everything at the discount store. They were, understandably, more interested in savings than in sentiment. They loved the novelty of the bright red tickets with the high list price crossed out in fat black crayon. Sometimes the discounted price was listed right below—dollars cheaper—and sometimes there'd be a code that the salesmen would be happy to explain.

A few months later, after the customers had become used to the new, wonderful world of discounting, the price tags changed: only one price, the Big B discount price, was shown. That was all right, too, because everyone "knew" it was dollars cheaper than the "list."

Big B was always crowded and drew people not only from the immediate area, but from surrounding towns as well. Customers loved its very vastness; it seemed to have something for every need. Most of the inventory consisted of "soft goods"— wearing apparel and the like—but Big B also stocked appliances, furniture, radios and TV sets, drugs, records, jewelry, and books.

For a time, Big B ads featured "white goods" or kitchen appliances. A while later, drugs were heavily promoted, and then, for some weeks, furniture, radios, and TV sets. Whenever Big B concentrated on one area, the stores in the county that sold these goods would feel the pinch. And the pinch proved lasting.

Most of the items featured in Harry Borax's ads were nationally advertised brand-name products, the kind of merchandise all the young couples in the area had learned from their magazines to know, love, and long for. It seemed that now they had a chance to buy these goods and save money at one and the same time. Those who had hesitated to buy before felt it would be positively imprudent to wait any longer; at Borax's prices, who could afford to wait? Those who did not need kitchen appliances, TV sets, or other "big ticket" merchandise hurried to the Big B anyway to buy their slacks, shoes, towels, drugs, blouses, and blankets. It was true that Harry Borax had no reputation to speak of and that the Big B itself was something of an unknown quantity, but the big brand names which were featured in the ads were all respected, and their respectability rubbed off on the Big B. Any store that could offer name-brand appliances at cut-rate prices, it was reasoned, would offer everything else at discounts, too. It was a point the Big B's ads sedulously drummed home.

In time the impact of the Big B could be seen on Main Street. A lot of the stores that had been around for a long while had closed their doors. Some of the older merchants just quit trying and retired. Some of the younger ones went to work for the big chains. A few merchants tried to survive by joining together to form a local chain, but their efforts were for the most part dispirited and lackluster. The area's one and only bookstore shut up shop. Drugstores that used to be open day and night lowered their shutters shortly after the sun had set.

Few people cared a damn. It seemed clear now that the local retailers, the independent Main Street merchants, had been over-charging for years, "getting away with murder" because of a "lack of competition." It seemed clear also that the manufacturers had been playing the public for suckers, overcharging on their products and setting their "list" price at whatever the traffic would bear. So ran the talk in Pigeonville.

The few independent stores that remained in town raised their prices, because they sold far less. Some of them prospered, for it turned out after a while to be amazing how many things the Big B did *not* sell. A lot of people were beginning to grumble that they couldn't find what they wanted at the Big B but, by and large, they bought there anyway, because it seemed just plain smart to buy at discount, and not to pay those big list prices others charged.

Soon Harry Borax looked out over a retail wasteland and knew that the Big B had done its job. It had, he said, "captured the market." It had done more than that: it had demolished it. It owned the bulk of the retail trade in Pigeonville and for many miles around. Harry Borax was satisfied and drew up his report.

He was, of course, no local citizen and would leave town just as soon as he had trained a local manager in the techniques of run-ning a discount operation. Borax represented a corporation that owned similar outlets elsewhere in the country and which, al-though a newcomer to the discount industry, already was grow-ing at a fast rate. He told headquarters that the area seemed ripe for another operation, maybe 30 or 40 miles from Pigeonville. Ground was broken for the new store a year later. This one also flooded local newspapers with advertising and was hailed as a blessing for the little people who wanted a break, pricewise. Once more the Big B chain slashed prices in their ads, sucked in an army of customers, and killed off local competition. In the process, it made a fortune.

Let's see how some discounters do that.

3

The Island of Loss in a Sea of Profit

> When a trade-marked article is advertised to be sold
> at less than the standard price, it is generally done
> to attract persons to the particular store by the offer
> of an obviously extraordinary bargain. It is a bait—
> called by the dealers a "leader." But the cut-price
> article would more appropriately be termed a "mis-
> leader"; because ordinarily the very purpose of the
> cut-price is to create a false impression.
>
> —LOUIS D. BRANDEIS (1856–1941), Associate Justice
> of the United States Supreme Court, *Harper's
> Weekly*, November 15, 1913.

HENRY R. PETERS, who owns and operates a drugstore
at 2917 Georgia Avenue, N.W., in Washington, D.C.,
has been a retail pharmacist for more than 15 years.
When he first started in business, he had two partners, both
doctors of pharmacy; one of them, like Peters, was also con-
nected with Howard University.

Peters, a Negro, is a civic leader, secretary of the District of
Columbia Board of Pharmacy, and much concerned with the
opportunities Howard graduates have to go into business for
themselves in his field. These opportunities have been getting
pretty scarce lately, in large part because of the impact of discount druggists. Peters says the graduates today either go to

16

work for a chain or get a job with an independent pharmacist who has been established for some years. It's hard for them to get capital financing to start their own retail pharmacies, not just because they're Negroes, but because the future looks grim to the lenders. As Peters puts it, "it seems like the retail independent pharmacist is on his way out unless something is done."

Peters' two partners are already out; the three together couldn't make a living. It happens, though, that Peters' wife is a pharmacist too and, together, working 16 hours a day, the couple continued to try and "give it a whirl and stick it out." Somehow, they managed to stay active in civic and professional groups. Peters seems pretty stubborn. "We as a group," he says, "have always wanted our own business, and we are going to want and fight for our own business. . . ."

One day, Henry Peters became sufficiently curious or irritated at the tactics of local drug discounters in Washington to seek one of them out. The man he visited was, he says, "one of the originators of discount operations here in the District." Why did Peters visit him? Quite simply, to find out about his discount operation, to find out how it worked.

"There's nothing to it," the discounter told Peters smugly. "All you have to do is get them in the store, and to get them in you use a few leader items and your problem is solved. *When you get them in, then you go to work on them.*" [1] [Author's italics.]

What is a leader that it can have so magical an effect? It is an item—almost always a famous nationally advertised, brand-name product—which a store is willing to sell at a very low markup or even at a deliberate loss, in order to accomplish two ends: to build traffic and to establish a "discounting image." Loss leaders (the term by which they are usually known) are essential to the discounting industry. Such deeply discounted items bring in customers who hope to get something for virtually nothing, and they help promote the image of the discount house as a place in which customers can *consistently* find discounts in *all* departments.

The "discounting image" that the loss leader creates is the key element in the discount store's profit picture. Once that image has been successfully projected, once a community thinks of the discounter as a retailer who consistently offers cut prices on all merchandise, the battle is won. The only thing that's left to do is to pick up the profits.

Famous brand-name products are used as loss leaders because these products have a reputation for integrity that many discount stores—particularly new ones—do not have. Not only does the manufacturer have a reputation that inspires confidence, but the magazines in which he advertises have a comparably solid reputation. Using these brand names for loss-leader purposes—using them, in short, *as bait*—the discounter attracts customers who otherwise would not buy in his store.

The use of the loss leader to bait customers is, of course, not new to U.S. retailing. Many department stores and conventional retailers use loss leaders also. Supermarkets have used them consistently. As a matter of fact, loss-leader selling probably goes back to the days of the American pack-peddler who preyed on frontier housewives a hundred or more years ago. Carrying a few brands of merchandise of known quality, he unloaded tons of junk on families too far away from stores to be able to say no.

All this, however, seems a mere prelude, a muted amateur rehearsal, to what came when prosperity and a saturated marketplace turned discounting into big business in the period following World War II. Those who entered the discounting industry then recognized that the public had a lot of "disposable income" left over after necessities were bought. Impulse buying became a habit. The stage was set for a loss-leader operation that would make the techniques of yesteryear look as innocent as those of Girl Scouts selling cookies. The discounter recognized that the lure of a bargain was irresistible to men and women with a few extra dollars to spend. He fed their greed and profited by it.

The difference between most discounters and those conventional retailers who may also use the loss leader is this: the latter use it mainly to bring in customers, to jog a flagging market. A great many discounters, on the other hand, use it deliberately to represent their stores as "discount houses" in which *all* merchandise carries similar low, "discount-type" markups. The loss-leader item is advertised not only as bait for traffic, but *primarily* to create a discounting image for the store. Store-owners who use it say, in effect, "Here's a terrific bargain on a big brand name. Come on in—our store is full of such discounts." Once customers do come in, such a discounter "goes to work on them."

Do discounters use this weapon of the loss leader as part of the basic technique of their industry? We have heard from Henry Peters' discounter. John A. McCandless, vice president of the Neisner Bros. variety and discount chain, calls the loss leader *"the foundation of the discount business"* [Author's italics], and Samuel J. Rosenstein, former chairman of Towers Marts International, has said he doesn't think there's a single discount store in the United States that does not use it.² *The Discount Merchandiser* quotes Lawrence Altman, president of the Jubilee Cities discount chain, as saying that he intends to use appliances for this purpose. "As a matter of fact," says Altman, "we plan to own and operate our own traffic appliance departments. [Traffic appliances are those that bring in store "traffic."] It will simply be a loss-leader operation. We are going to take a percentage of the store items that will identify value and use them as giveaways to build an image." ³

Could there be a more frank statement concerning the kind of tactics in use throughout much of this industry? Altman's statement appears in the pages of the discounters' own trade journal, where the public, of course, is not likely to find it, and it is made ingenuously, as though the loss leader were a thoroughly respectable form of merchandising, like decorating windows for Christmas. The fact is that loss-leader selling—while engaged in by many discounters and conventional merchants as well—is regarded as offensive, unfair, and reprehensible by many responsible persons. "If you want monopoly, then loss-leader selling is a way to obtain this," said former Federal Trade Commission Chairman Charles March. "Loss-leader selling is one of the most remorseless enemies of healthy competition." [4] Today's FTC Chairman Paul Rand Dixon also calls it "an unfair practice, an unfair method of competition." [5]

When Altman speaks of loss leaders, it is worth while to look again at the significance of his phrasing. He intends, he says, to use as loss leaders those items *which identify value* and he intends to *give them away to build an image.*

Justice Louis Brandeis called the leader a "mis-leader" and said its very purpose "is to create a false impression."

"The dealer who sells a Dollar Ingersoll watch for 67 cents," Justice Brandeis wrote more than 50 years ago, "necessarily loses money in that particular transaction. He has no desire to sell any article on which he must lose money. He advertises the sale partly to attract customers to his store; but mainly to create in the minds of those customers the false impression that other articles in which he deals and which are not of a standard or known value will be sold upon like favorable terms. The customer is expected to believe that if an Ingersoll watch is sold at thirty-three and one-third per cent less than others charge for it, a ready-to-wear suit or a gold ring will be sold as cheap." [6] *

Is there any reason to suspect that any discounter has had any desire consistently to sell articles on which he loses money? To ask the question is to answer it.

Some discounters claim that the term loss leader cannot be applied to their advertised "bait" merchandise. They like to define loss leaders as products that are sold at below-wholesale

---

* In a day when the nation's liberal conscience was awakening, Brandeis was among those who led the fight against the trusts and the monopolies. Price-cutting, in its infancy in his day, already disturbed this great liberal. Throughout his 23 years as an Associate Justice of the United States Supreme Court (1916–1939), he championed the individual against combinations of wealth and power and fought for minimum wages, shorter working hours for women and children, and conservation. His investigations and thinking influenced the LaFollette and Stanley anti-trust bills and he was consistently against price-cutting, which he saw as a ruthless and unprincipled technique of organized monopoly, meant to lure the consumer to his own destruction.

prices. Their gall is really incredible; they seem to feel that the public is so ignorant of basic business arithmetic that it believes a discounter could make a profit on items sold either at the whole-sale price or only slightly above it. It is obvious that every store has an overhead, and that each item has a sales expense. It costs so much to run the store, pay employees, and meet other ex-penses, such as rent and insurance, and it costs a certain amount of money to sell a product, in terms of display space, salesmen's time, and other factors. Discounters occasionally assert that they can operate successfully on a storewide policy of a 10-to-20-per-cent margin. E. B. Weiss's thorough study, *Marketing's Stake in the Low-Margin Retailing Revolution*, says flatly: "The off-list operator can—*and does*—earn a profit on the markups of from 5% to 20%" and it refers elsewhere to "discount margins of 22–24%." Stephen Masters, one of the pioneers in the discount-store industry, told a subcommittee of the U.S. Senate in 1958 that "A true discount store is one where every product is sold at a discount." He then explained selling at discount to mean this: "[It] does not mean that merchandise is arbitrarily *marked down* from list or fair-traded price, but rather that all merchandise is *marked up* a fixed percentage above its actual cost." [Author's italics.] In other words, Masters seems to be saying that dis-counters don't concentrate on discounting, but on maintaining lower markups, a practice which would offer the products to the consumers at a cut or discount price.

But it is highly unlikely that a store can survive and prosper on a storewide policy of a 10-, 15-, or even a 20-percent margin and that any item sold for that amount or less is an item on which the store makes so small a profit that the item is, in effect, a loss leader. The profits in a discount store come from other sales. One South-ern discount operator told the U.S. Senate that "There are places making 1,000 percent on some merchandise and selling some be-low cost." [7] Manfred Brecker, vice president of S. E. Nichols, a variety chain that recently went into discounting, says: "Hard goods are the traffic-building department. You build an image that way. If you can do that and have soft goods working for you, you can make money." [8] This seems to mean that the discounter can make money by giving away some items, as long as he marks the others up high enough.

How High Is High?

These facts are generally contested by discounters and by their apologists. They continue to talk of low margins and markups *throughout* their stores, based on the "mass merchandising methods" they claim to have discovered. Just recently, however, their claim of low markups across the board was put into question. How this came about is an interesting story in the annals of American retailing. It not only reveals much about discounting, but it raises some serious questions about our own gullibility.

For several years, the United States Senate and the House of Representatives have patiently probed the U.S. marketplace and, in the process, the discount store. Quietly but persistently, their subcommittees have collected a great deal of testimony from discounters and their opponents. A large portion of this testimony is technical and detailed. In much of it, the discounters have been on the defensive. One would, therefore, assume that the discounting industry would marshal all possible arguments to bolster its cause. Its members have spent a great deal of money fighting those who question discounting tactics; Ruder and Finn, Inc., one of the biggest U.S. public relations firms, was even hired to help fight the battle against legislation that many discounters regarded as hostile to their interests. But while discounters have gone to great expense in enlisting enthusiasts, *they have not bothered to present the complete facts about their pricing policies.*

All they would have had to do was to present to the Congress a list of all merchandise sold in a few discount stores, along with the markups on all these items. If even one or two discounters had produced such a list, the industry could have made some sort of a case. It could have proven that storewide policies of low margins exist—and much of the public debate about discounting might have ended.

But trying to pin discounters down to facts and figures, says Senator William Proxmire of Wisconsin, is like "trying to nail a custard pie to the wall." I have found my experience to be the same as the Senator's. I recently studied 2,521 pages of testimony before House and Senate committees, searching for such evidence. Those 2,521 pages represent just about *six years* of testimony and cross-examination—six years during which discounters could have proved their case. *But not once, in all those pages, did they come up with full and complete disclosure of all markups in even a single discount store!*

In all those years, only a few discounters and a few of their apologists offered any figures at all. These few figures did nothing but raise the question of how high markups were elsewhere in the stores. One discounter offered figures on 39 items in his store; another on 72 items, and a third on *four* items. In addition, a Washington official came up with a selective list *of one-time purchases* of 119 items that, in one place or another throughout the country, could be bought cheaper at discount houses; since no one was disputing that savings are possible, especially on loss leaders, his testimony did not seem much to the point, nor was he able to show that the same or similar prices prevailed in these stores on another day. Some more figures were offered by a few other discounters, but none even remotely approached full disclosure. Finally, a Congressman offered two sets of figures he himself had collected while out shopping, one on 10 items and the other on seven.[9]

Senator William Proxmire is one legislator who found this lack of disclosure vexing. On April 29, 1964, he rose in Congress to say, "Until recently I have searched in vain among the voluminous propaganda issued on behalf of the giant discount chains for one solid attempt to deal in hard facts and cold statistics." He then let loose his announcement. "I am pleased," he said, "to tell Senators I have finally found a nugget." That nugget is "The

Marrud Study," and it goes far to demolish the discount industry "image."

Marrud, Inc., is a discount drug chain that operates in almost 200 discount stores throughout the country. It is a lease-department operator. (We shall discuss lease-department operations in detail later on in this book; it is enough now to point out that many discount stores consist chiefly of leased departments, each run by separate owners. Although the stores may appear to be under one management, this is not always the case. The effect of this for the buying public may be that of turning the shopper loose among a number of profit-hungry merchants without his knowledge, rather than just one.)

The "nugget" to which Proxmire referred is a 48-page study of Marrud's operations, published in *The Discount Merchandiser*. The editors of that trade journal called it "the first documentary study ever published on how a discount drug department does business." The purpose of the extensive study, said the magazine, was "to provide an anatomy of the sales and profit structure of the discount drug department so that there would be a body of reference to serve anyone who needed these vital facts."

What did this Marrud Study contain that was so unusual?

The statistical portion of The Marrud Study, which covered 4,261 products, offered detailed gross-margin figures on 3,765 of these. The figures covered a 17-week period early in 1963 and constituted full and frank disclosure for this one chain.

As Nathaniel Schwartz, editor-in-chief of *The Discount Merchandiser*, put it, "It's the first time in history that anyone has accomplished such an anatomical study, item by item, of any sector of the discount business." How did he see its significance? He wrote, "We think that The Marrud Study represents more than just a fascinating document on how a drug department lessee does business in over 200 discount stores," and "it is simple to appreciate that The Marrud Study can be of vital help to discounters themselves in their own business. Those who never had the facts and figures, *now have a model of what is generally happening*. Those who have their own statistics have a yardstick against which to measure their performance." [Author's italics.]

If the study provided figures of what was generally the case throughout the discount-store industry, as this seems to mean, then it assumes a significance far beyond the discount drug field alone. If the study was "a model of what is generally happening," as the editors seemed to feel it was, then it proved conclusively that (a) average markups were *not* maintained at either the 5–20% or the 22–24% levels Weiss suggests as profitable and (b) that merchandise in discount stores was marked up very flexibly indeed, with the top range way, way above anything many of us might expect to find at a so-called "low-margin retailer."

The Marrud Study also showed:

• The average margin at Marrud was actually *higher* than that maintained by independent, conventional drugstores with a small volume of prescriptions business (the type of drugstore most comparable in this respect to most Marrud outlets).

• The average margin at Marrud was only a very small percentage below that maintained by the average of *all* U.S. independent pharmacies and drugstores, many of which maintain extensive and valuable prescription services.

• Less than 10 percent of all Marrud products carried margins in the 22–24% "discount" range or below, suggested by E. B. Weiss and so often by discounters.

The Marrud Study showed that the *average* margin was 33.4 percent. This proved to be almost 2 percent *higher* than that of independent pharmacies that maintain a small prescription business. The reputable *Eli Lilly Digest* (1963), which surveys pharmacy figures, included a group of 84 stores whose prescription income was under 15 percent and whose gross margin was 31.5 percent. It is this group of independent drugstores that seems most comparable to Marrud in this respect, for the Marrud chain at the time had only recently added registered pharmacists and prescription service and did not maintain them in all its outlets. What's even more interesting is that other drugstores, which maintained even more extensive prescription services than the 84 mentioned previously, also operated on a lower average margin than did Marrud, the biggest discount drug operator in the country. For example, the Lilly survey showed that another 137 drugstores, which had 15–20% prescription business, maintained average margins of 32.3 percent (1.1 percent lower than Marrud's average) and that another 188 drugstores, with 20–25% prescription business, maintained a 33.1 percent average margin, again below Marrud's average. This means that a total of 409 pharmacies some of which derived as much as 25 percent of their total income from prescription service maintained lower average margins than outlets run by Marrud, Inc.!

A drugstore that does almost 25 percent of its business in prescriptions would seem, of course, to be much more valuable to the community than one that cannot cater as much to the community's health needs. Because pharmacists are expensive (as Marrud's president notes), one would assume that such drugstores would have shown a higher average margin than Marrud. *The reverse, however, was true.*

Even when we take an average of *all* the pharmacies and drugstores throughout the nation, we see that the average margin was only 3 percent higher than Marrud's 33.4 percent. Marrud, it should be noted, compared favorably only with the very top of the Lilly range. There were 335 drugstores that derived more than 60 or 75 percent of their incomes from prescriptions service and maintained gross average margins of over 40 percent, but these cannot be accurately compared to Marrud outlets. Marrud also compared favorably with markups maintained at one supermarket chain, the figures being provided in The Marrud Study, but these do not seem to this writer as pertinent as the Lilly data. Marrud, after all, is a discount *drug* operation, and its markups should be contrasted with those of drugstores, not of supermarkets, whose main business is food.

So much for *average* margins, which are supposed to cover operating expenses and profit. When we study the margins on individual items at Marrud, then other data come to light. The

3,765 items analyzed in The Marrud Study revealed the following:

• For each item that carried a "low-low" discount-type margin, *more than eight* carried higher margins.

• Less than 10 percent (8.1%) of all items sold by this discounter fell below Marrud's 25–34 % margin range.

• Of 3,765 products from which to choose, shoppers could get E. B. Weiss's "discount margins" of 24 percent or less on only 304.

• Of the 3,765 products, 2,373 carried markups ranging from 53.8 percent and up.

• Almost 1,000 products (923) carried a gross margin of upwards of 45 percent. This means they carried markups of 81.8 percent or more.

The following is the table from which the above figures were taken. Originally published in *The Discount Merchandiser* and later inserted into the *Congressional Record* by Senator Proxmire, the Table is here adapted to show *markup* figures as well as the margin figures provided by The Marrud Study. (Readers are urged to refer to page 167 for an explanation and analysis of the differences between margins and markups.)

TABLE

On 65 items, Marrud's margin was 65% and over (markup: 185.7% and over)
On 164   „   „   „   „   55%–64%   „   122.2%–177.8%
On 694   „   „   „   „   45%–54%   „   81.8%–117.4%
On 1,450„   „   „   „   35%–44%   „   53.8%– 78.6%
On 1,088„   „   „   „   25%–34%   „   33.3%– 51.2%
On 259   „   „   „   „   15%–24%   „   17.6%– 31.6%
On 45   „   „   „   „ below 15% or a markup of below 17 %

The Table shown above continues to have great significance to the shopper. As we've seen, comparable 1963 Lilly figures showed that many independent non-discount drugstores maintained lower average margins than did this drug discounter. Translating the Table's margin figures to markup, we see that only 304 items at Marrud were marked up below 33.3 percent.

What happened to all those "low-low" discount markups? And what ever happened to Stephen Masters' suggestion that all items in a discount store should carry discount-type margins?

It is hardly surprising that *The Discount Merchandiser* seemed startled at Marrud's profits. "The amazing figures tell the story of Marrud's accomplishments," the magazine said. "In 1963, the profits of over $800,000 were actually greater than the total sales achieved in 1956."

In an interview with Marrud President J. E. Margolis and three of his vice presidents, the editors of *The Discount Merchandiser* brought out the following comments, which help us to understand the workings of a large chain such as this one:

"... The average woman customer," said the executives, "comes in with the intention of saving two, three, five or ten dollars, not five or ten cents on a tube of toothpaste. But if these departments are doing their share to bring customers in and the merchandising efforts in the overall store are handled correctly, we will do our share—and more—at the same time giving the operator a much bigger return per square foot than practically any other department in the store. *We help create for the operator the image that his is actually a discount store.* When the customer knows he can buy a tube of well-known toothpaste in a drugstore for 69 cents and in our store for 46 cents, he knows he is actually saving something. *But in soft goods it is most difficult to determine what the value is in terms of the price...*" [Author's italics.]

Elsewhere in the same issue of *The Discount Merchandiser*, the Marrud executives said, "... The drug department especially is being used as a football. In many instances we have to discount 20 to 25 percent across the board on our fastest-moving items and actually sell a number of items at absolute cost. In addition, we supply many items *for loss-leader advertising...*" [Author's italics.] [10]

Creating an "image" of the store as "actually a discount store" —that is said to be the main job of a department that supplies items for loss leaders. At the same time, as we've seen, such a department must be filled with "profit-boosters," as high-margin products are often called. Whether a local discounter surrounds every loss-leader or low-margin item with eight profit-boosters, or with nine or ten, is beside the point. The fact remains that those shoppers who expect to pay only a small markup when buying from one of these "low-margin retailers" are often likely to be disappointed. Those shoppers who come in expecting to find "discount margins of 22–24 percent" across the board are living in a dream world. They just don't know the nature of the price-mix.

4

The Switch, the Nail-Down, and the Spiff

> *Caveat emptor*, the Romans said—let the buyer beware. There's nothing at all new about bamboozlement. Only the words have changed...
>
> —*from a Sears, Roebuck advertisement.*[1]

A L SAMSON * had always taken pride in the meticulous care he gave to his half acre of lawn in Philadelphia, but now that he was over 65, he decided he'd better stop shoving a hand mower about. He kept his eyes open for a good power mower.

One day he saw an advertisement in his newspaper, featuring a Toro power mower at a local discount store, reduced from $139.95 to $99.50. Samson decided he could afford that discount price. He went to the discount store and asked for the Toro.

"Sorry, we're all sold out of the Toro," the salesman told Samson, guiding him to a display of power mowers bearing an off-brand name. "But I can sell you this model for the same price. It's just as good as the Toro."

Not many of us know much about power mowers; they are items we might buy once or, perhaps, twice in a lifetime. To Al Samson, the off-brand looked pretty much the same as a Toro.

* The name "Al Samson" is fictitious in order to protect the privacy of the individual involved.

He paid $99.50 and took it home. Then his troubles began. Right off, he had difficulty starting the motor, and when he finally got that working, he found out the mower just would not cut grass. He inspected it and noticed that the revolving blades were not aligned properly. He took the machine to a nearby mechanic who specialized in servicing and repairing power mowers. Samson told the mechanic of his difficulties, and after looking it over briefly, the mechanic added that the mower blades were also dull and needed sharpening. He was told to come back next day.

When he did, the mechanic told him to throw the mower away and get himself a good one. "There's no use sharpening these blades," he said. "They're soft metal. These are shoddy materials and shoddy workmanship."

Al Samson had been baited-and-switched. The discount store had baited him with its ad for a Toro "discounted" from $139.95 to $99.50, and then had switched him to a cheap import. Of course its profits on the $99.50 off-brand were bigger than any it might have made on the Toro, even at the full $139.95 price. Al Samson had discovered, along with many other Americans, that one can pay extra when one buys at discount. In the case of Samson, that "extra" came to $99.50!

In the old days of retailing, it was a salesman's job *to sell*. A store's advertisements brought you into the shop and face to face with the salesman; it was then up to him to persuade you to buy the product the store advertised. That was in the quaint old days.

Salesmen today often aren't supposed to sell you the advertised merchandise that attracted you to the store. In some discount stores, at any rate, their job is to *un*-sell you. They are well-paid professionals whose job all too often is to disparage the famous brand-name items the store advertised. If they don't, they don't get far in the business. They have been told that the famous national-brand product that the store advertised is "nailed down," "nailed to the floor," or "nailed to the shelf." If they sell it, they may be reprimanded or even fined. If they have a record of selling you what you ask for, they will certainly get fired. If, on the other hand, they successfully argue you out of buying the products featured in the store's ads, they are marked for promotion. They've shown that they are the kind of men the boss looks for. And if they switch you to another product, this kind of discounter rewards them with a "spiff"—a special bonus.

Does this sound topsy-turvy? It may indeed—unless you're one of these discount-store owners. Then it makes good sense. Does baiting-and-switching really go on throughout the U.S.A. today? To ask that question, said one witness before the U.S. Senate, is like asking whether the Pope is Catholic.[2]

Baiting-and-switching has many variations. The particular deception practiced on the gentleman who needed a lawn mower is perhaps the most common, garden-variety swindle: baiting the victim with an advertised-brand name at a discount price, then switching him to a cheaply made off-brand. Sometimes, however, a discounter practices "a bait and a step up," in which he lures a customer with a dirt-cheap brand-name item, then unloads an expensive off-brand model on him, suggesting it's far better. This trick is called "putting the customer on the elevator."[3] The shopper has, of course, been baited and switched in both cases.

Attorney T. A. Rothwell differentiates between the two basic aspects of bait: bait advertising and bait merchandising. We discussed bait advertising in the previous chapter. Its purpose is to lure you into the store. Its aim is to create store traffic and, above all, a "discounting image." Once the shopper gets inside, *bait merchandising* all too often takes over. The aim of this is to switch you.

How does the salesman do this? There is, after all, probably no living soul who is willing to admit that he can be switched. Indeed, those who've heard of the practice believe they know how to shop "with their eyes wide open," determined to resist the salesman's arguments, if he tries any funny business. Yet salesmen continue to switch customers successfully every day; there are stores that would be out of business very quickly if they always had to sell what they advertise for the prices at which they advertise.

The U.S. Federal Trade Commission's *Guides Against Bait Advertising* (reprinted in full in the Appendix to this book) can serve as an extremely valuable shoppers' handbook to deceptions they may encounter in a discount store, although it is meant to guide retailers generally against practices forbidden by the FTC. It lists several ways a salesman can bait and switch you. It even includes ways in which a shopper can be switched *after* he's bought the item he wanted and after he's left the store. Here is a rundown of techniques described by the FTC, shorn of the Commission's formal language:

1. There are salesmen who will often simply refuse to sell the brand-name product advertised—or even to show it or demonstrate it. This is what happened to the New York City Juvenile Court officer who tried to buy his wife a discounted Hoover vacuum cleaner in the incident we reported on page 4.

2. If the customer insists on being shown the item, the salesman may disparage it, either by words or by deeds— or he'll run down its guarantee, credit terms, availability of service, repairs, or parts. "Sure you can have it, mister, if you insist on it," he'll say, "but we've been getting so many complaints about it that I don't like to sell it. Also, it's almost impossible to get parts for this model."

3. A customer may just not be able to find the product in the store. It's either "all sold out" 10 minutes after the store opens its doors (as was the case with Al Samson's Toro power mower) or the store will have just one or two models on hand, neither of which will suit the customer. It's not unusual, for example, for a store to buy a few $5 brand-name shirts at retail, advertise them at a discount price, and use them to switch customers to off-brands worth far less. He doesn't have to worry about selling those name-brands;

he made certain that the few shirts he bought were in odd sizes, which would fit about one man in a thousand. An even more brazen use of this technique was shown on page 8, which reported the case of the Connecticut discounter who regularly advertised Florsheim shoes for sale—although he had only *one pair* in his store.

4. Where a chain has several stores in one market area, a customer coming in for an advertised brand-name bargain may be told it is available, but only at another outlet. Of course, the chain's ads say nothing about this.

5. If a customer resists the switch obstinately and insists on buying the "discounted" brand-name product, the salesman may take his order and, after doing so, announce that delivery will take a few weeks, or even a few months. That usually breaks down the last bit of shopper resistance. "All right," the customer says with resignation. "Show me a brand you can let me have right now."

6. Stubborn customers, who insist on being shown the advertised brand-name product and even having it demonstrated, are often shown a beat-up demonstration model. As the Federal Trade Commission puts it, it will be "defective, unusable, or impractical for the purpose represented in the advertisement." In plain language, it'll be a lemon. It may be an ancient model or it may be a battered one. It may, occasionally, be a tired second-hand one. It will, in any case, be guaranteed to make a shopper gasp. All a salesman has to do is demonstrate this clinker, muttering disparagements of the brand name all the while, and even the toughest customer is unsold.

7. A salesman, says the Federal Trade Commission, may not try and switch you immediately. To create an impression of honesty and legitimacy, he may write up your order *and take your deposit.* Only after he has done that will he start the switch. This deceit is often very effective, for the customer is disarmed and unsuspecting. It even makes the salesman appear conscientiously dedicated to your welfare.

"Gosh!" he'll exclaim suddenly, after he's written up your order. "I could kick myself! I completely forgot to show you the models we got in just today. They're no more expensive than the one you just bought, but they're much better. All kinds of new improvements on them. See if you don't agree. I'll be happy to rewrite your order and credit your deposit to the better model!"

8. There are even ways of switching the customer *after* he's made his purchase. One way, says the FTC, is simply not to make delivery within a reasonable time, or make a refund. Customers who complain are told they were warned delivery might be slow and are then offered immediate delivery of a substitute off-brand model. This ruse usually works—after a family has been waiting a few weeks for a TV set or a major appliance.

9. Another way in which a salesman can switch a customer after he's left the store is to deliver a *defective* model of the brand-name product to his home. Of course the customer will howl, but the store will simply tell him, "Our salesman warned you that this brand isn't all it's cracked up to be." It then offers to exchange the defective model immediately for an off-brand that is "much better." The defective name-brand goes back onto the floor, to be demonstrated to the next sucker and to legitimize more of the store's bait advertisements.

The Federal Trade Commission tags a special warning note to its *Guides Against Bait Advertising*. It's an important note, one we would do well to keep in mind when we think that everything's on the up-and-up where we shop. The Commission says:

"*Sales of advertised merchandise do not preclude the existence of a bait and switch scheme. It has been determined that, on occasion, this is a mere incidental byproduct of the fundamental plan and is intended to provide an aura of legitimacy to the overall operation.*"[4] [Author's italics.]

A Runaround on Wheels

Arnold, Schwinn & Company are the manufacturers of the well-known Schwinn bicycles. Like many another manufacturer of products primarily meant for youngsters, Arnold, Schwinn has found that its bikes make ideal "bait" for cut-price and cut-throat merchants. The company recently provided the Congress with five examples of how bait-and-switch artists use Schwinn bikes to lure in trade, then disparage the bikes and sell off-brands.

1. In Florida, a customer who asked for a Schwinn was told: "Yeah, but it will cost you $80 or $90.... Why, they are so high-priced—we had lots of them, and you know we took a lickin' to get rid of them during Christmas—I did not want to stock them. The only thing is with Schwinn that they use English parts and put it on their bikes, that's all...." [Ray Burch, the company's marketing manager, told Congress that "the Schwinn model the customer was interested in had the suggested price of $58.95—not $80 or $90 ..."]

2. In Detroit, a customer who asked for one of the advertised Schwinns was told:

"I'm glad you asked for a Schwinn—come here and I will show you one. Look at this front fork, it's just welded on. Look at the cheesy chain guard. This sells for $47.95. What you are paying for is only the name. Let me show you a good bike for that price." [Says Burch: "The Schwinn bicycle was the only make on the market at that time equipped with a solid forged steel fork and a chain guard strong enough to support the weight of an adult standing on it (for demonstration purposes)."]

3. In Chicago, a customer who tried to buy an advertised Schwinn reported that the salesman tried to switch him to another brand, and "when I insisted on the Schwinn he even went so far as to tell me that if it was his decision to make he would pass up the sale entirely because he was absolutely sure the boy he was buying the Schwinn for would have nothing but grief with the Schwinn."

4. In Stamford, Connecticut, another bait-and-switch operator told the customer:

"It was impossible to service the Schwinn bicycles because
the gear shift was made in Austria and you could not get replacement parts for them. He said Schwinn bicycles were outra-
geously expensive. He said he would order one if my husband
insisted but said I was foolish." [Says Burch: "The fact is that
Schwinn is the one bicycle on which replacement parts are
always available . . ."]

5. In Philadelphia, a customer who tried to buy a Schwinn
reported this experience:

"When I entered this place I asked for a Schwinn bicycle and
the sales person showed me the one and only one he had on
display. He at once told me that he was sure I did not want the
Schwinn for $59.95." He tried to switch the customer to another
bike at $39.95, saying it was a better buy, and that some of the
foreign imports were even a better buy than the Schwinn.[5]

We are not concerned here with whether Schwinn's bikes are
good, better, or best—or whether they are a good value at the
manufacturer's list price. The point is that they are recognized,
famous brand-name bicycles. They are known to the public and,
judging from their sales, are trusted by the public. Indeed, the
best evidence of this is that the bait-and-switch operators use
Schwinn, and not off-brands, for bait. The parent who comes in
to buy a Schwinn shows, after all, that he has a certain faith in
its quality and value. Unfortunately, he or she all too often knows
very little about the features of a product such as a bicycle and
can, therefore, be switched easily by what appears to be a sincere
and well-meaning salesman.

Case histories in the files of New York's Bureau of Consumer
Frauds and Protection illustrate further problems consumers
face. One, for example, tells the story of a Long Island shutter-
bug who attempted to buy a PC X-100 strobe for $8.88, this
being the price advertised for this piece of equipment by a
major New York discounter. "I placed a $3 deposit on the order,"
he wrote the Bureau. "Before the order was taken, I was shown

another unit bearing the designation PC X-200 as well as the PC X-100 and was told to buy this one, as it was 'much better' at $19.95. Since the only visible difference was the number, I [asked for] the lower priced unit. I [then] was told that they had sold out, except for the sample unit, but that additional units would be available 'in about a week or 10 days—we will notify you.' I asked for the sample unit. My request was refused, because 'we need it to show other customers.' " This Long Island man never did get the unit which the chain had advertised at $8.88.

In late 1964, the Bureau received another complaint, this time from a Brooklyn, N.Y., customer, enclosing an advertisement placed by another big discounter in New York City. This ad offered a brand-name movie camera with grip at $29.99 and another brand-name 8mm movie camera for $129.99, "way below original wholesale cost." Upon asking for the lower-priced unit, the customer wrote the Bureau, "I was told by a salesman that the price in the newspaper was an error and that the store had none of the cameras. However, another camera salesman told me that I could have one at $129.99 in a sealed box and that there were just none of these on the floor. I requested to speak to the store manager." The customer then was told again that the newspaper in which the advertisement had appeared had made "a mistake." He was even shown a telegram, from the newspaper's advertising department to the store management, saying that the prices in the ads had erroneously been switched. The first unit should not have been priced at $29.99, but rather at $129.99, and the second unit should have carried the lower, not the higher, price.

Was this an innocent mistake on the part of the discounter and of the newspaper? It may well have been; composing rooms do, of course, make typographical errors. Yet such mistakes have been increasing in recent years, according to New York Assistant Attorney General Levy, and they seem to follow the same pattern. An advertisement featuring a big bargain appears in a major daily newspaper, but the bargain price proves to have been

an error, presumably made by those lax compositors. A telegram
is dispatched to store management, admitting to and apologizing
for the error. (It of course also helps substantiate the uninten-
tional nature of the error.) The telegram in the above-cited case,
which I examined, was sent out at noon on the day on which the
advertisement appeared, many hours after this morning newspaper hit the streets. As Barnett Levy notes, hundreds of thousands of people may have seen that early edition and many of
them may have responded to the ad. The discount store has
drawn a sizable morning crowd, thanks to this mistake. "Such
composing room errors have increased so much in recent years,"
says Mr. Levy, "that in 1964 I met with representatives of several
newspapers to advise them of the Bureau's growing concern."

Presently under investigation by the Bureau is the case of a
customer who responded to a February 1964 advertisement,
which featured a toy train set at $6.88. This was such an unusual
"discount" that the man hurried to buy it. As he tells the story,
the discount-store salesman informed him that the advertisement
was a mistake and that the $6.88 "special" was not a train *set*,
but a toy train engine. "I then asked to see the engine," he says,
"but was informed that they were 'all sold out.' " What ensued
after this disgusted customer wrote to the Bureau demonstrates
how long it may take a customer to get satisfaction, even with
an organization like Barnett Levy's to assist him.

On March 31, 1964, the Bureau informed the discount-store
management of the customer's allegations and asked for a reply.
Three months later it still had not received an answer. On June 30,
it wrote once more, noting that no reply had ever been received
to its first letter. Two weeks passed before the store answered;
its attorney wrote to apologize, saying that the first letter from
the Bureau had apparently "got lost" and asking for full details.
The Bureau provided these and, in August, the store's attorney
wrote once more, now asking for further additional details so
that he could complete his investigation. He also assured the Attorney General's office that his store never advertised items for
sale unless it had "a quantity sufficient, according to our experi-

ence, to meet the expected demand." In late August, the Bureau supplied the additional data. More silence followed. On December 18, 1964, Assistant Attorney General Agnes T. Leen again wrote the store, asking for a reply. By this time, ten and a half months had gone by. As of this writing, the discounter has still not replied to the requests for information, nor explained the strange matter of the missing train set and engine.[6]

We may never know for certain whether these were honest errors; all we know is that the errors accrued to the benefit of the stores involved in them. The errors brought in customers. Those customers who wrote to the Bureau of course had not allowed themselves to be switched, if that was indeed the purpose of the original ads. Yet many consumers inadvertently permit this switching. In the case of the Schwinn bicycles, the bait-and-switch nature of the offer was clear and the danger to the public acute.

Of course a customer who lets himself be baited-and-switched is somewhat at fault for permitting himself to be argued into an off-brand. He should see, but often does not, the clue that tells him a fraud is being worked. This clue is the fact that, while the salesman disparages the product in the store, he praises it in his bait ads and will, for that matter, continue to advertise it as bait even after the individual customer has been switched.

One thing is clear from the evidence about bait-and-switch practices: the discounter who follows such practices has only a parasitic interest in brand names. He uses them, with no thought whatever for the merchandise itself, for the well-being of the companies that sell them, or for the prosperity of the workers who manufacture them. He has, of course, even less interest in the retailers whose stock in trade—famous brand-name products—he renders valueless. Certainly he has no interest in the consumer, whom he patently regards only as fair game for exploitation.

Few legal remedies exist for the consumer. Indeed, as we shall see, much of the official climate in government is predisposed toward the discounter. The Federal Trade Commission Act makes it impossible for private parties to seek relief. Senator A. S.

Mike Monroney reports that "The Federal Trade Commission testifies it is four years before they could get any action and have testified they could give no real hope under the present law—unless we [i.e., Congress] presume to let them stop it without due process. They have no hope of stopping this kind of bait advertising and bait merchandising and refusal to sell the advertised product." [7]

In the absence of legal protection and relief, it is up to each one of us to protect himself. How we can do so will be discussed in the last chapter of this book. Some guidelines, however, are implicit in this chapter. *Caveat emptor*—let the buyer beware—has again become the watchword of the intelligent and informed American shopper. Perhaps we should not be too surprised. We live, after all, in a time when, all too often, sharpies are touted as industry statesmen, labor-union racketeers are promoted to defenders of the working man, and fast-buck operators hide effectively behind the respectability of a Brooks Brothers suit and tread, not on ice, but on Bigelow carpets.

In our age of bigness, we respect wealth and frequently do not care very much how it is achieved. Too many of us half-envy those "who get away with it." Too often we ask not what is unethical, but only what is illegal. And we ignore as unimportant those laws that are poorly enforced. It is not surprising that we are being played for suckers in the marketplace.

5

Price Tags and Turkeys

> "When *I* use a word," Humpty Dumpty said ... "it
> means just what I choose it to mean,—neither more
> nor less."
>
> —LEWIS CARROLL, *Through the Looking-Glass*

FOR some years, my family and I have been spending our summers, or parts of them, near a small village in upstate New York. Nearby lies a large town, whose 30,000 inhabitants enjoy a median family income of almost $6,000. It is a reasonably prosperous city and, as might be expected, the shopping hub of the entire area. The average citizen spends slightly more on clothing and accessories than the average urban New Yorker and about $90 a year more on general merchandise; in 1958, when the State last surveyed these facts, the town supported 60 apparel and 17 general merchandise shops.

The city's prosperity and the fact that it attracts trade from many miles around served, of course, as a lure to the discounters. So, in addition to some fine old houses dating back to Revolutionary days, the city now sports a brand new discount house. It's an ugly, warehouse-type building surrounded by an enormous parking lot, situated just outside of town. You can't miss it; its name, in big letters, is visible from far away.

This outlet is part of a big discount chain. My wife and I

42

shopped there one Saturday afternoon during the summer of 1964, to see what its policy of "extra discounts" might mean and to find out what merchandise was being offered. What we learned from this visit helped clarify the word game some discounters practice.

We expected to find "comparative price tickets" on the store's merchandise; as it turned out, they didn't exist. That is to say, none of the merchandise that we saw in the store (and I believe we inspected most of it) showed *two* prices: a "high" price, supposed to be the "list," followed by the store's own supposedly discounted charge. Here, we saw only the store's own price. There's no question about it: on most goods, that price was low.

This discount store, in other words, labels its products just like any other store anywhere. How, then, does the shopper know he's getting "discounts"? The answer is simple; as Lewis Carroll put it, "What I tell you three times is true." They told us about the discounts almost continuously. Throughout our lengthy visit, a reassuring female voice, emanating from hidden loudspeakers, spoke on and on of a storewide policy of extra discounts (whatever that meant), of at least 20 percent off on every item, and of quality brand-name products displayed in all departments.

The fact was that well-known brands were conspicuous by their absence; aside from some Fruit of the Loom shirts, I spotted hardly any names that I could identify. Most of the merchandise seemed to be manufactured for the discount chain itself—"private brands," in other words—and much of it was of otherwise mysterious origin. As for the 20 percent off on everything, that was hard to check, because comparative prices were absent; I did, however, spot a brand-name baby powder that had a manufacturer's price stamped on it and which the store had discounted, but the discount was about five percent, not 20. As for "extra discounts," I tried to imagine what that might mean. Discounters often talk of maintaining 20-percent margins, favorably contrasting these with the average retailer's; "extra" discounts seemed to imply that the chain went the 20-percenters one better and offered all their goods for sale at cost. Still, since the store seemed prosperous, such a practice appeared unlikely.

There was hardly a thing in the store that seemed to be a genuine discount item, except perhaps the can of baby powder, some other drug department "sundries," and some books. A typewriter for sale near the check-out counter was priced at nearly $50 and certainly wasn't worth a dollar more; the salesgirl I asked said she wasn't sure whether this was discounted (despite the voice on the loudspeaker saying everything was an "extra" discount). As for the books, most of these looked shopworn. There were, perhaps, a half dozen recent publications offered at discount on the day my wife and I visited there, but there didn't seem to be more than one or two copies of each title, and the inconvenient location of the department did not attract much trade. On the whole, the discount chain's outlet here appeared to specialize in "soft goods" that shoppers find hard to evaluate and which so often carry very big hidden markups in discount stores.

This store was really little more than a low-end merchandiser, as the trade calls stores selling cheap products at cheap prices. There were shoes selling for around $3, but these looked as though they'd fall apart at a touch. There was nothing that a bargain hunter like my wife could identify as a genuine bargain; in fact, despite the loudspeaker's syrupy assurances that everything was discounted, much merchandise was sold at "list." (My wife, for example, found some wrinkled, shopworn Butterick patterns, sold for exactly the price printed on the package.)

Finally, insisting that we buy *something* while there, we picked up a package of typewriter paper, so that I could write some more of this book. While it seemed a nicely ironic touch, the joke later on proved to be on me, for after I opened the plastic in which the paper was entombed, this "standard office paper" turned out to be a quarter of an inch short at both the top and the sides. It struck me at the time that this might be one of those economies that mass merchandisers claim to have developed to save consumers money. Some months later, I was reminded of this when

New York Markets Commissioner Pacetta told me about a Brooklyn discount store that had advertised 1,000-sheet rolls of toilet paper at drastically cut prices; when his diligent inspectors actually counted the sheets, they came up with far fewer than 1,000 on each roll. Both purchases proved to be mere paper discounts in all senses of that term.

Keep in mind, however, that most persons who shop at this upstate New York discount outlet which we visited go there in expectation of genuine discounts; while they are in the store, this lie is constantly drummed into their ears and, presumably, their minds. The store deliberately misrepresents itself, and the customers are deliberately deceived.

If this store cannot genuinely be called a discounter, despite its name, then what is a discount store? Obviously, a store that consistently offers real discounts. It is in differentiating a real discount from a phony one that we need guidance.

"To be a genuine bargain," says Paul Rand Dixon, chairman of the U.S. Federal Trade Commission, "the offering price must be a reduction from the price being charged by the advertiser's *principal competitors*, those who sell in competition with him *in his own trade area*." [1] [Author's italics.]

The FTC stresses that an item that has been discounted from $2 to $1 is *not* a discount at all if the same item is not selling for $2 in the discounter's own trade area. It isn't enough if some store miles away sells it for $2; the discounter's own "principal competitors" must be selling it for the higher price before the $1 price becomes a true $1 discount.

"I thought I was dealing with reputable people," said the Manhattan automobile salesman when he swallowed the price line on the tag attached to a fan at a discount house. [See page 6.] As many of us do, he believed what was in front of him, in black-and-white, in print. Even shoppers who may have doubts as to quality have few doubts, if any, about the truthfulness of a store's price tags. We generally accept the tag at face value and, if it carries a comparative and higher list price, we assume blithely that this is what we'd pay for the article else-where. We believe what the tag says: that the higher price is the one charged by the independent retailer around the corner, or the department store down the street. We believe also that the higher price is the one that the manufacturer set for his product. If the discounter does not show a high "list" price, then we assume nevertheless that the store's own price represents a discount. Didn't the girl say so over the loudspeaker, doesn't the store's name include the word "discount," and don't all the store's ads speak of discounts as well?

When a discount store abandons comparative price labeling, when it starts listing only one price (its own) and no longer refers to a list, recommended, nationally advertised or compara-tive value price from which it is allegedly discounting, then it has reached a certain phase in its development. It has so firmly established its "discounting image" in the community that it need no longer *show* comparative prices; it is enough for it to *suggest* that these exist, by its name, via advertising, or through other similar devices. It thereby also avoids running afoul of the law, for as we noted, the FTC has strict criteria regarding the adver-tising of comparative prices.

Too much of discounting, however, is a word game and the words mean whatever the discounter wishes them to mean. A recent Sears, Roebuck & Co. advertisement, which appeared in various national magazines, sheds light on this. Sears called the word game a lot of "hanky panky" meant to "create value by playing with words." Here is what Sears says:

"1. *List price.* This is the 'value' the manufacturer or retailer puts upon the product. It's easy to abuse. Too often, they put a high list price on the product so it can be marked down to *look* like a bargain.

"2. *Nationally advertised price.* This is the price the manufacturer puts in his advertising. Sometimes it's fairly arrived at, sometimes it's inflated. How can you tell? You can't.

"3. *Discount price*. It's supposed to be a bargain. Is it? Remember how easy it is to set a phony list price and then cross it out.

"4. *Comparable value*. Hardest of all to pin down. Are the terms being 'compared' identical? Very seldom. Usually the comparison, even if it's honest, is loose guesswork.

"5. *Recommended price*. Set by the manufacturer, another name for list price. Too easy to make it high so the store can mark it down.

"6. *Manufacturer's suggested price*. Words again. Same as *list price* and *recommended price*. May be legitimate, but subject to the same kind of hanky-panky." [2]

The Sears list is a good guide and one that shoppers might do well to place in their wallets or purses. For many consumers, the appearance of that Sears ad may have been the first hint that a discount often is no discount at all. The fact that a manufacturer will even supply discounters with inflated list prices, so that the store can then "discount" them, is of course disgusting; perhaps, however, it should come as no surprise, for the manufacturers who do this are often the complete captives of the discounters, dependent upon them for orders, and willing to prostitute themselves for the sake of such orders.

Giving the Customer the Bird

On November 21, 1963, E. J. Korvette, Inc., opened a large outlet at 1998 Bruckner Boulevard, The Bronx, N.Y. Like many discount centers throughout the country, this Bronx operation included a food supermarket. Its opening created quite a stir, and thousands were drawn to buy its Opening Day bargains. This was not surprising since Korvette is generally regarded as one of the largest and most famous chains in this field.

Among those visiting that day were two inspectors from the New York City Department of Markets, Ognibene and Gerstner by name. They came to have a look around and maybe to buy a few things. Their tour led them to the meat department, where they decided to examine the price labels. Turkeys were on sale at 35 cents a pound. Ognibene and Gerstner did some fast multiplying, bought five turkeys, paid for them—and summoned the manager.

On the first turkey, E. J. Korvette, Inc., had overcharged them $2.04; on the second and third, $2.05; on the fourth, $2.09, and on the fifth, $2.10. Ognibene and Gerstner issued a civil violation to the meat-department manager, who on December 10, 1963, was fined $100 ($20 for each of the five turkeys), after pleading that the overcharges resulted from the inexperienced help the store was forced to hire for the Opening Day crowds.

Commissioner of Markets Albert S. Pacetta decided to keep an eye on E. J. Korvette, both at Bruckner Boulevard and at its fashionable Fifth Avenue location in Manhattan. Here's what happened:

On January 6, 1964, his inspectors visited Korvette's on Bruckner Boulevard and discovered misleading advertising on cheese. Korvette coughed up $50 for this penal violation on February 19, 1964.

On April 28, 1964, they visited the same outlet again and this time discovered that the store was handing out short weight on candy. On May 12, 1964, Korvette was fined $10 for this civil violation.

On April 27, 1964, the inspectors visited Korvette's big Fifth Avenue "department store" and bought some bubble-bath preparation bearing Korvette's own brand name, *Kor-Val*. *Kor-Val* seems like a contraction meant to convey the idea *Korvette value*. Precisely what kind of value this private label represented in this one case we shall now see. On 24 packages of Kor-Val bubble bath, the inspectors found a total of twelve and three-sixteenth ounces short weight! That is less than an ounce per package but, taken together, comes to three-quarters of a pound! Short weight is a civil violation and, once again, E. J. Korvette, Inc., paid a $10 penalty, levied on May 12, 1964.

On August 22, 1964, its Bronx outlet had a run-in with an

alert shopper, a Bronx housewife, and a few days later, with two Markets Department inspectors.

The housewife in question tells the following story. She and her husband, a taxi driver, had visited the Korvette store on Bruckner Boulevard on August 22 and had selected an 11-pound, 15-ounce turkey from the meat department case. As she reports it, this turkey was marked at 39 cents a pound, and the total price was listed at $5.84. Most shoppers would have left it at that, but this lady decided to multiply. The figure she came up with was $4.59—$1.25 less than that printed on the discounter's price tag.

"I brought the matter to the attention of a clerk in the meat department," she says, "who said she would check and let me know. She returned with the turkey and stated it was incorrectly marked at 39 cents a pound and should be 49 cents. However, I pointed out to her that there were many other turkeys of approximately the same size and identical brand name (House of Raeford) which were also priced at 39 cents a pound. She then referred me to a man in charge of the meat department and when I repeated the aforementioned facts to him, he also advised me it was an error. I told him I did not believe it was an error, since there were many other birds of like size and brand name which were also priced at 39 cents per pound. He then came out to the turkey bins and proceeded to remove all of the birds marked 39 cents a pound."

"I told him that, since the merchandise was marked 39 cents a pound, that he was obligated to sell it to me at that price and that I did not intend to pay any more. As there were quite a few customers listening to this conversation, he said, 'Lady, if that is the turkey you want, you can have it for 39 cents a pound and I will have the price put on for you.'

"I waited around for a while, but no one brought out the turkey. I rang the service bell again and the bird which I had previously selected was handed to me with a correction, indicating the price had been altered to 49 cents a pound and the cost was $5.84!

"I became quite upset at this point and asked to speak to the manager of the store. Finally, after waiting around for some time, a man appeared at the window stating his name was Sid Brown. He gave me the same line about an error in pricing. I repeated the entire story to him which I had related to the other employees, and also informed him that I had been promised the bird at 39 cents a pound. However, he kept on insisting that the price was 49 cents. Needless to say, I did not purchase the turkey and left the store in sheer disgust."

All of the above allegations were included in a letter that the lady in question states she wrote to Korvette management at its corporate headquarters address. They are quoted from this letter and are supported by her husband, who says he was present throughout; both provided the author with sworn statements in this matter. The lady ended her letter to E. J. Korvette with the statement that she was mailing a carbon copy of her letter to the Department of Weights and Measures "so that they might investigate the matter." [She says that her letter to Korvette management was never answered.]

The carbon copy of her letter reached the desk of Commissioner Pacetta. His inspectors arrived at the Bruckner Boulevard outlet on August 28, six days after the lady had been there and four days after she had written, warning Korvette management that she was alerting the authorities.

"To our amazement," Pacetta says, "when our men bought seven turkeys there, they were overcharged from 93 cents to $2.48 on each of the birds." Commissioner Pacetta issued seven summonses, one for each bird, to both the discount store and to its meat-department manager. Such summonses are returnable both at the Department of Markets and in Criminal Court.

On October 28, 1964, E. J. Korvette, Inc., of 1998 Bruckner Boulevard, The Bronx, pleaded guilty to seven counts of overcharging, before the Bronx Criminal Court. The charges against the meat-department manager were dismissed. Criminal Courts Judge Ambrose J. Haddock levied a fine of $25 per turkey, for a total of $175, an amount hardly meaningful to a corporation of this size. The results of this criminal proceeding were reported to the New York City press by the Department of Markets, but none of the city's newspapers found space enough to report the findings to the public.

A week after Korvette's Bronx outlet was served with these seven summonses, the same two Market Department inspectors who'd bought the seven turkeys returned to the discount store, to see if there were any further violations. This time, they were given short weight and overcharged on flounder. They reported also that there was a fast scale that didn't register at zero. On September 29, 1964, the concessionaire who ran the fish department was fined $15 for giving short weight on filet of flounder and another $10 for the fast scale.[3]

The Deteriorating Safeguards

Why are so many of us taken in when it comes to a discounter's price tag? A United States court of appeals referred to this puzzle in giving an opinion on the deceptive representations made by Giant Food in its advertisements (reported on p. 2). The court suggested that the public's gullibility stems from a fast-buck mentality, a wish for something-for-nothing.

"The vice inherent in the representations," the court said, "is the inability of the 'gullible' price-conscious consumer to control his urge to make what he erroneously may believe is a good buy."[4] This suggests that the sight of a crossed-out high figure, or the word "discount," is enough to sweep away all the good common sense we use in other areas of our lives. It suggests that we simply cannot resist a bargain and that many discounters, knowing this, make use of it.

Of course the lady in The Bronx was right when she said that "many shoppers do not take the time to calculate their purchases." The reason they don't stems from the whole history of the U.S. retail marketplace.

The story of buying and selling in America was described very tellingly by Justice Louis Brandeis in his 1913 article, "Cut-

Throat Prices: The Competition That Kills," which *Harper's Weekly* published. Brandeis discussed the growth of consumer safeguards. And it is precisely in this growth of safeguards that we will find the roots of our own current "naiveté."

"Primitive barter," Brandeis wrote, "was a contest of wits, instead of an exchange of ascertained values. It was, indeed, an equation of two unknown quantities. Trading took its first great advance when money was adopted as the medium of exchange. That removed one-half of the uncertainty incident to a trade; but only one-half. The transaction of buying and selling remained still a contest of wits. The seller still gave as little in value and got as much in money as he could. And the law looked on at the contest, declaring solemnly and ominously, 'Let the buyer beware.'

"Within ample limits the seller might lie with impunity; and, almost without limits, he might legally deceive by silence. The law gave no redress because it deemed reliance upon sellers' talk unreasonable; and not to discover for oneself the defects in an article was ordinarily proof of negligence.

"A good bargain meant a transaction in which one person got the better of another. Trading in 'the good old days' imposed upon the seller no obligation either to tell the truth, or to give value, or to treat all customers alike. But in the last generation trade morals have made great strides. New methods essential to doing business on a large scale were introduced. They are time-saving and labor-saving; and have proved also conscience-saving devices.

"The greatest progress in this respect has been made in the retail trade; and the first important step was the introduction of the one-price store. That eliminated the constant haggling about prices, and the unjust discrimination among customers. But it did far more. It tended to secure fair prices: for it compelled the dealer to make, deliberately, prices by which he was prepared to stand or fall. It involved a publicity of prices which invited comparison in detail with those of competitors; and it subjected all his prices to the criticism of all his customers.

"But while the one-price store marked a great advance, it did not bring the full assurance that the seller was giving value. The day's price of the article offered was fixed and every customer was treated alike; but there was still no adequate guarantee of value; both because there was ordinarily no recognized standard of quality for the particular article, and because there was no standard price even for the article of standard quality.

"Under such conditions the purchaser had still to rely for protection on his own acumen, or on the character and judgment of the retailer; and the individual producer had little encouragement to establish or to maintain a reputation. The unscrupulous or unskilful dealer might be led to abandon his goods for cheaper and inferior substitutes. This ever present danger led to an ever widening use of trademarks. Thereby the producer secured the reward for well-doing and the consumer the desired guarantee of quality. Later the sale of trademarked goods at retail in original packages supplied a further assurance of quality, and also the assurance that the proper quantity was delivered. The enactment of the Federal Pure Food Law and similar state legislation strengthened these guarantees.

"But the standard of value in retail trade was not fully secured until a method was derived by which a uniform retail selling price was established for trademarked articles sold in the original package. In that way, widely extended use of a trade-marked article fostered by national advertising could create both a reputation for the article, and a common knowledge of its established selling price or value. With the introduction of that device the evolution of the modern purchase became complete. The ordinary retail sale —the transaction which had once been an equation of two unknown quantities—became an equation of two known quantities. Uncertainty in trade is eliminated by 'A Dollar and the Ingersoll Watch,' or 'Five cents and the Uneeda Biscuits.' "

Here we have all the great advances in consumer safeguards of which America may be proud: the creation of the one-price system, guaranteeing every customer an equal deal, the establishment of brand-name prices, assuring standard values. Haggling and barter had been eliminated from the marketplace.

Now let's update Brandeis' history, written more than a half-century ago when retail morals, at least, seemed very different from those of today.

In 1961, after the postwar period of discounting's fastest growth, marketing columnist E. B. Weiss wrote that "we have been moving out of a one-price era for well over a decade.... Today, only a minor percentage of brands are retailed under a one-price philosophy. By 1965, the total will be much smaller." [5] As early as 1957, Weiss offered this opinion: "A whole generation, several generations in fact, have been thoroughly conditioned to 'haggling' and extreme price flexibility." [6]

In other words, the evolution described by Brandeis appears to be endangered. Despite gains in consumer protection, embodied in various laws, the retail market today appears to be entering a demoralized condition where practices engaged in by discounters and some others place consumers at a serious disadvantage and where legal remedies no longer seem sufficient. "The constant haggling about prices" that in Brandeis' day was ending is back with us full force. Once again, many a seller "gives as little in value and gets as much in money as he can." Once again, "a good bargain means a transaction in which one person gets the better of another." Once again, unscrupulous dealers "abandon quality goods for cheaper or inferior substitutes." The individual shopper is often at the mercy of those he trades with. There is often too little legal relief for the customer; he can often only hope that the authorities will send out inspectors who—if they find proof of false advertising or are overcharged—can act on the matter.

Today what discount stores offer us so often are mere paper bargains, discounts in words alone. As one camera retailer put it before Congress, all such a discounter need do is "take merchandise which should formerly sell for $10 . . . arrange for the manufacturer to put a fictitious price of $19.95 on it, and then . . . come out with a big sign and say [he is] cutting the price 40 per cent." [7] It's "the old system," says Senator William Proxmire, of crossing out a phony $88 price and labelling the merchandise at $50. "The feeling you get," Proxmire adds, is "that you get a big reduction in price, but actually [it] is a misunderstanding on the part of the purchaser." The consumer doesn't understand that price tags can be printed anywhere and may carry any price at all.

"Shy away from prices far below those offered by firms you know to be reputable," warns the Better Business Bureau. "The chances are that such prices are completely insincere—just bait to hook you." [8] BBB adds elsewhere, "Steer clear of anyone who advertises 'fantastic' or 'amazing' bargains. As a rule of thumb, you can take it for granted that the wilder the promise, the smaller the value you receive." [9] As for fictitious list prices, BBB warns, "When used in advertising it is often a price at which the merchandise does not regularly and normally sell. Often used as a basis of comparison with a sale price to misrepresent that the difference in the two prices is a 'saving.' " [10]

These warnings, meant to alert the public to all frauds at retail, are worth pasting in one's hat together with the Sears, Roebuck list of discounting price-tag terms. They can save us money every time we shop.

6

Who's in Charge Here?

> I have not found that people go into business for
> holy or moral reasons.
>
> —SAMUEL J. ROSENSTEIN, former chairman of the
> board, Towers Marts International [1]

W HEN I buy something, I like to know with whom I'm
doing business and that they take an interest in me as
a customer," a young New Jersey housewife told me
recently. "Even when I'm in a very big store, I want to have the
feeling it stands behind what it sells. Also, I like a store where
the customer—me—comes first."

This housewife, whose husband's $12,000-a-year income makes
her more affluent than most, has a point of view that the majority
of us share. Her expectations seem reasonable and reflect traditional demands. This is so particularly today, as the wealth of
products available makes it difficult for us to gauge quality and
value; most of us will, after all, admit that we cannot find our
way through the tangle of synthetic fabrics and the maze of
electronic gadgetry. More than ever, we want to rely on the
individual merchant to guide us in our choice and, more than
ever, we want to rely on his integrity. The Better Business
Bureau agrees. "Remember," it cautions consumers, "that a good
reputation is the result of fair play, and deal only with people
who have such a reputation." [2]

56

Good advice—but unfortunately almost worthless today. Such admonitions applied to a time when the customer dealt with a merchant and a store that he knew, at least by reputation. Those days are past. Today, discount houses are often run in such a way that you can never be sure with whom you're doing business, from whom you're buying, or even to whom you are giving your money. The fact that you are inside a particular discount store, with four walls around you and a roof over your head, does not mean that you are doing business with a responsible store management that you know and can identify. As a matter of fact, no management at all may exist—at least not in the way you expect it to exist. Nowadays *Caveat emptor* may apply not only as we cross the parking lot to enter some discount houses, but also as we cross each aisle inside, to shop in another department.

The startling truth is that in large numbers of discount stores many departments are run by different concessionaires. Shoppers are often unaware of the prevalence of such concessionaires and, in any one store, are unaware of their existence, from counter to counter. This is not to say that there is anything clandestine about leasing; the operation of leased departments in discount stores is a completely accepted feature in the industry and well known to the trade. Many department stores have gone in for it as well; indeed, there is nothing new about leasing except its extraordinary growth. *The Discount Merchandiser* frequently publishes lists of leased-department operators, and the handbooks on discounting carry such information as well. Only the general public seems to remain unaware of the phenomenon. The consumer often thinks that, because he shops in the discount house in his area, a reputable retailer who owns the store and its departments is at the head of it. Perhaps there is, but it is just as possible that he acts merely as a landlord to a collection of concessionaires, few or none of whom the public may know by name.

An example of the leased-department operator is Marrud, Inc., the largest discount drug chain in the country, which runs the drug departments in about 200 stores throughout the U.S.A. We've already seen the nature of its markups in that 1963 survey and how it was able at one and the same time to boast of a low *average* margin, while maintaining unexpectedly high margins on most categories of merchandise sold. We've already seen that the customer who shopped at a Marrud discount outlet in the expectation of finding only rock-bottom "discount-type" margins may well have been disappointed. At a discount center composed largely of similar leased-department operations, he might well encounter comparable disappointments as he tours this bazaar, counter to counter. Each might well have similar "mixes" of prices and margins.

American Stock Exchange Investor magazine calls the leased-department operators the "unsung merchants" (meaning *unknown* merchants) of the discount industry. They account, says the magazine, for much of the industry's fantastic growth in recent years.[3] In fact, if it had not been for such leased departments, discounting might well not have enjoyed the rapid growth it did.

According to *Barron's*, the authoritative financial weekly, "lessees [that is, the leased-department operators] generally work on higher markups"—this, "despite pressure from store managements to offer traffic-building bargains." An interesting aspect of the *Barron's* article, entitled "Smart Operators," is the fact that those leased departments that are required by their landlords to cut margins to meet competition from other discounters often find themselves without any profits at all—another indication that talk of selling successfully on "low-low" discount-type markups may often just be talk. "Your profit margins are already paper-thin," *Barron's* quotes "a scarred veteran" as saying, "and when that happens they disappear completely." Many of the leased-department operators who have failed in the business have, apparently, failed for this reason.

Despite the hazards, concessions can be a get-rich-quick scheme, for as one department rakes in the profits, another can be opened at low cost, and a huge chain can be formed speedily. Further, what hazards do exist are minimized by being spread throughout the chain; if one department, in one discount center, fails, the losses can be made up elsewhere, where the departments are successful. *Barron's* points out that getting into the discount house concessionaire field may seem deceptively simple to the lessee since it takes only about a fifth of the money needed to start a conventional retail store. "The merchant contracts for a specified amount of floor space, installs or buys from the store a few simple fixtures, lays in a stock, and is ready to do business . . ."

Fast growth seems to be the rule. One leading operator of leased men's and boys' wear departments in discount stores did $1,400,000 worth of business in his first year; after eight years, this chain operated in 104 discount stores and enjoyed a sales volume of $30,000,000. An operator of 60 discount-store jewelry departments made $550,000 in sales in his first unit, during the first year of operation. One of the biggest discount-store chains, which has almost all departments leased out, boasts that it can open a 100,000-square-foot unit for what marketing authority E. B. Weiss calls "an unbelievably low investment of $125,000." [4] A good example of growth in this business was provided by testimony given before a U.S. Senate subcommittee by Joseph A. Marcus, president of GEM International, Inc., St. Louis, Missouri. Marcus traced the rapid growth of his organization over less than 10 years. "GEM began as a single store in Denver, Colorado, in 1956," he told the Senators. "At the present time GEM has 34 stores in 22 cities and 14 States. At the present time it has over 1,600,000 members. Since only one member of a family needs to qualify, GEM can be said to represent 1,600,000 families or roughly better than 3 percent of the total families in the United States. [By "members," Marcus means customers, for GEM is a "closed-door" operation, in which customers need to buy membership.] GEM is what is known as a horizontal operation; that is, it leases out to independent operators each of its merchandising departments. At the latest count, GEM had 238 such operators or lessees." [5] Marcus makes the point that GEM's lessees are mostly small businessmen.

There is, nevertheless, an element that seems disturbing to the author in the operation of leased departments. That element is, of course, the largely unknown nature of the transactions that some customers are likely to make. Very often, large discount centers spring up virtually overnight in a community, thanks to the existence of large discount leased-department chains equipped to stock a large store with great speed. Community housewives are led to believe (by the existence of *one* store name) that "a new retailer" has come to town; in point of fact, what has come to town to stay is a caravan. Does the average shopper know from whom he is buying? Often, he does not.

More recently, many discount houses have been buying up their lessees, or at least the more profitable ones. This is not just because the profits from these departments have set many landlords' mouths awatering, but because ownership allows for more maneuverability. *The Wall Street Journal* quotes one discounter on the subject: "If you own the departments you can operate a single department at cost or at a loss to promote the whole store, while a leased department would never stand for this." [6] Ownership, in other words, lets management operate even more extravagant loss-leader promotions by running, say, an entire appliance department on a loss-leader basis, and marking up the merchandise in all other departments to compensate.

The battle over whether to lease or operate departments inside discount houses continues in the discounting trade press. Leasing was particularly useful in the beginning, for it enabled many a discounter to open one outlet after another with razzle-dazzle rapidity, capturing the best locations around the country. As these outlets have become established, the trend toward owning rather than leasing grows. A recent Dun & Bradstreet survey of 55 discounters reports that only 14.5 percent acquired any leased departments in 1963 and that 13 percent said they would buy out the lessees who handle furniture, liquor, and gifts during 1964. "The departments offer a wide possibility of profit margin maneuverability as well as being big drawing cards," says *Home Furnishings Daily*. The reason given for cutting down on leases: "an inability to locate a proper lessee who would assure a high margin and a desire for overall control of operations." [7]

Still, the lease operator remains a big part of the nationwide discounting picture. Some traditional retailers like Woolworth, who have recently entered the discount industry with their Woolco Stores, reportedly plan to lease many of their major departments. They are motivated not merely by the fact that leasing is a cheap way toward fast growth, but also because the lease operators know more about the very specialized business of discounting than they do. They recognize, says *Fortune* magazine, that "discounting is a distinctive form of merchandising and merchants brought up in conventional retailing frequently have a hard time unlearning their old habits and attitudes." [8] This is certainly true. As Nathaniel Schwartz, editor-in-chief of *The Discount Merchandiser*, wrote in a signed editorial in April 1963, "Discounting is a new retailing university but the people in it are learning their subjects very fast." The first thing that freshmen coming to this university from a conventional college must do is to unlearn old attitudes.

Bait for the Belly

If the lure of a bargain seems hard to resist, the appeal of bargain food, of cut-price groceries, is overwhelming. More and more discount stores, therefore, have recently added food departments to their operations. Many of these are leased out wholly or in part to concessionaires. They prove effective bait for the rest of the discount center.

The Discount Merchandiser puts it bluntly. It says discounters are not satisfied with getting customers into their stores every two or three weeks; food, they realize, will bring shoppers in two or three times *weekly*. The food supermarket, says the magazine, is "a potent magnet of attraction" and once a discounter has that magnet, he can "draw them in with groceries and then sell them everything else." The editors predict that a third of all discount houses in the country will shortly be adding food departments.[9] Indeed, the drawing power of cut-rate food cannot be overestimated, says E. B. Weiss. He believes that "no

other promotion produces the day-in, day-out traffic to the
degree true of food—especially when food is offered at low
prices." That these low prices are often a gimmick is clear;
Weiss says the discount outlet "can afford to take a loss on food
because it earns a good profit on its non-foods. . . ." [10]

The Discount Merchandiser studied three food discounters in
depth and presented its findings before a Denver convention of
the National Association of Food Chains. Despite the fact that its
own survey showed that two out of the three stores *lost money*,
the magazine, astonishingly, continued to claim that cutting
prices on food could be a profitable business. *The Discount
Merchandiser* then proceeded to admit that most discounters
believe "a lot of groceries have to be given away and counter-
balanced by the merchandise sold for a profit," adding that "it
stands to reason that the more goods you have around on which
to recoup your losses, the more staying power you will have. . . ."

It is obvious that different types of food operations—ranging
from huge supermarkets to small, neighborhood groceries—have
different pricing policies. Discount-center food operations, however, do not compete with small merchants as much as they do
with the huge (non-discount) food chains. To do so and to serve
what appears from the trade press to be their primary purpose—
attracting shoppers to the rest of the discount center—such "food
discount" stores are often just loss-leader operations, profitable
because consumers in most cases will buy high-markup merchandise while they are in the discount center. *The Discount
Merchandiser* suggests that discounters are smart if they own
their own food departments, rather than leasing them out, because then they can make sure their losses are offset "by the
profits of the 50 or 60 other departments in the general merchandise area." The future, it says, also lies in a reverse twist:
food discounters are adding general merchandise, which gives
them greater "flexibility" and gives their food prices "a sharper
bite."

Some general-merchandise discounters, then, are going into
the food business because they know that food brings customers

in more often; some food discounters, at the same time, are going into general merchandise because they know that it's in high-markup general merchandise that the big profits lie.

Food discounting as practiced by E. J. Korvette, Inc., was the subject of a late-1964 article in *The Wall Street Journal*. It reported that, while Korvette sales jumped to more than $485 million during fiscal 1964 (up from 1963's $330 million), the chain reported only a very small rise in operating profits. Part of the reason apparently lay in the losses Korvette had deliberately taken in food discounting. Joseph H. Lamm, the company's executive vice president, was quoted as saying that the chain had tried an "experiment" of "giving food away" (presumably in order to draw customers into the store's other departments). Says *The Wall Street Journal:* "when Korvette stopped offering these loss-leaders, customers stopped coming." [11]

According to Lamm, Korvette's food sales in fiscal 1964 were about 15 percent of its total volume. Since it seems Korvette made no profit on this 15 percent, we also know it had to make up this loss elsewhere, if it wished to make an over-all profit. And the chain did make a profit. Once more we see how one department or one section of a store can serve to build a "discounting image" for the whole. Food prices are readily comparable; any alert housewife knows what chickens or frozen peas are selling for throughout her neighborhood. Of course she will avail herself of the "low-low" prices being offered at the food discount store; food, after all, is a major family budget item and there is no question that this housewife will save money if she shops for food at discount. Psychologically, however, she may make an unwarranted assumption: that the rest of the discount center, selling non-foods, will offer her bargains comparable to those she encounters in food.

7

Cherry-Picking on Main Street

> Anything that suggests a fast turn-over, or anything
> we can build into a fast turn-over we go after.
> —MANFRED BRECKER, vice president, S. E. Nichols
> Co., New York City [1]

O N April 6, 1964, I did some "comparison shopping" in
East Berlin, that gray, dead city lying on the builders'
side of the *Schandmauer* (Wall of Shame) from prosperous, lively West Berlin. The Germans incarcerated behind that
wall seemed drab, exhausted, and monotonously alike; those few
walking the street who weren't in some sort of uniform were uni-
formly threadbare and poorly clothed. The food, apparel, appliances, furniture, and other merchandise that I inspected in the
stores was cheaply made and all of it was overpriced. In the window of one East Berlin appliance store, I saw kitchen ranges
and washing machines just like you'd find in the U.S.A.—30
years ago. Yet these grotesques were brand new, right off the
assembly line of some Soviet Zone factory. It was clear that the
production planners in East Berlin do not consider the customer
to be "king," nor do they even concern themselves with his
tastes. They don't have to, for they have a monopoly right
through to the retail outlets, which, like the factories, are also
run by the State. Workers lucky enough to be able to afford the

sky-high prices either buy those quaint washing machines, or do without. As for the stoves, which looked as though they'd come off a set for *The Grapes of Wrath*, those East Germans who don't like them presumably are told to go and barbecue their Sauerbraten.

Farther down the street was a State-run *HO* food store. I studied its window-display, then stepped inside. It offered a selection that seemed meager even for a village, yet this store serves a main street in the capital. And what a choice it offers!

One window was entirely given over to sausages in glass jars, all of which would have been condemned by the U.S. Food and Drug Administration. The lids looked rusty, the glass seemed dirty inside and out, and the sausages swam in a scummy fluid that would have repelled even the hungriest worker. The price of a jar represented several hours' working time for an East German.

On another main thoroughfare, there was a gift shop in which I bought a carton containing 12 boxes of wooden matches, each decorated with poorly printed pictures of Soviet statues. I still have trouble getting a light from them; either the thin wooden match breaks in half upon striking, or the sulphur tip snaps off. Yet these matches, which at least did not cost much, were the only items it made sense to buy, even as a "souvenir"; everything else, from ladies' scarves to fountain pens, was priced far too high, and was of equally dubious quality.

As I walked out, heading back to West Berlin, I thought that what I'd seen was current proof that there is no such thing as a benevolent monopoly; all are rapacious. In that totalitarian state, monopoly control of the manufacturing process and of the retail marketplace is an accomplished fact. There are few shops, and there are few factories producing consumer goods. There is virtually no selection, because it apparently makes no sense to the East German bosses to produce a wide range of appliances, when one type of stove and washer will do for everyone. Quality also plummets because it does not count. The only thing that matters is that big profits go to the "capitalist bosses"—in this case, the Communist state. Workers have no choice but to buy and, when they buy, they have no choice either, for no selection is offered and one cannot shop around. As I passed through Checkpoint Charlie at the Friedrichstrasse, the Moscow-run monopoly was to my back. I was glad to get out of that repressive atmosphere. A few days later, I was glad to get back to the U.S.A., where things are different.

But how different? In which way? And for how long?

Great Expectations

Americans of course have a vastly higher living standard than East Germans. Indeed, except for such cultural items as books, Americans spend more money in most areas of life than any other people.

If yours is an average American family, you spend $558 a year on clothing, $277 on furniture, $91.59 on personal care supplies, $74.69 on major appliances, $42.25 on TV sets, $33.33 on such household textiles as sheets and blankets, and $15.10 on housewares.[2] If you are a more or less typical American shopper, you have certain expectations about what you want to get for your money.

You expect to get value and good quality at a fair price. You expect a wide selection, not only in terms of sizes, but in styles, colors, designs, performances, and brand names as well. You expect a variety of products from which to choose within each product category. You expect to be able to satisfy your family's diverse and individual tastes.

There are also certain things that you expect from your retail merchant. You expect him to maintain a sizeable inventory, so that he will not be all sold out of the product you want. You expect him to take the diversity of your family's tastes and needs into account. If you are shopping for a radio, you do not wish to be shown only three or four models, none of which may suit your purposes. If you are shopping for shirts with tab collars, you expect your merchant to carry them, and not to stock merely button-downs. Quite understandably, you are irritated at being shuttled about, from store to store, looking vainly for exactly what you wish, be it a blouse, a skirt, a toy, a ball of yarn, a radio, a shirt, or a leather chair. You expect *not* to have to settle for less.

These expectations are neither arbitrary nor unreasonable. The "average" American family that spends more than $500 a year on clothes has a right to be considered important customers. When a store does not have what you want, when our "affluent society" offers a poor selection of cheap merchandise, when you cannot get the service your expenditures entitle you to, then it is only natural that you are annoyed and, perhaps, troubled and disturbed.

"What seems to be happening?" you ask. "Why can't I find exactly what I want? What's wrong with the merchants, anyway?"

These questions are good and valid ones. Something is indeed "happening." There are distinct reasons why we often have trouble finding what we want, and there is indeed something wrong with today's merchants.

One good reason is that the discounting industry has grown up. Why we often can't find what we're looking for is the result of a widespread discount-store policy called *cherry-picking*, and what is wrong with so many of today's merchants is that they're dead or dying.

Cherry-picking (or "creaming," as discounters sometimes call it) is the policy of selling a great volume of a small selection of high-turnover merchandise. It is a policy, in effect, that offers consumers little choice and that concentrates only on fast-moving, high-profit goods that are constantly in demand by an overwhelming majority of consumers. *Fortune* calls it a policy of "thick on the best, to hell with the rest." It is one of the aspects of the disease that infests the U.S. retail marketplace today.

In the olden days of retailing, a man who elected to open up a shop chose (whether he liked it or not) to go into public service.

Perhaps he was an ex-GI who stumbled across a 10-block area without a shoe store and hoped to find his pot of gold at the corner of Elm and Main. Perhaps he was a young college graduate clutching a degree in pharmacy or a bibliophile longing for the life of a small-town bookseller. Whoever he was and whatever were the motivations that led him into retailing, the minute he opened his door for business he found himself saddled with a public responsibility.

It went far beyond giving good value at a fair price, something a man might do out of cupidity, simply as good business. The retail merchant's public responsibilities include providing the community with the products it needs and wants. The young man entering the retail trade soon learned that he not only performed a selling or distributive function, but a buying function as well. In his own way, he helped support thousands of manufacturers and tens of thousands of products. He helped support the hundreds of thousands of workers who produced these products and he helped contribute to the support of the countless American communities that lived off their manufacture.

In addition, this retailer learned that he was expected to play a significant role in his own community, not just as a substantial taxpayer, but as an active participant in its civic and political life. He learned that a man who owns a retail store is a target for every fund-raiser in town and is corralled as a matter of course into business, civic, fraternal, veteran, church, welfare, and political associations. As an independent store-owner, he soon found that he could not escape these community responsibilities as easily as could many a local manager of the nationwide retail chain outlets, who could plead that he was merely a glorified clerk serving distant, indifferent employers.

Strange as it may seem, the young retailer also learned that he had a cultural role to play, whether he himself was cultured or not. This role is most easy to identify in the case of the bookseller; his inventory reflects and often shapes the intellectual tastes and levels of his community. In a medium-sized or small American city (where a bookstore already is about as unusual a sight as an outdoor café), the bookseller's influence may be considerable. Yet even the furniture dealer finds that his activities have a cultural effect, if we consider a standardization of styles and tastes unhealthy and regard a diversification of the same as culturally desirable. Mass-produced "Early American" and bogus "Danish modern" furniture are already as much a dreary part of the American home as look-alike ranch houses and split-levels are of the American countryside. Many people regard such uniformity with misgivings and see it as a disturbing few steps from living in cadence. "Marching along together" may have already gone a bit too far.

The roles that the independent retailer plays and the responsibilities he assumes, as we have described them, represent the ideal. It goes without saying that some "modern mass merchandising experts" have no interest in these roles or responsibilities, or in anything other than a fast turnover of merchandise that offers them big profits.

This may become more true as chains grow increasingly powerful and take over more and more of the retail market in our communities. The bigger some discounters become, the less interested they often are in serving the public in the traditional manner of retailers. It is true that, in the continuing evolution of the discount store, many of the big discount houses today look more like conventional stores than they did in the past. Some have added credit facilities, and others chandeliers and rugs. While here and there a particular local discounter adds window-dressing to his operations, the fact is that in the essential area of serving a distributive function in our society he may cut down sharply.

It is obviously far more profitable for such a discounter to stock only items for which there is a large and constant demand than it is for him to service a community by stocking in addition a variety of items that sell more slowly. It is more profitable to sell 500 lawn chairs of the same design, make, and standard of quality than it is to sell 50 each of 10 different types and styles. As far as this discounter is concerned, the standardization of tastes in

America may be the best blessing to be visited upon the Republic.

Many operators of discount houses see nothing whatever the matter with cherry-picking and often admit to it. To them, the efficient and profitable operation of their business provides their sole reason for being. Conventional business ethics and the notion that a retailer must also meet a larger responsibility to his customers are sneered at. Such discounters speak contemptuously of the conventional merchant as being hobbled by his ethics and, therefore, "inefficient." They regard cherry-picking (as they do loss leaders, etc., *ad nauseam*) as evidence that they are "modern mass merchandisers," in tune with the times. The president of a Pennsylvania discount operation, for example, describes his company's policy of discarding all "slow-moving" merchandise as the "key to the merchandising of our operation."

"We don't have many slow-moving items in our stores," he is quoted as saying by *The Discount Merchandiser*. "... In simple terms, we try to handle only basic merchandise." [3]

In the organization of any one particular discount store, cherry-picking can mean stocking as small a selection of fast-moving goods as possible in each merchandise category. In furniture, it may mean offering a minimum selection of, say, bedroom sets, not a full choice. In dinnerware, it may mean stocking only a few of the most popular patterns, not a complete line. In shoes, it may mean offering a few fast-sellers, not a full selection of styles. Often it also means stocking mostly high-profit merchandise. The difference between selective and full-line merchandise is indicated by Marrud's, which stocks an average of only 4,261 items, [4] versus the average of 12,000 carried by *non*-discount drugstores. According to trade sources, there are some U.S. drugstores that carry as many as 24,000 items. Some of these are not essential to health (such as a dozen or more brands of toothpaste in assorted sizes), but many are. Says one New York City pharmacist of my acquaintance, whose estimate of his own corner store inventory runs to 12,000 items, "The full-service drugstore carries thousands of items not because we want to, but in order to serve our customers." It is argued that the discount drugstore has no such obligation, since it specializes in offering low prices rather than the type of full service many independent pharmacies offer; this is true, to my way of thinking, only super-ficially. If what happens in practice is that the discount drugstore often kills off the local "full-service" pharmacy, then, in my view, it has a *moral obligation* to assume the "full-service" functions of that drugstore. If it then does not do so, the families in the com-munity suffer as a result. (It should be noted that one section of The Marrud Study asks "how much creaming?" The Study offers statistics to show that Marrud "does not prune its inventory to the bone," for many of its items move very slowly indeed. Yet it is my contention that these figures are inadequate because they fail to provide a comparison with independent drugstores. Trade sources say that average inventories appear to run between 10,000 and 12,000 items; The Marrud Study said that Marrud carried 4,261 items.)

Home Furnishings Daily gives an example of cherry-picking by saying that a store might carry "a Universal coffeemaker, or a General Electric iron, or a Sunbeam mixer, and a few other pieces that have had great demand . . . but nothing more." [5] But cherry-picking doesn't refer only to selecting the most popular nationally advertised, famous-brand names; it refers to a general, storewide policy of minimum selection, and it applies to off-brands and private brands as well. It is basically a merchandising policy, perhaps best described by its alternate name, creaming: a policy of selling *only* what sells best. The discounter's stock, of course, is enormous, but that is only because he has captured so much of the retail trade. In many cases, his over-all selection may be wretched, as so many discriminating shoppers have found.

To see cherry-picking in action in one particular area, let us return to the upstate New York discounter my wife and I re-cently visited and look at its "book department." According to my rough count, it consists of about 100 titles (not counting paperbacks sold at *list* prices). These included a handful of best-sellers that were discounted, and a larger selection of old titles that obviously had been around for some time. This latter, rather shopworn, group consisted chiefly of "turn-over" items like cookbooks, home encyclopedias, guides to baby care, popular medicine books, juveniles and mysteries, with a few classics thrown in to spice the selection.

The bestsellers that this outlet offers are, naturally, a big source of income for local independent booksellers. These are the men who "make and hold customers" for books, reports Joseph A. Duffy of the American Booksellers Association, New York City. Discounters, says Duffy, who carry "only bestsellers and the fastest moving staples" do not support the American book industry. They raid it. In doing so, they "cream" the bestsellers on which the independent bookstore depends for so much of its income. Such independent stores need popular mass literature to pay for the rest of the books they carry. When a discounter's cherry-picking policies remove this source of income, the independent retailer is left with only the slower-moving titles to sell. He soon goes out of business, as so many already have, or he cuts down his stock of worthwhile literature, trying to compete with this discounter by selling sensational books, sex books, and other fast-moving titles not yet taken on by discount houses. Certainly the independent bookseller cannot continue to maintain a large inventory of slow-moving books of cultural value when faced with cut-price competition, unless he is located in a large city like New York. There are independent bookstores in New York City that now discount current bestsellers by as much as 30 percent. By and large, however, these are a special breed of bookstore: they specialize in publishers' overstock (as many discounters do) and do a heavy volume of their business in these. A large percentage of their profits is derived from such remaindered titles, offered at low prices, to be sure, but nevertheless carrying a profitable margin. The difference between such stores and discount book departments seems to me to be that they do not in any way suggest that the bargain books are "discounts," that is, lower in price than they would sell for elsewhere. A more conventional bookstore, on the other hand, does not follow such practices, simply because the book-buying public in smaller cities and towns is in itself too small to support a high-volume business in remaindered titles.

"Without personal bookstores," says Joseph Duffy, "many fine books would not be published and will not be available to the public even through our free-library system. New authors will be too much of a gamble for the publisher to consider. The books essential to students for special work, and those on philosophy, education, economics, sociology, and other special subjects, will have too small a sale to make it worth while for a publisher to invest his money in them." What will happen then? The book-buying public will just have to forgo its literary pleasures, in favor of other pursuits. One is reminded that when Conrad Hilton bought Chicago's Palmer House, he transformed a bookstore that was losing money because of cut-price competition into a bar. The bar has been making money ever since.[6]

The implications go further than even Duffy suggests. After a time, of course, publishers are reluctant to print books such as he describes without raising their prices to compensate for their decreased sales. The state of the publishing industry already attests to the effect of the profit squeeze. Mergers and consolidations are the rule, and the trend is towards bigness and ever more reliance on school textbooks, which have an assured market, rather than on the introduction of new literature. While total book sales rose 5 to 10 percent in 1964, to about $1.8 billion, more than half of this figure is accounted for by textbook and encyclopedia publishers, as well as by home-study and programmed learning courses, which are the assured bestsellers in the book industry today. The question asked by Marya Mannes in her book's title *But Will It Sell?* is more than ever the dreary one asked whenever a young talent, especially in fiction and in poetry, offers his wares to Parnassus. There is no dearth of good-will toward good literature; there is merely a terrible dearth of book-loving independent bookstore owners, who will buy first novels, support new authors and even new publishers, and push books by recommending them to their customers.

What is happening to books is happening to much more

homely items. Lee Waterman, president of Corning Glass Works, Corning, N.Y., has pointed out, for example, that a two-quart casserole is the best seller in that field, but that there are of course families that need three-quart casseroles. Corning and other manufacturers produce these three-quart casseroles, but many discounters won't stock them. They sell too slowly. In vain does the manufacturer protest that there is a market, albeit a small one, for these items and that the big family has as much right to a casserole as the small one. "The neighborhood retailer," says Waterman, "realizes this [responsibility]. The turn-over merchant does not." [7] Waterman says that soon the three-quart casserole won't be available anywhere. Obviously, the independent retailer can't—and won't—stock only the slow-moving items; he needs the "best sellers" in the pots and pans department to pay for them.

Replacement covers, handles, and other items traditionally a part of a manufacturer's kitchenware line also hold no interest for the discounter who follows a policy of cherry-picking. They take up inventory space and turn over slowly, and he prefers to leave them to the small independent who, of course, sells them only sporadically. The market for them begins to disappear and soon they themselves disappear.

Cherry-picking practices are, at times, somewhat bizarre. Certainly they are highly arbitrary. Close by our home, there is a discount drug store, its windows jammed with cut-rate hand lotions, cleansing tissues, and electric toothbrushes, all bearing nationally advertised brand names and clearly "bait" for bargain hunters. Inside, the store is jammed with its own-label merchandise. A neighbor of ours told us she recently went there, hoping to buy a specific against menstrual cramps, expecting to find it there because the store is owned by a pharmacist and claims to compound prescriptions. He suggested she try aspirin, but when she insisted on one of the specifics instead, he told her he did not carry them. It seemed odd to her at the time, since they obviously have a market. Then the answer dawned on her. "I suppose," she said to us, "it's because not all women use them and those who do only want them a few days out of the month. He probably doesn't want to clutter up his store with such products." There is another reason, of course. They probably do not permit him the high hidden markup he gets on some of the rest of his merchandise.

At the upstate New York discount store to which I referred before, the customer who wants to buy a business suit is similarly out of luck; after a half hour of searching, I couldn't find any. There were slacks, shirts, and leather jackets by the dozen, and it is true that most country folk in the area find more use for blue jeans than for blue serge. Yet the store is located outside a sizeable town with a business community, and local businessmen dress for the office just as any Chicagoans or New Yorkers do. Such a businessman cannot buy his suits at the discounter, so he must turn elsewhere. The independent men's wear merchant, however, has had his faster-moving casual clothes taken from him. What is this merchant left with? He is forced to concentrate on suits and high-quality slacks and sport clothes. And now because his sales are slower, he must charge more on each of these in order to stay in business.

Sporting-goods dealers report much the same happening to them. If a customer wants low-profit items like hooks and sinkers, he goes to them; if he wants rods and reels, he patronizes the discounter, hoping for a price break. A lot of discounters, however, stock only a few makes, and the customer often may find the selection poor; if he turns to the independent sports store, he finds that they can survive only by stocking the high-priced rods and reels, which such discounters don't want.

A Look at the Future

What does this mean to the consumer in search of value? Donald Dayton of Minneapolis's Dayton Co. predicts: "The retail revolution of today will end with two successful operations at opposite ends of the spectrum, the quality, fashion-right stores at one end, the discounter at the other—and trouble for the merchant in between." David Williams of L.S. Ayres, Indianapolis, paints an even darker picture. "The store in the middle can't survive," he says.[8]

Those Americans who live in large cities may feel this pinch taking place more slowly. New York City in particular will probably continue to support many independent small and medium-sized shops, because of the wealth and diverse tastes of its citizens. Yet it is important to note that even New York City has seen the number of its retail outlets *cut in half* since the advent of discounting. In New York's suburbs, the situation facing the consumer is almost identical with that facing Americans living elsewhere in the country. The development Donald Dayton describes is almost a *fait accompli* today. This is true even of some large cities, such as Chicago, where a large percentage of the total volume of retail shopping is done in suburban shopping centers, heavily dominated by discount chains.

Caught in the squeeze of the shrinking marketplace, the consumer is faced with the question of whether *he* can survive. For vast numbers of Americans, particularly those who live anywhere but in the largest U.S. cities, the reality of shopping boils down to this: You can buy what you need at the discount house and risk getting low-quality goods, or you can go to the nearest specialty shop. There you may find a blouse that used to be sold by a neighborhood merchant for $4 now selling for $6.50. That same high-quality blouse is very probably not available at the discount store. That discount store may offer you an "even better" price. A blouse there may sell for $3.00 and show a $6.50 "list price" on it. But too often it will not be worth $6.50, nor even the $3 at which it is now priced.

"The public be damned" seems to be the slogan both in the *HO* stores in East Berlin and in many a discount store on Main Street, U.S.A. In both places, the public pose is that of the public benefactor. *Decipimur specie recti*, said Horace: We are deceived by an appearance of right.

8

Monopoly in the Making

> Americans should be under no illusions as to the
> value or effect of price-cutting. It has been the most
> potent weapon of monopoly—a means of killing the
> small rival to which the great trusts have resorted
> most frequently. It is so simple, so effective. Far-
> seeing organized capital secures by this means the
> cooperation of the shortsighted unorganized con-
> sumer to his own undoing. Thoughtless and weak,
> he yields to the temptation of trifling immediate gain;
> and selling his birthright for a mess of pottage, be-
> comes himself an instrument of monopoly.
>
> —JUSTICE LOUIS D. BRANDEIS [1]

WHEN Sam Nides opened his appliance store in Denver,
Colorado, in 1947, that city was just entering a decade
of rapid growth. Nides had faith in his future, stocked
his store with top-quality brand-name products, and adopted a
policy of offering customers maximum service. As his wife
Nessie recalls, Sam Nides believed "that the basis of the appliance business was good will and service to the consumer." This
philosophy—which seems so outdated today—was still very much
alive in 1947, and Sam's attitude caused Nides Appliances, Inc.,
to prosper, particularly as Denver grew by 1950 to a population
of about 564,000.

Then, Sam Nides died. His passing might have meant the end
of Nides Appliances, had it not been for his wife, a woman of
remarkable energy, managerial ability, and dedication. Nessie
Nides was the daughter of an immigrant who arrived in the
United States with nothing more than the clothes on his back
and who from 1922 until his death in 1933 built up a successful
business in Denver as a retailer of automobile tires. When her
father died, Nessie Nides did what she was fated to do seven-
teen years later when her husband passed away: she took over
the business, running it until Sam Nides married her. "I've seen
the retail business through many cycles," she says, "through good
and bad years." It is not surprising, then, that she made a big
success of Nides Appliances, all on her own.

She also believed in service to her customers. It was, for one
thing, a sound business policy. People who bought an appliance
from her wanted prompt and courteous delivery, good installation, and immediate attention if anything went wrong. As appliances became increasingly complex, her customers wanted a
guide through the maze of pushbuttons, and Mrs. Nides hired a
home economist to educate them.

She came to be known, respected, and well-liked by thousands
of Denver citizens, as well as by the trade. She loved the con-
tacts and associations the business gave her. She loved the challenge of her job and honestly believed that her appliances helped
her customers (as she puts it) "to find a better way of life." In
short, Nessie Nides was a dedicated woman. She organized the
Denver chapter of the National Appliance Retail Dealers Association, was active on the industry magazine, and in 1963 was
elected to the national board of the NARDA.

By 1960, the city's growth and the growth of discounting met
head-on, with the expected result. Price-cutters, smelling volume
in the Queen City, increased in the Denver market. Customers,
says Mrs. Nides, still wanted service and even demanded it from
her, but they "became enamoured with the 'lower-than-cost' lure
advertising on name brands by the discounter."

By 1962, after losing money for two years, she says she "saw the handwriting on the wall." She had only two alternatives: to go out of business, or to join the discounters. She decided to quit.

It would not, she thought at the time, be hard to find someone to buy her store, but as it turned out, she couldn't. One large-volume appliance dealer whom she approached told her he himself would quit the business if he could get his investment out. "I'm lucky to just be making a living," he said. Another told her he was losing money on everything he sold and was surviving only on his service business, repairing appliances that had been bought elsewhere. Finally, Mrs. Nides sold her stock and just closed shop. "Believe me, I salvaged very little."

"This was just one more store closing as far as statistics are concerned," she says, "but to me, I think you will agree, I have lost a vital part of myself. Thirteen years of running a business in which I took great pride.... Now the lost feeling of where to go and what to do." [2]

The Growth of Retail Monopoly

The developments that killed Nides Appliances were the same that have in the past several years turned many another American city into a retail jungle where only the strongest and biggest can survive. What does this mean to us as consumers? Where will we be shopping a few years from now? From whom will we be buying? Who will control the merchandise that is offered to us, the quality and value we get, and the price we will pay? How much competition will there be?

The answers to these questions are right now being fought out in a bloody retailing revolution that makes us, the consumers, the booty or prize of war. The casualties are heavy, and the opposing armies are sometimes hard to tell apart, for they both wear the uniforms of Free Enterprisers, march under the banners of More Competition, and patriotically wave the flag of Public Benefactor.

Those are mighty attractive blandishments to Americans. We have been reared to appreciate the success of a competitive, free-enterprise economy. No one needs to convince us of its value. We know from practical experience that we are best served as consumers when more manufacturers and retailers vie for our favor; when there are more stores, not fewer; when more retailers fight to win us as customers, not fewer; and when those retailers are part of our communities and responsive to the wishes of our communities.

We know from our historical experience what happens when monopoly takes over. We know the techniques of monopoly. We have even seen it play the public benefactor—until it wins monopolistic control.

"One of the most effective means employed by Standard Oil Company to secure and maintain the large degree of monopoly which it possesses," wrote Mr. Justice Brandeis in 1913, "is the cut in prices to the particular customers, or in the particular markets of its competitors, while maintaining them at a higher level elsewhere." [3]

The monopolistic trusts of that unlamented era cut prices to kill off competition by companies that were less well financed. Once they were out of the way, prices were maintained at more profitable levels. Those very customers who greeted Standard Oil's lower prices as kindly benefactions from Wall Street suddenly found themselves shelling out sky-high prices—or else. All that was left for them to do after they had awakened to the reality of price-cutting was to say, with Kipling: "With all our most holy illusions knocked higher than Gilderoy's kite, we have had a jolly good lesson, and serves us jolly well right!"

Few Americans would exchange their present highly competitive economy for the system under which Standard Oil flourished. We have rejected a rapacious, uncontrolled "competition" that served only to kill real competition and create monopolies. We have done a good job of preventing the formation of monopolies in manufacturing. In the process, we have neglected the retail marketplace and may be allowing a new type of monopoly, a Retail Monopoly, to be formed there. It is right now taking shape, and it may already be too late to stop it.

"Yes, the independent retailer is doomed—as an independent, that is," says E. B. Weiss. By no later than 1973, Weiss predicts, 75 to 90 percent of all merchandise will be sold through huge chains.[4]

An exclusive club is forming. Like most exclusive clubs, it will be located in a big financial center like New York City, and its members will be the "fat cats" of industry. Their wealth and power, their influence over purchasing policies and thus over manufacturers, will determine both what you will buy and where you will buy it.

Business Week joins E. B. Weiss in making much the same predictions. There are, it says, "fewer stores to share the pie" and those stores that remain get bigger in size but decrease in number.

In fact, the number of stores serving each American has been dropping at a fantastic clip. Right now, hundreds of thousands of the nation's 1,547,000 proprietors of independent retail businesses are fighting what appears to be a losing battle against heavily financed armies. Ten years ago, Americans could shop in 100,000 radio-TV stores; today they have a choice of only 19,000. Fully 81,000 stores in this one field alone—about 8,000 a year or 700 a month—have been killed off.[5] The death rate is just about the same as the one J. Edgar Hoover gives for homicide in this country.

These casualties aren't only in the radio-TV field. They occur throughout your marketplace, no matter where you live. Representative Thomas M. Pelly of Washington reveals that businesses are failing at the rate of over 1,200 per day—50 an hour— "10 while I am talking to you," he told the assembled Congressmen.[6] Of the 4,752,000 business units in the United States, independent retailers—sole-proprietor stores—are the numerically largest single unit, 1,547,000 of almost 1,800,000 retailers. The effect of their failures is staggering.

If these paragraphs were read by some doctrinaire Communist in Moscow, he might easily come to the conclusion that the U.S.S.R. is indeed in a position to bury the United States economically. He'd cheer at Representative Pelly's statistics and at his reference to Tacoma, Washington, as "a virtual [retail] graveyard." [7] He'd note with amazement and delight that even New York City, with its high income and a tri-state megalopolis to service, has felt the impact of this creeping death. In 1950, its citizens could shop in 153,000 stores, but 10 years later the number had plummeted to 66,474 serving 8,000,000 people.[8]

Our Red reader would pop his eyes at testimony before the United States Senate that "small businessmen are dying at a rate topping anything since the Depression." [9] He would gasp at Small Business Administration figures that report that the failure rate is the highest since 1939, and he would goggle at Representative James Roosevelt's statement that 20 businesses go out of existence for each one whose death is recorded. "In other words," the Californian says, "it is a fair estimate that over 300,000 businesses went out of business last year alone." [10] With 1964 marking another 13,809 officially recorded bankruptcies, this would mean that an estimated 276,180 actually closed their doors in 1964. Despite the fact that this shows a decline over 1963, it remains a disturbing figure.

The Communist functionary would cheer at the news that within a dozen years (1947-1959) the birth rate for new stores in the U.S.A. dropped from 106.5 to 80.4 per 1,000 Americans. He would note statements by New York marketing authority Victor Lebow to the effect that "the small retailer lives in an atmosphere of catastrophe today" [11] and by Representative Ray Madden that "the American system of product distribution is in the process of being disintegrated . . . [and] steadily undermined." [12]

What conclusion might he come to? Certainly it might seem to him that the United States is hellbent for a new Great Depression, that income must be so low and sales so poor that shops are slamming shut their doors faster than Khrushchev was able to pound a table. And he would be dead wrong.

Income and sales have never been better. The gross national product rose to $623 billion during 1964 and may be expected to reach $655 billion in 1965; personal incomes are in excess of $500 billion, and consumer spending has reached $400 billion. Give or take a few million, retail sales stand at nearly $250 billion a year. The cash registers have never been busier.

Is there a paradox here? How can business be better than ever while businesses collapse faster than at any time since the thirties? How can retail sales be higher than they have ever been, while at the same time retailers apparently cannot make a living and survive?

The answer lies in what we have termed the shrinking marketplace. Just exactly what has been happening was explained very bluntly by Editor-in-Chief Nathaniel Schwartz of *The Discount Merchandiser*. In an editorial, he announced that "the most important trend in retailing in the U.S. today ... [is] *the trend toward concentration, with fewer and fewer stores— the bigger mass merchandising units—getting more and more of the shopper's spending dollar*." [13] [Author's italics.]

Here are some of the Census Bureau figures that Schwartz cites to support his statement:

- While grocery store sales rose from $24.7 billion to $43.7 billion between 1948 and 1958, 10,000 groceries *a year* were killed off, making 100,000 fewer stores in all. Big corporate chains pre-empted the field.
- As retail trade went up $69 billion in the entire retailing field, "the sales shift was to the bigger stores."
- Four percent of those stores, doing a yearly business of a half million dollars or more, controlled 44 percent of the total retail volume!

Thoughtful citizens are increasingly concerned. One of them is the President of the United States. On February 1, 1964, Lyndon B. Johnson told the Congress that "There are some 200,000 grocery stores, but we know that $1 out of every $2 spent for groceries goes to fewer than 100 corporate chains." E. B. Weiss says that 50 giant retail organizations will soon control 50 percent of the nation's retail volume in practically all merchandise. No

matter what you buy, half of it will be from this small number of
national chains and on their terms.

Others also peer into the crystal eight-ball to see the future
of the U.S. marketplace. Senator Vance Hartke says that
"the simple truth is that the basic competitive strength of the
American enterprise system is once again being challenged,
undermined, and eroded." [14] Congressman Pelly quotes discount
chains as saying that within 10 years *all* retailing in the country
will be controlled by fewer than 100 companies.[15] And Leroy
Pope of United Press International says "Discount store enthusiasts say their movement is going to take over 80 percent of
the retail business in the country before 1970." [16] *American
Stock Exchange Investor* magazine predicts that the huge discount combinations will control 90 percent of all retailing by
1970 and 50 billion of your shopping dollars by the end of the
century.[17] Says Sol W. Cantor, president of Interstate Department Stores, "Today we are seeing the formation of chains in
the discount industry which tomorrow will be the giants of
retailing." [18]

The trend is without question toward mergers and combinations, a movement that both in the short and in the long run
can be nothing but disastrous to the nation. That these mergers
may be tending toward monopoly (without necessarily violating
today's inadequate antitrust laws) is a fact that has, apparently,
escaped the Antitrust Division of the U.S. Department of Justice. Its staff, educated to see restraint of trade among manufacturers, often seem woefully behind the times. In the face of what
is going on in the marketplace, one would wish that the government department extended its action to the trend toward the new
"Retail Monopoly" as energetically as it has acted against monopolies in manufacturing. They do not do so, apparently, because
they do not understand the workings of a discount store. Backed
by various economists, theorists, and bureaucrats who defend discounting as "healthy competition," they think of the discounter
merely as an aggressive, imaginative entrepreneur, running rings
around the old fuddy-duddies who are regarded contemptuously

as managing "Mom and Pop stores." This ignorance works only to the advantage of the discounter. While the Justice Department watches for malefactions among manufacturers, the chains keep growing. This is not to say that this growth is in any way illegal, for much of it admittedly comes from internal growth and not via combinations and conspiracies that run afoul of existing laws. Yet we have seen how certain "modern merchandising practices," engaged in by many discounters, *do* have the effect of killing competition through price-cutting. This, in Justice Brandeis' words, leads to "monopoly."

Is this good? Is this for the public good? Are there benevolent monopolies? It seems a major national tragedy that the dangers inherent in this monopolistic growth are not apparent to many responsible persons in government, in education, and in the press. The voices raised to warn are throttled, and those courageous legislators who have addressed themselves with vigor to this problem are berated as being prophets of gloom and doom.

Yet there are still those who do speak out. A good many members of Congress are among them. They are liberals and conservatives alike, men like former Senator Hubert H. Humphrey and Senators Eugene McCarthy of Minnesota, Hugh Scott of Pennsylvania, William Proxmire of Wisconsin, A. S. Mike Monroney of Oklahoma, Daniel K. Inouye of Hawaii, Jennings Randolph of West Virginia, Frank Carlson of Kansas, Thruston B. Morton of Kentucky, Karl Mundt of South Dakota, Milton Young of North Dakota, and others. Together with many Representatives, they are concerned about the steamroller that is in the process of flattening competition in the marketplace. Other Americans, like Indiana University's Dr. Charles Mason Hewitt, Jr., have warned of this kind of rapacious throat-cutting. "Unrestrained competition creates monopoly," he said, ". . . the cards are stacked against the independent businessman, no matter how efficient he may be." [19]

By and large, that independent businessman *is* efficient. Those who charge him with being inefficient are those who consider the growth of discount chains to be an example of the rewards of efficiency, when that growth is often due—as we have seen—to other factors, including misconceptions on the part of the public. To cite just one example, a merchant of my acquaintance recently went out of business after 14 years of running a greeting-card and toy shop in his neighborhood. He was put out of business—driven out—not by a "more efficient" toy operation, but by discount centers that sold toys as bait for the rest of their stores. Because he specialized in toys, he was of course unable to subsidize losses sustained in selling them by high hidden profits on other merchandise. The discount center was able to do so. Toys that were advertised nationally on television proved to be irresistible bait. Of course such stores did not offer the shopper any service such as my friend did; shoppers had to hunt for their own toys at the discount center, stand in line with them at the checkout counter, and take them home without gift-wrapping. The independent merchant, on the other hand, served as a counselor and spent time with each customer, advising him as to the toys that were appropriate to various age levels. After that, he gift-wrapped the product and, of course, personally guaranteed satisfaction. Once the discounter appeared on the scene, however, shoppers stopped buying, for they now suspected my friend of being a thief who charged far too much. Nothing could be further from the truth. This merchant maintained an average 40 percent margin, and there were very few items on sale in his store that carried higher markups. The discount center, on the other hand, gave away toys at wholesale prices and made up its profits elsewhere, on items that carried sky-high margins. After a while, he closed up shop and went to work for someone else. "Independent retailing is dead," he says with bitterness. "So is individual initiative in America."

Today's marketplace penalizes the small retailer for honestly fulfilling the function of the retailer serving his community. In many communities, he is at the mercy of those discounters who are solely interested in the financial growth of their enterprises, the public interest be damned. This seems to me a completely reactionary, monopoly-building business philosophy and one that reflects thinking that is somewhat to the right, politically, of Torquemada. This type of rapacious, uncontrolled competition has been rejected by Americans resoundingly—except, apparently, in retailing.

"When the big get really big," said Vice President Hubert H. Humphrey while still a Senator, "they want to eat up the little fish." [20] There is not much that the small fish can do about it. Fighting the huge discount chains with their immense wealth and loss-leader promotions, says Humphrey, "is rather like playing in a poker game with a man who has Fort Knox, Kentucky, at his back door, and you are sitting there with the proceeds from a popcorn machine. You can put up a good show for a while, but, eventually, it gets a little rugged." [21]

More and more as a nation, we seem to champion the goals of the rich and powerful and to accept these goals as being in the best interests of our country. The small independent retailer and the manufacturer who supplies him are left unprotected against loss-leader price-cutting. On the other hand, many richer and more powerful retail chains are virtually immune from assault by the discount houses.

Big chain stores that sell their own products almost exclusively and manufacturers who sell direct to the public via door-to-door salesmen (e.g., Fuller Brush, Avon cosmetics) are protected against having their prices cut. Let us contrast this with the reality facing a small neighborhood bicycle-shop owner. He needs famous nationally advertised bicycles like Schwinn, but it is these very bikes that are so often used for loss leaders or to "bait-and-switch" the shopper. Not only is he faced with this unfair competition, but he is also faced with competition by *non*-discount chains that are completely insulated against attacks by discounters.

Who are these competitors and what brands do they sell? There's the J. C. Higgins bike: no one can use that as a loss leader or cut its retail price, because the make belongs to Sears, Roebuck and is sold through Sears, Roebuck outlets. There's the Hawthorne bike; that's sold through Montgomery Ward outlets and is also immune to price-cutting. There's the Western Flyer, which is sold in the 400 Western Auto-owned stores, and is similarly protected. There's the Hiawatha bicycle, sold in Gamble-Skogmo's stores; it also is immune.

What does all this signify? It means that the U.S. Government seems to maintain two standards regarding protection against price-cutting. A chain like Sears, Roebuck is permitted to sell its own brands exclusively in its own outlets, making it impossible for almost any other store to carry these same makes, and thereby insulating itself from loss-leader price-cutting. In this case, the manufacturer, producing exclusively for Sears, Roebuck, can in effect "maintain" his retail price; if an independent manufacturer who operates through independent retailers did that, or even tried to do so, he would be blasted for "illegal price-fixing." Even—or especially—in today's "affluent" age, the rich get richer, while the poor go bankrupt.

The Government argues loftily that *any* retailer can, of course, protect himself from price-cutting, by selling his own brand of bicycle. This is nonsense; a small neighborhood store can't afford to do so, doesn't have the many to go into exclusive manufacture, and absolutely *must* depend on famous national brands to make a living. Significantly, a Federal judge recently agreed. On December 29, 1964, Judge Perry of the U.S. District Court for Northern Illinois pointed out that the U.S. government was trying to penalize Arnold, Schwinn & Co. (which he referred to as "a microscopic Lilliputian") for not being able to use the marketing methods of giants such as Sears, Roebuck and General Motors. Sears can maintain its own retail prices by opening its own stores, while GM does the same by franchising exclusive dealers, but manufacturers like Schwinn are thrown to the cut-price wolves. Judge Perry rejected this economic thinking, so prevalent in the Justice Department. In doing so, he offered what we may hope to be a landmark decision. If applied elsewhere as well, it may reverse much of the chaos in the marketplace. It may prove to be a new civil rights decision, for retailers. Certainly it shows a refreshing and enlightened concern for the economically weak, offering them at least some of the rights of the powerful. (It might be noted, in this connection, that Henry Peters, the Negro Washington, D.C., pharmacist quoted earlier in this book, made much the same point in testimony before Congress. Legislation aimed at ending economic abuses sustained by independent pharmacists, he said, would be an essential part of a real civil rights bill, since opportunities for Negroes in business are at present even worse than they are for whites. If the Negro is to achieve economic equality, then the business climate must be changed, so that it at least makes sense once again for a man to open up a store and go into business for himself.)

What of the public? Is it well served when cut-price or "schlock merchandise" retailers use quality brands as loss leaders? Briefly, to be sure, there is the benefit of the cut price itself. Soon, however, this can prove illusory. Consumers, for example, are hardly served by letting the discounter sell bikes as loss leaders. For one thing, such a discounter is often unwilling to service the bicycle. "A bicycle is a vehicle," says Ray Burch of Schwinn. "As such, it needs to be properly assembled. In use it requires adjustment and repair. This is particularly true since bicycles are used primarily by children who often inadvertently abuse them. Moreover, as bicycles have become more complicated, the compelling need for proper adjustment when new and in use has gradually increased." The small independent retailer is prepared to provide such service. He is trained to do it. "But he cannot survive only on charges for adjusting gearshifts, tightening brakes, repairing tires, and fixing this and that," says Burch.[22] The great chains that are not bicycle dealers *per se* sell bikes in cartons and often couldn't care less about servicing them.

Perhaps there are people who think that a discount store that has killed off the local bicycle retailers will install a bicycle service department. This is not often the case; the discounter may well abandon selling bicycles altogether at cut prices, because a loss leader is valueless if the cut price cannot be compared to standard prices in standard stores.

Watches are other items that need proper care and servicing. Frequently discounters who sell watches fail to entrust this task to trained jewelers. The man waiting on you in a discount store jewelry department, says Leonard Sadow of Longines-Wittnauer, is often a fast-talking salesman who is interested only in the "spiffs" he collects as bonuses for selling "promotional" rather than "fine" watches. Such a discounter does carry a few fine watches, using them, says Sadow, "to give the impression of broad stock." These tactics have cut sharply into the retail jeweler's sales. Watches used to account for thirty percent of his income; today this portion of his income has dropped as much as fifteen percent. Yet discount stores are not equipped to retail watches properly, Sadow claims. They cannot and should not "be handled like a box of crackers in a supermarket." When they are, he says, customers just don't end up with "a satisfactory long-service time-piece."

Of course the customer still goes back to the retail jeweler—often to have him repair the watches he bought at a discount store. Too often he needs this service shortly after he makes his purchase. "The regular retail jeweler keeps his watch merchandise clean, adjusted, and well oiled and times the watch to the customer's personal habits," says Sadow. "He is, by experience and training, the proper distributor of good and fine watches. Many cut price outlets are not equipped nor are they interested in maintaining their watch inventory so that customers receive a properly operating watch." [23]

Just like the bicycle store, the independent jeweler cannot exist only on repairs and adjustment; when he closes his shop, where do we go? When we buy cameras, toasters, electric irons, lawnmowers, or major appliances like kitchen ranges, refrigerators, freezers, or washers and dryers, we require service and adjustments—and we require them, as we shall see presently, much sooner today than we did years ago. The independent retailer provided this essential ingredient; the discounter by and large does not.

Those discounters who do provide service sometimes charge

plenty for it. A lady I know in New York City recently bought an electric broiler from a Manhattan discounter, found it "smoking like a furnace" a week later, and had to bring it back for repairs. Their adjustments turned out to be unsatisfactory and, all in all, she took it back to the discounter four times. Each time, she was charged $1.50, and, by the time the broiler seemed as though it might broil without incinerating the apartment, she had paid six dollars for repairs. Her "discount" had disappeared—it had literally gone up in smoke. She would have been better served had she bought this small kitchen appliance at a neighborhood hardware store, where the sales clerk is often a trained repairman. Almost any neighborhood merchant is prepared to stand behind the goods he sells; many a customer has found that his discounter backs off from them as fast as he can.

The Watermelon Patch

"These characters are like a kid getting in the watermelon patch," said Vice President Hubert Humphrey of discounting in 1962, while still a United States Senator. "They come in and stick their hand inside the heart of the watermelon, take it out, and run. That is generally what a discounter does. He comes in, sets up his establishment, contributes nothing to anybody, including the Community Chest, the church, or the town, and even fights over his taxes. He comes in and tries to pick out the juicy part of the market, disrupts the normal practice of the community, and after he has made what he thinks is a killing, he gets out and runs." Humphrey, whose family owns a drugstore in Minnesota, adds, "Well, we can't do that. We are people that have our young born in these towns and bury our dead there and have our business there."

The Humphrey family has had its experiences with price-cutting over the years. Each Wednesday, young Hubert would be sent out by his father to make the rounds of the chain stores in town, to see how far drug items had been cut. The father then would always meet this competition, by cutting the price a few pennies further. "May I say how we were able to do it?" asks Humphrey. "I did not get paid any money, my brother did not get paid any money, my sister did not get paid any money, my father did not get paid any money. We worked sixteen hours a day, and I slept in the store. I do not like that. But in order to compete, that is what we had to do. It's a nice way to get experience—*period*. I did it for about eight years and I'm not for it."[24]

That might have worked in Hubert Humphrey's youth; faced with today's discounters, it may be necessary to work even longer hours to survive. The national sales average per day for independent drugstores is under $300, while cut-rate drug operators like Charles Fort of Baton Rouge, La., do $20,000 a day in volume.[25]

Fort's Food Town Ethical Pharmacies, it should be noted, claims not to be a discount operation, although it cuts prices and is apparently well known as a place where customers can get many drugs "off list." Says Fort, "Even though all our prices are 10 and 50 percent lower . . . we do not employ the term 'discount house' because, as a mass retailer, our prices are high enough to provide a very good profit before taxes." He cites average drugstores as doing $400,000 a year; "mass retailers and discount houses", $50,000,000 a year, and his own operation, $2,200,000 a year. A cut-price drugstore doing that volume certainly seems to be a "mass retailer" if not a "discount house"; Fort's criteria seem meaningless, for they suggest that a discount house can be identified by its inability to make a very good profit —a fact that the testimony of discounters contradicts.

Will the public find its needs answered, shopping in a few giant chains, when these are so often characterized by reduced inventories, high hidden markups, and lack of service?

The manager of a local branch of such a chain, says Senator Thomas H. Kuchel of California, "does not go down to the store at 3 A.M. to fill the prescription, or grant credit for groceries, or gasoline, or hardware items until a man can get another job. The local small businessman, an active and highly-regarded member of the community, does." [26] Even were he so inclined, there are many discount store managers who can not grant such credit or offer such services; they are often merely order-takers whose policies are set by mass-merchandising experts, a thousand or more miles away and too remote to know local needs.

It is interesting that such "Lilliputian" independent retailers as Nessie Nides, the Humphrey drugstore family, and others are regarded as "special interests" by many discounters. Numerically, they may form a large bloc, but in terms of power they are picayune and pitiful. The spectacle in Congress, where many discounters acted threatened by small retailers, seems to me perfectly ludicrous; it is as though the old Standard Oil Company shed tears, claiming to be at the mercy of the small gasoline dealers it was crushing. Furthermore, the discount industry seems in no danger, since even as numerous a group as the independent retailers have not succeeded in moving Washington, D.C., to come to their aid. Counting dependents, the nation's 1,800,000 retailers probably total 8-10 million persons and constitute the largest depressed population group in the U.S. today. If they all lived, say, in West Virginia, we may be certain that so large a number of voters would warrant immediate Federal aid. But they are scattered from Walla Walla to Miami, their voice is dispersed, and the fact that they themselves count as 10 million *consumers* is forgotten. In a time when all eyes are riveted on *Fortune's* list of 500 biggest corporations, they are too small to matter. We may only be moving toward the Great Society, but we surely are one already that worships size.

Non-Merchandising Retailers

One of the more disturbing consequences of "elephantiasis" in retailing is that, as many chains grow to near-monstrous proportions, serving the public in a retail capacity may assume second place. "The management of finances is becoming more and more important to some retail giants than the management of merchandising," writes E. B. Weiss in his analysis of the discount industry. "The promotion of real estate is becoming more and more important than the promotion of merchandise. The acquisition of other companies for corporate profit is becoming more and more important than the acquisition of merchandise for resale. Naturally, the executives responsible for these nonmerchandising functions move up on the organizational chart."

"Juicy net profit growth," continues Weiss, comes from nonmerchandising functions such as real estate speculation. Chains concentrating on financial management and not on merchandising are growing into huge, diversified, corporate empires. "The development of the holding company concept in mass retailing—which is a strong trend—involves corporate maneuvers that can throw off extraordinarily large net profits primarily through the exchange of pieces of paper." The future, according to this authority, will come not in the field of merchandising, but through acquisitions, mergers, and the holding company development. "Expansion," says Weiss, "must be financed. Big expansion demands big financing. And expansion by our retail giants will be big; very big . . ." [27]

The future the consumer faces seems less happy. As chains become super-chains, he is not likely to benefit. Like a character from a Kafka play, he all too often feels that there is nowhere for him to turn to seek relief. He is in a nightmarish dilemma and his only hope is that the nation may yet wake up in time.

It has yet to do so. The House Committee on Interstate and Foreign Commerce warns that, if the trend toward consolidation gets any bigger, "we shall find ourselves faced with the biggest concentration of retailing in the hands of a few giant corporations that this country has ever seen." [28] If this comes about, one witness told the Senate, "free enterprise in the United States will suffer a total eclipse of freedom." [29]

Those Americans who have been cheering the "new retailing revolution" will then have to carry a large share of the blame. Unfortunately, that group includes a large percentage of us consumers, seduced to our own destruction by monopoly's age-old device of the price cut.

9

Satellite Plants and the Quality Quandary

> There is nothing in this world that some man can-
> not make a little worse and sell a little cheaper and
> people who consider price only are that man's law-
> ful prey.
>
> —JOHN RUSKIN

ONE of the most difficult things in the world is to build up a market in as vast a country as the United States. It is not enough for a manufacturer to advertise his wares nationally; they must be *available* from coast to coast before such a market is his, and putting together so large a network of retail outlets takes years and a lot of money. The days when the man with the better mousetrap could sit back and wait are long gone.

Two friends of mine recently found this out the hard way. In the process, they learned to their consternation how discounting affects the marketing of new products.

These friends had perfected a product to be sold to professional and amateur artists, to anyone indeed who worked with oil paints. They incorporated themselves, established a small office, had containers for their product produced and labels designed and printed, bought a stock of the necessary chemicals, began production, and invested whatever they could scrape together in advertising. That was not much, of course, and they soon gave up a third of their business to a friend who put up

$5,000. With this amount—which seemed to them a sizeable bankroll—they started trying to sell.

In the beginning, they pounded the pavements, stopping personally at artists' supply shops, paint shops, and hardware outlets, and sold two or three containers here, three or four there. This failed even to pay their overhead, despite the fact that neither of them drew a salary. They realized quickly that they would have to sell a large volume for the business to get on even a modest footing, and this meant getting national distribution. There simply weren't enough customers in any one area to let them start small and build slowly.

They tried at first to get a national distributor to carry their product, but none would handle it until it was nationally advertised. They waited patient hours in the anterooms of the big chain buyers in Manhattan; they buttonholed manufacturers' representatives at trade conventions in New York, and they sat in the waiting rooms of Macy's and Gimbel's.

Almost everyone wanted only nationally advertised products. Finally, they went to a few of the big discount chains. They said, "Get it established first," and indicated that they might then place huge orders—at a price that they, the discounters, would dictate. My friends understood this to mean that this price would be quite low so that the product could be marked as "discounted" but still provide the chains with a good profit. At the same time, the few dozen independent stores that already stocked the product in New York warned that they would drop the item if it were sold in discount houses.

Meanwhile, their expenses mounted. The landlord, the utilities companies, the printers, the chemical and packaging suppliers all wanted their bills paid promptly. The two new manufacturers scraped up some more money, paid their bills, and quit trying. Today, one cannot buy their product anywhere. It seems a shame, because it was a good one.

Anyone who tries to launch a new product today quickly learns that almost no one wishes to take a chance any more on something that is not established. Conventional merchants find they can't afford to take the chance; most discounters won't take it as a matter of policy.

The cultivation of a national market is an expensive process. Manufacturers, working through wholesalers and jobbers, will very carefully build up the sales interest and support of a large number of retailers. Generally speaking, manufacturers prefer to market through many independent, small retailers, rather than through a handful of large accounts. The reason is obvious: they are less at the mercy of any individual. If they sell only through, say, two large chains and one drops their products, the manufacturers feel the pinch more sharply than they would if their sales were more broadly based. At the same time, widespread distribution through thousands of small stores benefits the economy, provides local employment, and assures support of new product development.

"A system which includes hundreds of thousands of independent retailers protects the consumers against monopolistic tendencies and resultant high prices," said Vice President Hubert H. Humphrey in 1963, while still a Senator. "I think that just speaks for itself. When you have a large number of outlets for products, you obviously stimulate commerce, you stimulate consumer desires, you stimulate the flow of goods, and you obviously protect what we call the competitive enterprise system. . . *

To get these thousands of retailers, the manufacturer may begin by advertising in trade journals; he may employ salesmen and demonstrators; he will certainly supply merchants with sales aids, educational and promotional materials, and display matter. In addition, he advertises nationally and usually underwrites part of the retailer's advertising when it features his product. Longines-Wittnauer Watch Company, of New York City, has spent more than $35 million advertising its watches in postwar years. Manufacturers of other products, for which there is a

---

* *Congressional Record—Senate*, 1963, p. 1968.

greater and more frequent demand, spend much more than that.

There is, however, one more thing that a manufacturer must do to assure broad national distribution for his product: *he must make it profitable to the retailer*. He must set a price that offers the retailer a fair markup, yet is low enough to make the product competitive.

All this takes years, often decades. When the process has succeeded, the manufacturer has a market; the retailer can make a living, and the consumer is able to buy the product.

It can all end overnight. The destruction of this elaborately wrought distribution network is the work of a moment. Sunbeam Mixmasters provide a number of illustrations.

• In 1956, Utah sanctioned price-cutting by making it impossible for a manufacturer to enforce his product's retail price. *Within seven months*, the number of dealers handling Sunbeam products dropped from 1,167 to 303.

• In Missouri, where the same thing happened, the number of dealers dropped from 2,125 to 334. Of those remaining, *four percent* had captured *eighty percent* of the remaining market!

• In New York City, factory sales dropped 17.68 percent in a year, after a price war handed three giant retailers 74.1 percent of the market within ten weeks! [1]

Sunbeam is no exception; price wars, price-cutting, and discounting can just as easily wipe out the market for a manufacturer of underwear. T. F. Southgate, Jr., vice president of P. H. Hanes Knitting Co., Winston-Salem, North Carolina, in 1962, and now sales manager of Quality Mills, Inc., of New York, says that a similar thing happened to Hanes a few years ago.

This price war started in San Antonio, Texas. A "closed-door" discount house (to which one needs a "membership card") obtained some Hanes underwear and advertised it at radically cut prices. "Other retailers in the area were forced to meet this competition," Southgate says. The defenders of discounting will say that this development is to the good, since the public benefits when discount houses "drive prices down." Let's see what happens in actual fact.

"In time," says Southgate, "because of our lack of control

in this market, practically every good account in the city dropped Hanes underwear. We had spent many years of hard work and a great deal of money in trying to build up a market for our products in San Antonio, only to see it all go down the drain because of unscrupulous action on the part of a newcomer to the retail field. I might add that after the discounter had accomplished his purpose of using our brand as a loss leader, and after other retailers had seen fit to drop the brand, the discounter discarded our brand and then turned to another well-known advertised brand seeking to do the same thing with it." [2]

Senator Hugh Scott of Pennsylvania describes what happens in the process: "The promotional efforts of the resellers dwindle and wane, for the sale of the product has been made no longer profitable for them. Reaction to destructive discounter competition at the retail level is varied. Some retailers drop the line; others give it less display space and less sales effort; others put the price-cut item under the counter and concentrate on the sale of not yet price-raided substitute items. Even retailers who merely attempt to maintain a retail price that covers their cost of the product come to be regarded unfairly by their customers as profiteers. The consumer often comes to feel that the manufacturer has been greedily overpricing his product, while the incentive of independent resellers to continue merchandising the product has been destroyed. In both cases clearly the goodwill of the public for the product is destroyed. In any event, at sharply varying retail prices, confidence in and demand for the product will not long prevail. A retailer will not continue to function as a mere displayer of the unfairly discredited product, as a mere showcase, a convenient backdrop, against which the price-baiting discounter can perform . . ." [3]

What's in a Name?

The dictionary defines *despoil* as "to strip of what is of value" and, in this sense, the price-cutters of today despoil the marketplace as ferociously as any Viking ever did the coasts of England 1,200 years ago. The thing of value that is wrested away in

these assaults upon products is, more than anything else, a product's brand name or trademark.

What is this that it is of such importance? Shakespeare said: "Who steals my purse steals trash; . . . but he that filches from me my good name robs me of that which not enriches him, and makes me poor indeed." This applies to today's manufacturers as well as it did to *Othello*. For it is the trade name that the manufacturer has carefully built up over the years and that his network of retailers serves. If Sunbeam produces a new product, it does not have to build up a new retail network to market it; Hanes may come out with a new type of men's underwear, but its retailers are prepared to stock this as well. Advertising sells a product, to be sure, but one of its main purposes is to instill confidence in the brand name.

Companies such as King-Seeley spent years and a great deal of money trying to protect their brand—or trade—names. In the case of King-Seeley, the manufacturer was unsuccessful, and the company's Thermos Bottle became a generic term and no longer needs to be capitalized. The makers of Kleenex, Jeep, Technicolor, Laundromat, Pyrex, Fiberglas, Formica, Dacron, Orlon, Teletype, Dixie Cup, Levis, Vaseline, Kodak, Coca-Cola, Frigidaire, Victrola, and Polaroid all know the value of a trade name; all fight to protect their right to the names they established. They know that these names are vital to their success.

The discounter knows this also. It is no accident that trademarked, famous brand-name merchandise is used as loss leaders. How could a store establish a discounting image if it offered *unknown* merchandise at cut prices? To be attractive, the bait must be properly set and the lure must twinkle.

Today, there is very little that a manufacturer can do to protect his brand name from being despoiled by loss-leader operations. Regulatory agencies in Washington watch such moves carefully. Sometimes they act as though the manufacturer sells his own good name to the retailer along with the dishwasher or pair of socks the store has bought. In 1936, the United States Supreme Court answered this claim in its *Old Dearborn* decision (299 U.S. 183): "We are here dealing not with a commodity alone, but with a commodity plus the brand or trademark which it bears as evidence of its origin and of the quality of the commodity for which the brand or trademark stands. Appellants [retailers] own the commodity, they do not own the mark or the goodwill that the mark symbolizes. And goodwill is property in a very real sense, injury to which, like injury to any other species of property, is a proper subject for legislation."

The benefits flowing from a brand economy used to be apparent to most U.S. economists and market analysts; today, ironically, their advantages are more recognized abroad, where brand names are in the process of being built up. Thus, even a Soviet Russian economist, V. A. Nikiforov, points out that trademarks force competing manufacturers "to undertake measures to improve the quality of their own [products]" and generally raise "the quality of production." In line with that statement, the U.S.S.R. currently is reported to have about 50 different brands of radios and phonographs, 35 of TV sets, and 20 of refrigerators.[4] Where they seem to be building up a brand-name economy, we in the U.S.A. are letting many discount practices tear ours down. And it is all being done in the name of free enterprise and competition!

When manufacturers find their brand names despoiled and their markets raided, they need to turn elsewhere for profits or go out of business. Often they decide that, being unable to lick a discounter, they must join him. John A. Gosnell, general counsel for the National Small Business Association, Washington, D.C., actually predicts that famous brand-name manufacturers who today do a side business of supplying many discounters with private-label and off-brand merchandise "may be facing the decision of whether to abandon their nationally advertised trademarks."[5] Such a decision might, for example, be forced upon a manufacturer whose profits have been reduced by the reduction of his retail outlets; by dropping his trademark, he would be able to save the expense of advertising nationally and he would no longer have to stand behind his products. When manufacturers begin to produce for the big discount chains, they soon become captives. *Home Furnishings Daily* reports that one big chain buys enough "to justify national-brand manufacturers making special models" to its specifications. These, says Earl Lifshey in his column, are sold under the manufacturer's *regular* national-brand label. The specifications are, all too often, much lower. "And while some manufacturers—G.E., for instance—decline to go in for that sort of thing," Lifshey adds, "the potential volume is so big many can't really ignore it." [6]

The FTC's "Fashion Show"

An example of what may happen was provided by a 1961 action brought by the U.S. Federal Trade Commission against a leading discount department store chain, three independent retailers, and ten clothing manufacturers. The matter is of interest to the consumer and pertinent to this book in that it shows how the FTC acts in cases involving the public interest.

The FTC charges accused all parties of entering into "an understanding, agreement, combination and conspiracy between and among themselves," allegedly to "deceive and mislead the purchasing public or cause the purchasing public to be deceived and misled through false and deceptive advertising and misrepresentations."

According to the FTC, the alleged conspiracy worked this way:

Three fashionable men's clothing retail stores on the West Coast agreed to let the department store chain purchase and resell a small quantity of men's furnishings that the chain had actually bought from the three shops. It was agreed that this merchandise could be resold by the chain with the labels of the fashionable shops attached.

The chain then allegedly entered into separate agreements with the three shops, regarding additional merchandise. This merchandise had "purportedly" been ordered by the fashionable shops from the manufacturers involved in the complaint. These agreements, said the complaint, allowed the chain also to resell this other merchandise with the labels of the three shops attached.

Subsequently, the chain allegedly entered into agreements with the manufacturers listed in the complaint, ordering men's clothing made to its own specifications and arranging for the manufacturers to attach the fashionable shops' labels into this merchandise. It then advertised this merchandise for sale, as though the merchandise had all been sold at higher prices by the three shops. Actually, the FTC charged, only the small amount originally purchased by the chain had been stocked by the three fashionable stores; most of the merchandise had never been stocked or offered at these shops and, therefore, the "Original Prices" as claimed by the chain in its ads were never applicable to this merchandise.

Just what did the chain offer in its ads? According to the FTC charges, which provided three sample newspaper ads, it claimed that "hand-tailored suits" originally priced by the three fashionable shops at $95-$135 could now be bought "only" at the chain's outlets for $46-$56. It claimed that "men's deluxe sport jackets" priced originally at $55-$75 could be bought for $21.97-$29.97. It claimed that shirts originally priced at $6.95-$12.95 could now be bought "only" at the chain's outlets for $3.99-$5.99. The advertisements, as the FTC reprinted them in its complaint, used such language as "the finest men's apparel ... millionaire's menswear sale ... luxurious dress shirts." The ads also said, "You see the original labels and price tags ... you get this luxury apparel at sensational ... savings!"

Such ads, the FTC charged, tended to mislead and deceive the public into "the erroneous and mistaken belief that the said statements and representations were true and into the purchase of substantial quantities" of this merchandise. The ads also, said the FTC, "unfairly diverted" a lot of business to the chain and its manufacturers and thereby damaged competition. The technique involved consisted of advertising fictitious high "original" prices and thereby offering the public big, but meaningless, savings.

It certainly would be very tempting to buy $135 suits bearing the labels of well-known, fashionable retail shops for a low bargain price of $56. Customers responding to those ads had good reason to be delighted with the "discounts" involved; after all, they could (as the ads proclaimed) "see the original labels and price tickets."

This case was ultimately disposed of by means of a "consent order" under which the chain, the three fashionable retailers, and the manufacturers agreed to "cease and desist" from such practices. It should be noted that none of the respondents in the case—that is, none of those charged by the FTC—ever admitted (or, for that matter, denied) the allegations. They simply agreed to stop doing things that they never agreed they had done in the first place.

Some charges, however, are tried in court and thus become part of the public record. To cite one example:

District Attorney Frank S. Hogan of New York City recently charged a number of other manufacturing executives with perjury in connection with a similar case, this one relating to S. Klein, the big Manhattan cut-price department store. In 1961, the Better Business Bureau of Metropolitan New York questioned some Columbus Day Sale advertisements, in which Klein's offered for sale clothes bearing the labels of a "renowned Broadway clothier" at reduced prices. The merchandise carried the price tag and label of Phil Kronfeld of Broadway and 49th Street, New York. BBB told D.A. Hogan that much of this clothing had *not* come from Kronfeld's store, and had been shipped to S. Klein directly by various manufacturers, *with* the Kronfeld label sewn in. When a Grand Jury summoned executives from the men's clothing manufacturing companies involved, these executives denied the charges. They claimed they did not know their merchandise was meant for Klein's and also insisted that the Phil Kronfeld store, not S. Klein's own buyer, had selected the merchandise.

It was the opinion of the District Attorney and of the Grand Jury that these denials were lies, and that purchase orders presented by some of the witnesses, which purported to have been made by Kronfeld, were phony. Eight executives were subsequently indicted and arrested for perjury, and five of them were also accused of forgery and of presenting forged evidence to the Grand Jury. As of this writing, six have pleaded guilty and been given suspended sentences; one is awaiting trial. The charge against one has been dismissed. (It's interesting to note that one of the defendants listed in the indictments was the secretary of one of the companies that signed a consent order in the FTC case mentioned earlier.)

S. Klein itself was not charged in any way; the perjury convictions of the manufacturers' executives made it impracticable for the District Attorney's office to investigate the affair further by calling upon these executives as witnesses.

Klein's itself was in trouble on another occasion in connection with an advertisement of May 31, 1963, which offered as a "Special—just 7 flawless 1 carat diamonds" with "14 karat gold mounting of your choice at no extra cost," all for $542. The Jewelry Department of Klein's was a leased department, run by another corporation. Following the purchase of one of the diamonds advertised, S. Klein and the corporation that ran the Jewelry Department, together with two of that corporation's personnel, were charged with violation of section 421 of the Penal Code of New York, on a count of untrue and misleading advertising. The charge against the leased department and its personnel was dismissed because the ad appeared under the name of S. Klein, and it was felt that there was not enough evidence to show that the others had authorized or even knew about the ad. A trial took place in January, 1964, and a decision was handed in February, 1964. The verdict: Klein's was guilty. It was found that the diamond advertised as 1 karat was in fact 3 points short of 1 karat. A $50.00 fine was imposed.

Unknown Quantities

The destruction of a manufacturer's national retail network does not inevitably lead him to enter into arrangements with discounters. Some manufacturers resist this energetically. One such manufacturer, for example, used to produce a high-quality slide projector. "It had all the fine reputation that they have been putting into their optical lines for years," says Leon Hartman, who operated a camera store at 126 E. 44 Street, New York City. He and other camera retailers stocked the projector and sold it by the thousands.

As Hartman related it before Congress, discounters then descended on the market. Manufacturers who were the captives of discount houses cranked out cheap slide projectors and the company had the choice of lowering its own quality standards to meet that price competition, or quitting. It meant, says Hartman, "putting in inferior components." The manufacturer, Hartman reports, "simply said, 'Nothing doing.' They said they were going out of the slide-projector business and that is exactly what happened." [9]

Others, who do not wish to associate their own names with lower quality line products, resort to boosting their declining independent retail sales by supplying stores with off-brand or private-label merchandise. The use of such merchandise by the big chains is steadily increasing. Their rapid expansion, their desire to nail down the best locations across the country, and their feverish policy of capturing retail markets through price-cutting have in many cases used up much of the profits made in their formative years.

Said Korvette's Jack Schwadron: "Our profitability has been hampered by the rapidity with which we have opened new stores. But we have finally been able to build the kind of base from which we can develop profitably into a nationwide company." To do so, says *The New York Times*, Korvette intends to concentrate on soft goods, "whose gross-profit margins outdistance that of hard goods." [10]

"There was a time, long before World War II, when retailers went in for private brands primarily so that they could have something to promote at a special low price during a sale," writes Earl Lifshey in *Home Furnishings Daily*. "In those days, no self-respecting buyer would think of murdering the markup on regular national-brand merchandise. But now . . . the No. 1 reason for private brands is . . . to provide the profit which has become so extremely elusive on the deeply price-cut national-brand products." [11] His observation is shared by others as well. J. Gordon Dakins, executive vice president of the National Retail Merchants Association, also points out the fantastic proliferation of private and off-brands, stressing that they offer higher profits.[12] And the trade press regularly reports on store buyers shopping the wholesale markets, looking for those off-brands that so conveniently offer big profits.

Goodyear Tire & Rubber Co., for example, according to *Business Week*, "fought the private label trend by jumping into that business with both feet." To do so, Goodyear uses its Kelly-Springfield Tire Co. subsidiary, which allows it to protect its own Goodyear name. *Business Week* estimates that four out of every ten replacement tires sold by all tire manufacturers carry a private label.[14] The number of brands was over 100 in 1963.

The private-label business is one that some manufacturers or retailers do not like to talk about. When Marion M. Brown of *Home Furnishings Daily* surveyed private labels in the bedding industry, he asked, "Are we opening up a Pandora's box?" and added that those who would allow themselves to be interviewed on the subject all asked not to be quoted by name. "Most producers seem eager to sidestep the private brand issue," he writes.[13]

It is easy to see why some manufacturers are leery about talking about this end of their business: the private-label items that they produce for a discounter must meet his price requirements and, therefore, may be of cheaper construction. "The purchaser thinks he's getting a bargain—but he's getting no more than he pays for," says King Features' Ralph de Toledano.[15] Some manufacturers who produce off-brand or private-label merchandise may not, of course, be in a position to stand behind their products. Much of this merchandise is produced abroad, particularly in the Far East, and a customer who is dissatisfied with his Chinese junk may have to go to Hong Kong to get satisfaction. At the same time, it is obvious that there is much good-quality and even high-quality off-brand and private-label merchandise available. Such is certainly the case with highly reputable retail organizations. As a matter of fact, private-label goods of this kind have often become equivalents to national brands, with all the characteristics of such brands. They are nationally advertised, produced consistently over many years, and are tested carefully. More importantly, they are recognizable to the general public. Often they are cheaper in price than equivalent national brands made by independent manufacturers. Some may even evolve into true national brands and no longer be sold exclusively by the retail organization that created them in the first place. Macy's, for example, recently announced that it plans to market its own label merchandise in other-than-Macy's outlets. Similarly, the off-brands and private-label merchandise offered by some major discounting chains may represent good value for the actual price being charged; often, however, this price is regarded erroneously by the customer as being a discount and, where it is listed as a low comparable value, it is difficult, if not impossible, for the consumer to evaluate it accurately.

There's still another type of merchandise that many discount stores sell; this is what the trade calls "schlock merchandise" or "borax." It is the kind of low-quality goods sold in a lot of bargain basements and low-end outlets in poor neighborhoods. Some of it comes from abroad and is distinctly inferior to domestic merchandise. Isadore Barmash (now with *The New York Times*) pointed out earlier, while with the *New York Herald Tribune*, that some "soft goods discounters" get their wares from the very same suppliers who feed the bargain basements; such discounters have expanded the bargain basement "to full-store scope." [16] Many a discount department store, Professor Edgar H. Gault of Michigan University wrote in *Michigan Business Review*, "is not really a discount house or a department store, nor is it a combination of the two. Actually it is a soft line, self-service store with more of the operating characteristics of a grocery supermarket than any other type of retailer. But the self-imposed name has customer appeal. It suggests the low prices of the discount house and the wide selection and services of a typical department store much as 'Ivory' suggests purity in soap. Therein is the retail illusion. . . ."

Gault goes on to say that the soft lines handled by such a discount department store "will remind the older generation of the bargain basement of department stores and other bargain and cut-rate stores of the 1920s and 1930s. The merchandise is cheap in quality and cheap in price. . . ." [17]

Many discount stores, then, are merely bargain basements expanded to full-store scope, selling low-quality "schlock" merchandise while drawing the public in with a few cut-rate national brands offered as loss-leader bait. Private labels may assist such stores in making up the loss sustained in that bait department.

Private brands also offer another advantage. Their use discourages price comparisons, or comparison shopping. Customers may lose faith in discounting if they find that the brand-name products at a discount store can be bought for the same price, or even less, at a conventional store. No such comparison shopping is possible on private-label merchandise such as soft goods and appliances. No real evaluation of comparative quality is feasible for the average shopper.

In order to make the private discounter labels more acceptable to the public, the discounting industry recently took steps to "certify" them. After undergoing tests at the hands of agencies approved by the discounters' own trade association, the National Association of Mass Merchandisers, products can receive an NAMM "certified quality" stamp. As of now, this program seems to cover only about 60 drug department sundries and vitamins, but NAMM reportedly plans to extend it to cover hard goods as well. [18] Whether this device will provide customers with safeguards remains to be seen.

"Fill-in" merchandise is another type sold at many discount stores. Joe Stone, the Manhattan Assistant District Attorney who has spent many years tracking down and prosecuting consumer frauds, tells me this is often the specialty of many of the kind of stores that resell clothes from conventional retail stores. Such a discounter may arrange to buy end-of-season and other discontinued merchandise from well-known retailers; he advertises and sells them at bargain prices, making the point in his ads that they carry the labels of famous shops. The consumer, of course, is delighted; what he does not know about is the practice of "fill-ins". It is not unusual.

What may happen is this: a discounter finds that he can't afford a big-scale and profitable promotion if he sells only the merchandise he got from the well-known shops. He needs more volume—in short, more merchandise to sell. And so he makes an arrangement with the shop to let him buy additional merchandise that the shop never stocked, with the label of the shop sewn in. In some cases, he may pay the shop a premium for the goods he actually bought from it; the *quid pro quo* is that the shop lets him sew their labels into the goods it never stocked. In such a case, of 5,000 garments bearing the store's label and now sold "at discount," only 500 or so may have ever seen the inside of the store involved; the other 4,500 are misleading. In one case of which Joe Stone has personal knowledge, the knavery went even further. The cut-price operator involved used one of his manufacturers' warehouses as a "depot" and returned to it any unsold garments after the special sale ended. There the fraudulent labels were removed and new fraudulent labels, bearing another famous store's name, were sewn in, to be featured in a forthcoming sale.

Another case involving Joe Stone's office concerned a cut-price operation on New York's 14th Street. Now out of business, this enterprise had over the years operated under several names. The Better Business Bureau of Metropolitan New York complained to the D.A.'s office that it had been unsuccessful in trying to stop the store from making false "bait" claims in its ads. Assistant D.A. Stone and a detective visited the store management and warned that such practices would not be tolerated. After giving elaborate assurances that they would cease, the store brazenly continued them. Eventually, the corporation running the store was brought to court and fined $1,500; in addition, a furrier who ran the fur concession in the store was fined $250 for misrepresenting mink stoles and coats. Another company, a clothing supplier to the store, was also fined $250 for mislabeling suits sold by this "price-cutter." A men's suit, for example, advertised and labeled extensively as "Silk and Cotton" proved to be 75 percent rayon, 23 percent cotton, and 4 percent silk.

Even containers can prove to be misleading, according to Stone. He tells of a counterfeiter of disposable vacuum-cleaner bags who had sold about 7,800 boxes, each holding six bags, "mostly to discount houses." The office of District Attorney Frank S. Hogan was brought into this case by a complaint from the Lewyt Company, which charged "that a number of discount houses in New York County were selling LEWYT SPEED SAK FILTERS in boxes which were the exact replicas of the LEWYT box and which bore the trademark LEWYT." The counterfeiter subsequently pleaded guilty.

Even hang-tags on clothing have been counterfeited, and Stone tells of one counterfeiter who had produced 100,000 such hang-tags, changing them whenever the legitimate manufacturer changed his in an attempt at thwarting the counterfeiting. In revealing these and other cases, Stone says, "The entire concept of consumer protection is in its infancy. The philosophy of 'let the buyer beware' still prevails in many areas despite some laws to the contrary. At this time, governmental control is at a minimum." [19]

The Quality Quandary

As the decade of the 1960s opened, *Time* magazine reported, "Buyers loudly complain that familiar products are just not so good as they used to be—and the figures tend to bear them out. Pittsburgh's Better Business Bureau reported a 19% increase last year in complaints on defective merchandise...." The reason given: "...manufacturers have tried to save by taking a chance on materials that often turned out to be inferior." [20] According to *The Wall Street Journal,* consumers in 1959 spent *twice as much* on television and appliance repairs as they did ten years earlier; the total spent on repairs wasn't so very far below the total spent in buying the merchandise itself.[21]

One reason for this is obvious: when a particular discounter has killed off much of the conventional market for a product and has succeeded in capturing a manufacturer, he tends to keep asking for ever lower prices, and often for artificially high list prices as well. Those manufacturers who won't cooperate are simply told the discounter will abandon their product altogether. This is, of course, nothing short of blackmail. Some manufacturers prefer euthanasia and mercifully kill their products themselves. Others resist surrender, but watch such discounters assassinate their line. All too many take the only course open to them and, swallowing their principles as easily as phlegm, join such discounters in carving up the consumer.

In doing so, they must meet the demand for ever lower prices by cutting costs. This demands good old American know-how, and in recent years many have mastered the art. Here are some of the ways a manufacturer goes about trimming expenses:

• He can cut the number of inspectors along the assembly line, letting a lot of slipshod work go through. One foreman of my acquaintance some years ago had served as a quality control inspector for a manufacturer of tape recorders and reports as "unbelievable" the shoddy workmanship he was forced to let pass. When he objected, insisting that the low quality was neither in the consumer's nor in the manufacturer's interest, he was reprimanded for wanting to "slow down production." [22]

• He can hire cheaper labor, perhaps moving his plant to non-union areas or even the Far East. This might benefit Appalachia or Japan, but hardly seems calculated to benefit the long-range interests of the U.S. consumer—or the direct and immediate interests of the American worker and the community in which he lives.

• He can cut payroll and get 15 workers to do the job of 20, again at the expense of the local labor force, the community, and the consumer, who quickly perceives the reduced care in the reduced reliability of the merchandise.

- He can cut requirements as to dimensions of working parts, tolerances, and accuracy of fit. One modest example of this may be seen in the increasing use of self-threading screws on electric housewares. These screws can be tightened only a few times before giving up the ghost entirely.[23]
- He can substitute cheaper, inferior components and materials for the quality materials he previously used.
- He can reduce the number of protective coats of paint or varnish which a product receives—putting on just enough to make it glitter in the store while it is up for sale.
- He can cut down the number of fastenings, seams, weld spots, rivets, screws, etc., again retaining just enough to hold the article together until it is sold. (This is an easy economy for manufacturers of packaged soft goods since much of this merchandise is wrapped prettily in cellophane or encased in plastic and is not subject to close examination by the shopper.)

Senator Karl Mundt has pointed out that a product's value to the consumer is not reduced merely by ten percent if the prime cost of manufacture is cut by ten percent. The value is likely to be slashed in half, because the manufacturer must cut on quality control, since most of his other expenses are fixed. This, says Senator Mundt, results in "concealed inflation" for consumers, who pay more for less. He points out that "the people who buy flagrantly discounted goods are the people who can least afford to be cheated in the quality and value of the product they get."[24]

In Pocatello, Idaho, C. G. Billmeyer, a wholesaler, has this to say about some American manufacture:

"When as a businessman, I see the quality of the junk being pushed on the gullible public today, with the buyer getting nothing but price, I wonder just how long this system of manufacturing and selling will last. For instance, I just saw an electric range—brand new, made by one of the largest manufacturers in the country, so light and flimsy that it was practically worthless when it left the factory and before the poor housewife was forced to use it. The gauge steel and the very limited amount of insulation, etc., used is beyond belief. . . ." [25]

Across the country in New York, Leon Hartman claims: "It has become impossible for anyone to survive in our industry and still say, 'My shelves contain American products.' An American public has grown disgusted with the lowered quality of U.S.-made camera equipment. . . ." [26]

What is true of electric ranges and cameras is apparently true of other merchandise. What is true of New York City and Pocatello, Idaho, is true of the rest of the country as well. The quality of a lot of merchandise we buy seems to be steadily declining in virtually all product categories. As one appliance dealer, quoted in *Printer's Ink*, put it a few years back, "Quality stinks." [27]

Not all of it, of course. Oddly, the effect of cherry-picking, discussed in an earlier chapter, has been to *raise* the quality of some merchandise. We noted that some retail experts believe that the marketplace is evolving into one where only the high-quality store and the discounter are going to survive. As this trend seems to be developing, high-quality stores are increasing in numbers. There's no question about it: the American public—or substantial segments of it—wants quality. Those who want high quality apparently are willing to pay a premium for it. The "fashion-right" store, the department store "boutique," and the specialty shop provide them with much top-rate merchandise. The trend seems to be toward a certain amount of high-quality goods on one end of the retail spectrum, plus a lot of lower-quality goods at the other, with little in between.

This trend, apparently, was beginning to take shape as the decade of the 1960s opened. In its first two years, the trade press reported increasing evidence of poor-quality merchandise. Here are some items from the pages of *Home Furnishings Daily*:

• Home furnishings experts of the National Retail Merchants Association reported a steady decline in the manufacturing standards of furniture throughout the country. [28]

• Reports from appliance dealers placed the blame for poor sales on consumer dissatisfaction with product quality and with repair services. *H.F.D.'s* Manning Greenberg quoted "a key sales executive" as saying that chains had become so strong that they played appliance dealers off against each other. "They tell us what they'll pay for a carload," the executive said. "We don't tell them." [29] (Greenberg quoted this executive on the subject of "price-fixing": "... sure there's price fixing—by big retailers. They fix the prices for us. As they get bigger ... the problems [*sic*] gets worse." [30])

• Housewares experts reported that manufacturers delivered a great deal of inferior merchandise. The trade paper quoted Washington-area service men as saying that most electric housewares "are not made as good as they were five years ago. . . . The quality of construction has had to slip by the wayside in the continuing battle of competitive prices. . . ." An independent Philadelphia service man was quoted as saying "Electric housewares across the board seem to be getting shoddier all the time as manufacturers try to make up for the poor profit picture by cheapening their products. Products are made with every possible shortcut on quality, and these shortcuts hamper repairs and replacements and boost the cost of service. The use of riveting in irons is a good example of this." [31]

• Aluminum-furniture dealers reported that the minimum gauge tubing used "has come down progressively. . . ." This means that the aluminum was getting thinner. "Four to five years ago," said the trade paper, "it didn't often get below .058. Now, however, more and more poundage is being shipped in .035 and .032." The latter gauge, it said, "is just about the absolute minimum for adequate construction." Welded, instead of "drawn" tubing, was another shortcut that increased numbers of manufacturers were using. In addition, continued *H.F.D.*, manufacturers were using inadequately tested materials in webbing, which proved likely to sag when sat upon and would not return to its original shape.[32]

• Manufacturers in the curtain and drapery industries reported that mills from which they bought cut quality and that values were not what they were in past years. "Some buyers admit," says *Home Furnishings Daily*, "that they were to blame in part for the poor-quality conditions by forcing converters to give them the lowest prices." [33] The pressure, of course, emanates at the retail level.

• Small kitchen appliances or housewares were among the quickest to deteriorate. The trade paper reported "an extremely high rate of service requests and returns ... for name brand electric can openers." Toasters were also "a good example of how 'things have changed.' " The paper stated that "Those made several years ago require less service than the newer models and are, as a rule, of higher quality." Among the shortcuts noted: putting copper or brass wiring next to heating units (these tend to fuse when heated, burning up the connection) and the use of more external plastic, which is prone to breakage and damage.[34]

More recently *Consumer Reports*, the authoritative publication of Consumers' Union, said that defects encountered on washing machines "appeared due to slipshod quality control in manufacture." It surveyed 76,000 machines, found that none were trouble-free, and discovered that a distressingly high 60 percent (46,000 machines) needed repairs relatively quickly. The magazine went on to say that "the shocker is how *soon* machines start to cost fairly substantial amounts to keep them going." In their first year, 85 percent of the machines needed minor service, while 11 percent of the two-year-old machines needed repairs costing from fifty to one hundred dollars. Of consumers surveyed, 14,300 said their machines didn't complete the washing cycle correctly; 11,500 reported defective pumps; 11,300 complained of excessive vibration or noise; 10,900 said items had a habit of escaping from the tub and blocking the pump; 8,900 claimed their machines failed to spin; and 7,800 reported excessive water leaks and flooding.[35]

In the appliance-radio-and-TV business, says Chicago Consulting Economist Richard E. Snyder, "substandard merchandise" has caused the volume of repairs to rise 14.2 percent a year, against a rise in sales of only 2.5 percent.[36]

The list could go on indefinitely. Quality—that one ingredient without which no product can be called a good value—is being squeezed out relentlessly by the drive for ever lower prices, as well as by that other, better-publicized factor, planned obsolescence.

"I will give you a perfect illustration," says Representative John Dent of Pennsylvania. "I do not make any bones about it. My wife, like every other American wife, looks for 'bargains' and is fooled as many times as anybody else by the so-called discount ads. Recently she wanted and bought for herself—of course she was only the agent; I paid for it—she bought herself a dishwasher. Now I know that dishwasher's source. I know the company that makes it. But it is sold by this firm for about $60 less than their top-quality product sold through independent dealers. However, she bought it because of the discount. Within three weeks there developed a little leak in it. She called the store where she purchased the dishwasher and they sent their so-called service man down. He looked it over, told her what was wrong with it, but refused to touch the machine because, when my wife bought it, she took it home and—oh, Johnny-do-it-yourself —I installed it. Since I was not home at the time the leak developed, she called for a repairman. He would not touch the machine because he had not been paid to install it." [37]

One of the editors of *Printer's Ink* reported much the same kind of experience: "Last summer I had the misfortune to buy two nationally advertised air-conditioning units from a local discount house. One was installed a few days later but the second one, found defective by the installation man, was left in the middle of the bedroom floor until mid-September.

"Week after week I called the store and from the sales clerk up to the manager received nothing but disdain. And the crudeness of the sales manager at the main office was incredible. Promises of delivery on specific dates were not honored, and innumerable phone calls only resulted in my being kept on the phone endlessly. Not only will I never go to a discount house again, but never will I buy another product from the manufacturer of those air conditioners." [38]

Of course poor quality hurts most in big-ticket items like air conditioners or washers, but it can prove vexing even in small-cost purchases. Representative Ray Madden tells of his experience in Gary, Indiana, where for many years he had bought a special brand-name pair of socks from a local clothing store. He says he used to get two or three years' wear out of them. Lately, things have changed. "I discovered in the last four or five years [that] the heels would be worn threadbare after a few months. They had become shoddy socks of inferior quality. I told the store owner that I wouldn't buy any more of the socks. He asked, 'Why?' I said, 'They are not what they used to be.' He agreed. The retailer told me that the loss-leader merchants had run the Denver factory out of business. Because of the loss-leader practices on that brand of sock, legitimate merchants wouldn't handle it. Distribution and sales declined. Quality in the product went down and down, as the manufacturer cut costs to try and stay in businesss. Now he's out of business, the quality brand has gone, all because the manufacturer was forced to compete with himself on a loss-leader basis from store to store." [39]

Does the consumer really care? Does he in fact want better quality or does he prefer ever lower prices? The president of one electronic corporation believes most consumers want improved quality, while dealers ironically continue to offer only "bargains." [40] Others are not so sure; a nationwide survey reported by *Home Furnishings Daily* indicates the consumer wants both.[41]

The Design Lag

"The truth is we cannot, as a nation, maintain a discount shopping economy for long without discounting more important things," says Bert Corgan, past president of the National Association of Retail Druggists. NARD, naturally, is concerned most with the future of the independent pharmacist, but Corgan's argument is well taken: discounting eats into product quality, and finally, into the research and development activity that is supposed to produce new and improved products for the consumer's benefit.[42]

In the matter of new products, the nation has no shortage of brains: the Department of Commerce issues more than 1,000 new patents *each week* [43] and, although many or most of these presumably are in the lucrative defense fields, we can safely assume that a large number are also for consumer products. It is such patents that form the first link in a chain that contributes greatly to the growth of the U.S. economy. Even today, we cannot rely on defense production alone if we wish to maintain a sound national economy. What shall we do if peace ever breaks out? We shall then require an even healthier consumer-goods market, and a better climate for inventiveness and innovation.

Retailers have been complaining for years that they need dramatic new products to sell. Those of us who read the retailing trade press are informed that television was just about the last such product and that the most exciting new item to hit the marketplace recently is the electric toothbrush. Much of the reason for this "design lag" lies in the destructive effect of price-cutting on American distribution.

"The thousands of small merchants among which small manufacturers found distributors and dealers willing to gamble on their products and little-known brands are disappearing," says Herman T. Van Mell, vice president and general counsel for Sunbeam Corporation, Chicago, Illinois. "The giant chains only want to carry the assured best-sellers of the best known manufacturers. They hesitate to gamble on new products. The discount houses frankly say, 'We can't carry an unknown product —get it established first.' " [44]

This attitude hardly assists the development of new products by any except the biggest and wealthiest manufacturers. It does not assist the expansion of present product lines or further capital investment on the part of small consumer-goods manufacturers. What militates most against such new product development is, of course, their almost inevitable use as loss leaders, once they do get established. The manufacturer is forced to assume that they will have a very short life indeed.

Only the biggest and financially most powerful may be able to withstand this erosion of the marketplace. Only those few manufacturers wealthy enough to afford saturation advertising may continue to introduce new items without the help of large numbers of independent retailers. As we have seen, such items must be actively promoted: they do not sell themselves. Shelf space means little. Prominence of display alone is not enough. It is essential that the retailer do more than merely stock a new product. He must educate the consumer in its use, explain its workings, and take the time to talk up its benefits. National advertising can do much of this, but such ad campaigns are too costly for smaller manufacturers.

Independent retailers have traditionally performed this selling function and have thereby supported countless small manufacturers. Store owners have felt they had a stake in expanding a line that they had carried for a long time, and this feeling was encouraged by the personal relationship between buyer and seller. Lee Waterman of Corning Glass Works, which built a network of 300 wholesalers and 45,000 retailers over the years, insists quite rightly that this sense of responsibility toward new products is completely foreign to many, essentially parasitic, discounters. "We are dealing today," he says, "with a type of retailer who takes an entirely different view. He is not at all interested in contributing to the building of a new product line. He is very unhelpful at the time of introduction. He doesn't service it in terms of carrying the broad assortment." [45]

Such a climate is clearly not in the consumer's interest. The shrinking marketplace encourages not only the creation of huge near-monopolistic retail chains, but permits only a small oligopoly of manufacturers to survive. If the discounters' predictions that they will take over most of U.S. retailing come true, the buying power of the chains will be enormous. As or-

ders are then increasingly concentrated with those manufacturers whose greed or timidity has made them satellites of the
discounters, other manufacturers will cut their operations or shut
down. Where will the national growth rate be then?

Equally disturbing in the long run is the effect upon consumer tastes in America, as increasing numbers of the young are
conditioned to a happy acceptance of shoddy merchandise. We
may then expect that the economy will cultivate the Gross
National Consumer along with the Gross National Product.

Certainly few children today have any experience with toys
that are built to last; the model cars they buy fall apart as quickly
as real ones do, and the child feels this is perfectly natural. As
he watches the kitchen appliances and even the furniture dis-
integrate, he learns to do so benignly, regarding the process with
the same complacency as he does the setting sun. Indeed, he
learns to adjust his life to the low-quality products with which
he is surrounded and justifies the process of disintegration. It allows him, as he sees it, to have new things all the time—particularly since they are cheap in price—and his possessions become
like playthings to be discarded when boredom visits him. Unlike
his elders, who complain that things are not made as well as they
once were, he is satisfied and likely to remain so, since all
memory of durability and quality are sponged from his mind.
Happily he enlists on the side of those for whom obsolescence
is a way toward increased wealth; he looks forward to the new
models and new fashions in all sorts of merchandise, not merely
because of their newness, but because the anticipation is justi-
fiable, being necessitated by the decay of those products he
bought last year. He will not only surrender with resignation;
he will do so with enthusiasm, knowing little of an era when the
demands of the consumer were heard in the marketplace.

10

The Bargain Hunters

> There are a lot of completely educated people in
> the world and of course they will resent being asked
> to learn anything new.
>
> —ROBERT FROST [1]

WHAT is the American shopper like today? What are his
habits, expectations, psychological traits? What effect
has the phenomenal growth of discounting had on the
way we shop—and on the way we think?

Some of the answers to these questions are implicit in what
we have already seen. We have seen how shoppers—all of us
throughout the country—have been manipulated, propagandized,
and victimized by the use of many of the practices of discounting. We have seen how these practices have tended to erode
quality, cut into the availability of goods, and weaken competitive enterprise throughout our nation. We have seen the results
all around us. Now let us have a look at the shopper himself and
see how the vicious circle turns on the consumer, and what effect it has.

What are his habits today? Pierre D. Martineau, director of
research and marketing for the *Chicago Tribune* recently discussed "a very extensive new study" on the subject. It reveals
the following:

1. The average shopper is highly mobile and thinks nothing

of driving to as many as twelve shopping centers to buy what he or she wants. Local shopping is virtually dead.

2. Shopping centers—where discount houses dominate the scene—attract trade from well over 1,000 square miles. Old Orchard Center, near Chicago, for example, draws 44 percent of its customers from a 1,500-square-mile area, the outer limits of which are 30 miles away. Another 16 percent of its customers come from communities lying still farther out.

3. Store loyalty is collapsing to an extent that Martineau calls "shattering." Today's shopper, he says, "is no longer loyal to any store or center, but rather she is just loyal to shopping itself. . . . The almost moral restrictions of the past about store loyalty have been broken." He uses a somewhat exotic analogy to illustrate this, comparing the American shopper to the Polynesian wife who "may have five husbands and . . . doesn't know whose children belong to who, and everyone is very friendly and casual about the whole system." In exactly the same way, he says, today's shopper "doesn't feel guilty about anything . . . she thoroughly enjoys all the choice she has."

4. The "blue collar" shopper "has changed . . . is not the same guy." Such consumers have long ago satisfied both "needs and wants" and now want to satisfy their "wishes." They are not the prime market for the discounter. "Contrary to our preconceived notions," says Martineau, "we find that the discount stores draw just about as well from all income groups except the very top of the market. Ninety-two percent of these highly mobile shoppers who spend the most, who have higher incomes, also shop at discount stores . . . the older, more conventional stores still have to solve the problem which the discount stores have successfully worked out, *to capitalize on the very considerable amount of impulse buying which the shopper of today does.*" [2] [Author's italics.]

Today's family of four, *Time* reported on January 8, 1965, will spend about $8,650 during 1965; today's consumer spends 93 cents of every dollar he earns. The magazine quotes Macy's president, Jack I. Straus, as saying that the American public's ability to consume is endless. "The consumer," he says, "goes on spending regardless of how many possessions he has. The luxuries of today are the necessities of tomorrow." That this is regarded as glorious news by American economists and businessmen is obvious, and it is not my purpose here to question such current thinking. It is enough to point out that acquisitive shoppers, out primarily *to spend*, with the object of their spending playing a secondary role, do a great deal of impulse shopping.

As we shall see, there may be ways in which a very careful, well-informed shopper can get a bargain at a discount store— but impulse shopping is not the way to do it. Impulse shopping is unthoughtful shopping, uninformed shopping and, of course, often unnecessary shopping. Many discounters make sure the impulse is irresistible.

The Wish and the Paradox

It was once taken for granted that good value was more important than low price, that good value would cost more, and that one got what one paid for. That old-fashioned era seems to be over. Its last exponent of prominence was President William McKinley, who commented a bit stuffily, "I do not prize the word 'cheap.' It is not a badge of honor . . . it is a symbol of despair. Cheap prices make for cheap goods; cheap goods make for cheap men; and cheap men make for a cheap country."

At first glance, McKinley seems to have missed the point completely. In his day there were many Americans who would have been well served by cheap goods sold at cheap prices. His comfortable comment smacks of the remark that "the law, in all its majesty, impartially forbids both rich and poor to sleep under the bridges of Paris." What McKinley meant to say, however, is another matter. He presumably was speaking of good quality.

Not that today's bargain hunter won't insist she is looking for just that: a good value and good quality. As a matter of fact, the retailing and discounting trade journals are filled with reports that high style and deluxe models are exactly what the consumer wants. Largely, however, such reports oversimplify.

The American shopper currently has a somewhat contradictory attitude towards the conventional store, on the one hand, and the discount center, on the other. She expects low prices from the discounter and indeed frequents the discount store only because of that expectation. Low prices at a conventional store, however, cause her to doubt the quality of the merchandise being sold. The Kroehler Design Center, which surveyed "white collar family" women in Chicago, drew this conclusion: "The panelist reactions show that women still rely on price for quality criteria. *They do not yet have the ability to judge a value.* [Author's italics.] The majority feel that if a price was 'too low' the value was to be doubted, because the quality wasn't very good." [3] The fact that a low-price item, although of reduced quality, may serve a useful and satisfactory purpose and thus offer good value for the money does not seem to occur to these women when shopping in regular department stores.

Discounters, however, have convinced the bargain hunter that at their centers she can find that most perplexing paradox: top-quality items at cut prices. What is it that causes so many shoppers to swallow this? Each person I have interviewed in connection with this book, each person I have spoken with about discounting, has offered his own opinion, many of them to the point. One of the most interesting and provocative of the lot, however, came not from a retailing expert, but from Konrad Kellen, an authority on psychological warfare and a frequent writer in the field of propaganda appeals and mass motivation.

"Propaganda analysts know," he says, "that even the most sophisticated and suspicious people are inevitably misled by a particular type of misrepresentation which is neither a claim nor a statement of 'fact,' but a more basic misrepresentation of what a man actually is or does.

"If a man, for example, opens a stationery store, people may have a thousand doubts as to whether the stationery is good, or a bargain, or of the latest style. But they will not doubt for a moment that they can get stationery there. By the same token, if a man sets up a discount house, people may doubt whether the merchandise is good, the delivery speedy, the service adequate, the detour from their ordinary shopping route worth the saving. But that they can get a saving there, a discount, they do not doubt at all. People cannot imagine that a man who claims to be a stationer, a discounter, or a bond salesman, is not exactly that, no matter how they may suspect his other claims. People also cannot imagine that a man who calls himself a discounter may offer very few discounts."

What Kellen describes is, of course, not unfamiliar to us. We have seen how persons with no medical training have masqueraded for years as physicians, simply by calling themselves doctors and setting up a practice. They have successfully carried off their deception because the average person cannot conceive of such a thing being perpetrated. The man is a doctor, they insist; he himself says so, and so do all his patients. Similarly, it is hard for the public to believe that a discounter does not offer discounts throughout his store if he claims to do so. As a result, shoppers buy his "discounting image."

"Why is price-cutting so successful?" asks Kellen. "My guess is, without trying to become Freudian, that people on the whole buy more than they can afford and live beyond their means. This causes them to feel guilty about buying more. The discount store provides a way out of this guilt. Its alleged bargain entitles the customer to indulge himself extravagantly, to shop on impulse and to spend far more than he would otherwise; in fact, the bargain makes him a fool if he does not take advantage of it. Therefore, he wants to believe that the discounter gives him top quality at cut prices and does so consistently and across the board. And what he wants to believe, he believes.

"Finally, discounting permits the customer to see himself as adhering to the American ideal of being 'shrewd, smart, tough.' This trait is very deep in people. Even the greatest art collectors, for example, always like to stun their guests not just by exhibiting their Rembrandts but by boasting about how little they paid for them. Similarly, millions of Americans seem to be eager to provide themselves with an 'ego boost' by blandly informing their incredulous and envious neighbors that they bought this TV set, that washing machine, for 'half the price.' Thus the 'discounter' has an eager audience. But he sometimes has surprisingly few discounts."

Kellen points out that a person who, for example, set out to buy a low-price name-brand TV set and who left with one that cost far more, will often deny this to his neighbors and perhaps even his wife. "Our tendency is to exaggerate the savings we achieve or even to invent them if they don't exist," Kellen says. "We don't like looking foolish. In the process, we defend those who take advantage of our weakness."

How does a bargain hunter's mentality work when he enters a discount house? Of course it will vary from person to person. There is no way (and perhaps no need) to attempt a portrayal of the many different psychological reactions that will be at play. The following fiction is offered as one example only and will not necessarily fit the reader's personality; it is, however, by no means atypical.

Our bargain hunter has seen a bait ad for a brand-name suit and has made the decision to take advantage of the price. Perhaps he has put off the purchase for some time, because he felt no pressing need for the item or perhaps because, as Kellen said, he felt guilty about already living beyond his income. Seeing the bait ad, though, convinces him that it would be imprudent to wait longer.

He now sets aside time for a visit to a discount store. Perhaps it is downtown and he lives in the suburbs, or perhaps it is in another suburban shopping center, an hour's drive away. He must allocate time for the expedition. Now he has made two commitments, which may have been difficult for him: to buy and to go. To back down now would be difficult, for he sees himself in possession of that suit, receiving admiring looks and flattering comments. The old suit has already been allocated to charity, and wearing it another season seems a sin.

He drives to the discount store, maneuvers his car through the crowded parking lot, finds an empty spot, backs his car into it, walks over to the discount-house doors, enters, and is engulfed in a crowd of shoppers. The very inconvenience, however, serves to assuage his guilt about the money he will spend; it is proof of his willingness to undergo anything, in order to save. The very act of buying seems virtuous and righteous now.

Countering the inconvenience also are the many signs, each advertising a bargain. Our shopper's acquisitive senses are aroused, and his heart beats a little faster as he sees before him a sea of things that his family might use, all "discounted." He has difficulty making his way to the suit department without stopping first to shop the appliances, the radio and TV sets, the drugs and drug sundries, the sweaters, slacks, and toys. Finally, he makes it and asks for the advertised brand-name suit.

He finds to his considerable disappointment that it is all sold out in his particular size—the only ones left were tailored for trolls. No matter, for it is just a moment before he is convinced that one of the 1,000 other suits available will do just as nicely and give as much pleasure. As a matter of fact, he soon feels even better about having come, for the salesman has informed him that the unmarked suit he bought is actually made by a top brand-name manufacturer, who wishes to remain anonymous. It is a suit, says the salesman, on which the store can allow an even bigger discount than it could on the ones it advertised. All momentary hesitations are swept away *instanter* with this argument and the bargain hunter leaves the suit department with a reinforced sense of shrewdness and sagacity.

Suffused with positive feelings about the discount house in general, he sweeps up other merchandise on his way out and leaves loaded down not only with the suit, but with a bagful of other "bargains." When his wife meets him on his return, raising her eyebrows at the bulging shopping bags, he does not say, "I spent more than I planned to spend." He says, "Just look at how much I saved!"

Columbia University Professor A. R. Oxenfeldt comments: "It is possible to view the existing popularity of the discount house, especially among prosperous groups, as part of a national fad. One might say that the discount house created a new game whose object is to obtain the maximum below list prices. The satisfaction from effecting a savings seems to have been far greater in most cases than the size of the saving would justify." [4]

Among those most vulnerable to discounters' arguments, says Kellen, are intellectuals. "Intellectuals," he says, "are often among the easiest to propagandize, because of two reasons. First, they believe themselves to be invulnerable to propaganda—which is what makes them extremely vulnerable. Second, intellectuals believe they must have an opinion—any opinion—about everything. Preferably, that opinion must seem particularly shrewd. Because they understand next to nothing about how some discount stores are actually run, they readily accept the talk of low profit margins resulting from various economies. This makes sense to them because few have ever been active in manufacturing or retailing and suspect the business community in any case." Even if stung, such persons are unlikely to admit it and will continue their defense of the very store that took advantage of them for reasons of personal pride. While they may save face, they may also lose their shirts.

They will even give the discounter a helping hand. *Fortune* magazine, for example, surveyed some of the reasons why some discounters have abandoned comparative price ticketing, why they have stopped showing both a "high list" price along with their own allegedly discounted price. As one merchant explains it in the magazine, customers might find the item selling for less elsewhere and thus lose faith in the store's "discounting image." When no comparative price is shown, he says, a woman *tends to exaggerate the saving*. Whereas the discounter might have put a $6.99 "comparative value" price on a dress that he sells for $4.74, failure to do so will cause the shopper to think the dress is worth $10. "At *such* savings," he says, "she wouldn't be thrifty unless she did buy the dress." [5]

The Greed Game

What is it that the discounting has fostered in the American consumer if it is not greed, cupidity, the desire for something for nothing? We are tricked by price-juggling, misrepresentations, and loss-leader bait ads. The process debases our thinking and increases our acquisitiveness. There are discounters who admit this. A Federal Trade Commission attorney told me of the remark of the president of one discount house. "The woman shopper," he said, "enters our store with larceny in her heart, and we cater to her larcenous instincts."

Discounting, says one discount-store executive, is "a colorful business," [6] much of it run by men whom the editor-in-chief of *The Discount Merchandiser* has called "a rough-and-tumble, no-holds-barred group of retailers... mavericks, every one of them." [7] Ed Wimmer, whose column appears in the *Cincinnati Enquirer* and the *Dayton News & Journal*, says, "Today's boys and girls just haven't lived under anything even resembling 'free enterprise'... the discount-house, chain-store, trading-stamp rat race ... fouls the whole atmosphere they breathe...."

These youngsters are indeed being brought up in a society that quite complacently assumes that discount stores and, indeed, trading stamps provide them with "savings" and "free gifts." It is unfortunate that new shoppers, young couples, are the most prone to being duped. "A whole generation," we have quoted E. B. Weiss as saying, "several generations in fact, have been thoroughly conditioned to 'haggling' and extreme price flexibility." [8] This cynical uncertainty is particularly prevalent, however, among the young who were reared in the post-World War II discount era. Gimbel Brothers' president points out that, by 1970, there will be 24,000,000 new customers in the U.S.A., "enough to create a new city each year the size of Los Angeles and Philadelphia combined." [9] They will be ready for the discounter, and the discounter will be ready for them.

Not only has discounting succeeded in making all too many Americans greedy and unthinking, but it has sown the seeds of suspicion and division in the country. The discount-store enthusiast today is suspicious and hostile to the small retailer and prefers to think that a giant discount corporation has his interests more at heart than the neighbor who runs the neighborhood store. A Connecticut shoe retailer who has seen loss leaders cut up his trade pointed out before Congress that discounters make the consumer think the independent retailer is "unfair and unscrupulous." In effect, he says, the bait ads shout to the public, "This guy here has been sticking you for 40-some-odd years. Why don't you come over and buy from us?" [10] With what seems to me ample justification, he is hurt and outraged. The discounter who smears his reputation, after all, is the one who carries *one pair* of Florsheim shoes to justify his bait ads, which offer Florsheims at more than $8 off list.

Not only does discounting encourage the impression that the small retailer is a thief, but it prompts us to suspect the manufacturer as well. The only one who escapes our suspicion is the discounter himself, appearing as the champion of the consumer. Even among thinking people it has become axiomatic that all manufacturer-set prices are inflated and all retail markups except the discounter's are larcenous. It is odd indeed that we should champion those very huge chains that many think are moving toward a monopolistic stranglehold on our retail market and our shopping dollar. We just cannot seem to accept the simple truth that Hilliard Coan, president of Hills Supermarkets, stated when he said, "You just can't sell dollar bills for 79 cents and make money. If you can, there must be another gimmick somewhere." [11] Perhaps, in our complex world today, it seems *too* simple. Like those who try to beat the stock market or the horse races, we listen to those "in the know" and consult the tip-sheets looking for a mathematical formula for getting rich quick. In the retail marketplace, we think we've found it in discounting.

The Larger Interest

Discounting has more than a psychological effect on us shoppers. It not only can weaken our resistance to swindles and erode our values. It also produces far-reaching social effects on us as consumers and Americans.

"The public," says retailer J. H. Fultz of Moses Lake, Washington, whose analysis appeared in the *Congressional Record,* "loves price wars. They love the bankruptcy bargains those price wars bring on. They shed nary a tear for the businessman who has lost his shirt, nor for his employees who have lost their jobs. But this jubilation is the offspring of ignorance. Ignorance of the fact that with every bankruptcy their own job security is lessened just that much. Ignorance of the fact that with every decline of business prosperity in their community their own chance of a wage increase is lessened just that much and their own chance of even having a job is lessened. Ignorance of the fact that their property values have also dropped in a 'sick' community. Ignorance of the fact that the chances of their children getting jobs when they enter the labor market is also lessened . . .

"Any purchase made by a consumer which results in a loss to the seller is only undermining that purchaser's welfare in the long run by jeopardizing profits. It is jeopardizing jobs—his job. He is, in effect, 'digging his own economic grave' with every such bargain purchase . . .

"Dogs fighting in the street are offered more protection than our businessmen on that same street. Common decent people will protest at a vicious dogfight and stop it; but will the same people stop a destructive fight between two local merchants? They will not, because they do not understand or even see much of what is going on. They do not realize such tactics undermine their own welfare." [12]

Has discounting turned our largely middle-class American society into one of new class antagonisms? There are those who point to an atmosphere of suspicion and hostility. Retailers like Fultz are bitter about the consumer; the consumer, on the other hand, regards the independent retailer as a thief. Only the "below-list" and "cut-price" merchant can benefit.

"The public interest," Justice Brandeis told a House of Representatives committee in 1915, "is made up of a number of things. It is made up, in the first place, of the consumer—that he should get a good article at the lowest price that he reasonably can, consistent with good quality and good business. This is his interest as a consumer—that he should get a good article at a low price, and conveniently. There should be no doubt that he gets value and there should be no doubt that he will be able to get it without putting himself to extraordinary trouble in getting it. That is the consumer's interest.

"But there is another interest that the public has and that we should look for, namely the interest of the rest of the public, the dealer and his clerks, and the producer and his employees. We are all a part of the public and we must find a rule of law that permits a business practice which is consistent with the welfare of all the people." [13]

It is a measure of the times and of our values that such a large view touches so few persons. We are accustomed to being bribed *en bloc:* supports for the farmers, guaranteed wages for the workers, special appeals to nationality groups, and space-age installations to assist regions that somehow failed to reach the industrial age. We wish to have our own *special interest* as consumers catered to, and we see that special interest as lying only in low prices.

We overlook the fact that most of us consumers are producers as well. The industrial worker who bought himself an off-brand suit or, for that matter, a name-brand TV set, at a cut price, receives a strange benefit if he ends up losing his job. Indirectly, the destruction of the manufacturer's brand name and the erosion of his distribution network may well have this result. Exactly the same thing can happen to the consumer whose income is derived, either directly or indirectly, from retailing or wholesaling. He is shoring up his family well-being during the working day, while his wife may be spending his paycheck to tear it down, by contributing his money to discounters who may be ruining his employers.

"When a manufacturer gets hurt by retailer pirates who for their own gain usurp and damage the manufacturer's good will in his trademark," says an editorial in the *National Independent Labor Journal*, "then labor gets hurt in two ways—one, as a consumer; second, as an employee, because the welfare of the employee—the welfare of labor—is interdependent with the welfare of the employer." [14]

Less theoretical was the blunt statement of Toby Coletti, president of Meat Cutters Local 342, who said that discounters "threaten to turn food retailing *into a profitless or nearly profitless industry in which further improvements in wages and benefits would become economically infeasible.*" [Author's italics.] Coletti here clearly demonstrates a sound understanding of the interrelationship of industry and labor; he apparently has had his share of troubles with certain discounters. "They've introduced a number of practices long since eliminated by unions in the food industry," he reports, "including extended hours, split shifts, 80 to 90 percent part-time workers, and Sunday openings." His union, the 350,000-member Amalgamated Meat Cutters and Retail Food Store employees, as well as the Retail Clerks International Association, are both interested in the unionization of workers in discount-food stores. [15]

It is hardly surprising that there are discounters who hire scab and part-time workers, run retail sweat shops, and squeeze their employees for extra hours and extra days. Why in the world would such discounters act differently toward workers from the way they do toward the retailers they ruin, the manufacturers they raid, and the customers they delude? These are often no-holds-barred characters, as the editor of *The Discount Merchandiser* puts it. Price-cutting encourages the production of cheap off-brand merchandise abroad, particularly in the Far East, where coolie wages may still be paid. Such production may do more than discomfit a few manufacturers. It can eliminate job opportunities; it can cause the dismissal of superfluous workers and can delay pay increases for those who remain; it can erode the nation's productive future, as manufacturing facilities are curtailed or not expanded; it can cut down on research and development as funds for such enterprises become scarce; and it can eat into community life, as area after area slowly becomes slightly more hard-hit by the retail revolution of today.

What opportunity remains in retailing for young people out

of college or high school? They can certainly take a job with the big retail giants, with the huge discount chains, but is this gray-flannelism an answer? The young man who wants to start his own store, or the young woman who wants her own small shop, cannot simply be told that this vision belongs to a bucolic America that has passed. Can we with clear consciences tell them either to join a big chain or to learn how to master the shell-game, so as to end up being First Fagin in some unethical operation? Perhaps we can, but it is not the American dream—nor is it saying much about the vitality of our free-enterprise system.

We need to have broader values, values that are not restricted to immediate gain. It is not enough for us to want better quality in our products or better value in what we buy; we must act in order to obtain these results. Indiscriminate discount buying is not the answer. We need to ask ourselves what it is we really want—the good quality and value we claim to want, or the cheap prices our actions show that we want.

Perhaps good quality and good value are mere atavistic words we use because they are lodged in our national memory, just as we so often use the language of the rugged independent frontier American when about the boldest thing we'll do is cross a street against the light. As consumers, we very badly need to reassert our independence and recapture some of our old-time fervor against big trusts. We need to throw off our selfish, short-term interests and recognize the extent to which we have been, and are now being, used. If we don't do it soon, the stranglehold will have been established and all the more or less inevitable results of discounting, which we have noted in this book, will be an accomplished fact.

11

A Survival Kit for the Discount Jungle

> We must wage an unrelenting fight against the
> selfish minority who deceive ... the consumer.
>
> —PRESIDENT LYNDON B. JOHNSON, on the appoint-
> ment of Mrs. Esther Peterson as Special Assistant
> to the President for Consumer Affairs, January 3,
> 1964

THOSE readers who visited the 1939 New York World's
Fair may remember one of its minor attractions, a man
who guessed one's age and weight for fifteen cents and
gave away free canes if he guessed wrong.

Maurice Mermey, who was director of exhibits and concessions at this Fair, says it was amazing how many of those canes
one would see on a day's visit to Flushing Meadow. Visitors
who came to the Fair would puzzle about the canes and where
they all came from; later, if they passed the man's stand, the
answer became obvious. There they were, big bunches of them,
free if he guessed wrong. And, from the number of canes in
circulation, it was apparent he guessed wrong often.

The man didn't mind. He knew that the reason people would
spend fifteen cents at his concession lay in their conviction that
they could stump him. And so—although he was a real expert—
he often guessed wrong deliberately. Even if he gave away a
cane, he could still break even, for they only cost him 7½ cents

each. And he wanted to get a lot of them out and into circulation throughout the fairgrounds. They were his best ads, and he knew it.

Even in 1939, it was obvious that giving something away, apparently for nothing, paid off.

Today it is paying off better than ever. In the carnival atmosphere that is often so much a part of discounting, the "loss leader" is the "cane" that gets talked about. It announces the fact —and it *is* a fact—that one can get discounts at a discount store.

Ten Guideposts

Let's face one very unpleasant fact right at the outset: we are today living in a *Caveat-emptor* society, where each buyer must look out for himself. Should the shopper in such a society venture into the discount jungle at all? My own belief should by now be clear. However, in the light of what has been revealed, each reader should make up his own mind. Many will undoubtedly enter discount houses, hoping to do their shopping in a more informed manner.

The mathematics of discounting will show such shoppers how to do this. The effect of such informed buying will also be quite large. If consumers bought only genuine discounts (e.g., loss leaders), then many of the evils of discounting would quickly end. No longer would a discount store be able to take advantage of those consumers who did not buy loss leaders. It would rapidly be compelled to adopt the policies of many conventional retail merchants. Order might return to the chaotic retail marketplace and American shoppers might once again feel safe.

A few guideposts for shoppers follow:

1. For your own protection, don't let yourself think that you can outsmart the professionals who run the stores. Don't let yourself think that you can judge quality on more

than one or two types of products. There is no way for you
to do so on all or even a majority of the goods in stock.
Those shoppers who consider themselves experts on quality
and value are among the first to be fooled.

2. Be careful in buying soft goods. Clothing of all kinds,
draperies, linens, fabrics and similar merchandise are the
very items on which so many discounters rely for their profits. These goods often carry unexpectedly high markups,
so as to make up the losses in the store's "loss-leader" departments. Also, quality control experts believe that the
public is often unable to judge soft goods, simply because it
does not know many of the manufacturing standards involved. "Comparable values" are difficult to determine.

3. Be very skeptical about claims of big bargains, as they
appear on price-tickets, signs, and other displays. Resist the
human animal's automatic tendency to believe what is
printed on such tags and signs. Remember that price-tickets
saying anything a discounter wants them to say can be ordered from any printing shop in the country. Remember
that the product you see may carry a phony, inflated "list"
or "manufacturer's recommended" price, so as to allow for
an artificial discount on which you may save nothing. Keep
in mind that "comparable value" is impossible to arrive at
unless you know virtually every step of the manufacturing
process. If there is no comparative "high" price, don't just
blandly swallow a claim by a discounter that his price represents any kind of true discount.

4. Refuse to be switched. Don't let yourself be argued
into an off-brand, when it's the advertised and allegedly-
discounted name-brand you came to buy. Remember that
there's something basically dishonest about an operation
which will feature name brands in their ads to draw you
into the store, then disparage those same name brands once
you ask for them. Remember also that, while an off-brand
may be a good value, there's no way you can tell. If an
off-brand is recommended by a reliable merchant whose

reputation is known to your community for many years, it might be worth taking a chance. If the recommendation comes from a store that relies on bait ads to make up for the fact that it has no known reputation, don't take it. Chances are, the salesman's only working to get his "spiff"—that extra bonus he receives if he switches you away from the brand-name product.

5. Add up the extras. Discounters and their defenders like to boast that the discount stores have cut out the "frills," but sometimes they aren't "frills" at all. Sure, you don't need home delivery on a bottle of Bayer Aspirin, but are you prepared to lug an air conditioner home by yourself? Find out what if any extra charge there may be for delivery. Find out what if any extra charge there may be for the installation of an appliance. I personally compared the prices on a name-brand air conditioner at both a discount store and a conventional retailer and discovered that the discounter's price was higher, once I added delivery and installation. His "list price" was discounted, but the delivery and installation charges were inflated to make up for it. Neither delivery nor installation qualifies as an "unnecessary extra" or a "frill."

Service is another "frill" some discounters have discarded. It may be unnecessary on some items, but not on others. When I buy shoes for my children, I want to make certain that they are fitted properly and that I can get reasonably prompt attention. At a discount store, I might have no fitter at all waiting on my children, or have to wait unduly. Is it worth the wait—and is it worth taking a chance on a poor fit? Ask yourself and give yourself some frank answers.

6. Investigate credit schemes carefully. While some discount houses today are members of standard credit card plans (e.g., Uni-card), others maintain their own credit systems. The rates on these may be higher than elsewhere. [A University of Chicago Graduate School of Business study of 34 discount houses, as reported in *The Discount*

Merchandiser of April, 1963, shows finance charges ranging from 15.5 percent to 27.7 percent, or a mean of 20 percent.]

7. Check to find out what guarantees, warranties, and
service are offered. Find out exactly who it is that stands
behind the product, who will replace parts and for how
long, and what if any charges will be made. Find out who
will send a repairman around if anything goes wrong.
A good many discounters often fail to stand behind what
they sell, and those who buy from such stores may find they
must apply to the manufacturer for service or guarantees.
Sometimes, when a discounter has obtained his merchandise
through unorthodox channels, a manufacturer may refuse
to guarantee the item.

Find out also whether the discount store will refund your
money promptly and without an argument, if you find the
item unsatisfactory. I know of one lady who bought an
appliance from a New York discount store, took it home in
what purportedly was the original manufacturer's package,
and discovered that it did not work at all. When she returned it the same day, the salesman took out a screw-
driver, fooled around with the machine for a while, and
handed it back to her. She, however, insisted on her money
back, saying she did not want an appliance that had to be
repaired the moment it came out of the original package.
The salesman offered to replace it with another appliance
and argued with her for ten minutes—"until I got hopping
mad," she said. Finally, he refunded her money. When she
got home, she says, she found he had shortchanged her five
dollars.

8. Avoid unknown appliances. The same holds true for
radios, TV sets, cameras, watches, sporting equipment, and
the like. The manufacturer may be in Hong Kong (just try
to get service from him if the store disclaims responsibility).
The manufacturer may have gone out of business; you may
have a bargain on your hands, but no one exists who can

service it, or supply parts. Or the manufacturer may be impossible to locate, because he may now be doing business under another name. He may have produced the product you bought as a "one-shot," especially for the store. If contacted, he may often stall you or totally ignore your letters. Because he doesn't produce a nationally advertised brand, he may have no need to stand behind what he manufactures, or to concern himself with customer complaints.

9. Find out with whom you're dealing. Find out from whom you're buying. Make sure you know who runs the department at which you plan to shop. Is it the discount store itself?—or is it a concessionaire, a "lessee"? If it is a lease operator, find out who is responsible for the merchandise: manufacturer, discount-store "landlord," or lessee. Make sure you know which one of the three will stand behind the product.

10. *Comparison-shop.* We've saved this for last, since it is the only way you'll ever be sure you're getting a bargain in a discount store. It deserves a section all to itself.

Before we discuss this, I believe it is important for readers to know where to turn for help if and when they suspect they may have been cheated. A pamphlet issued by the FTC (reprinted in Appendix 3 to this book) goes into some methods; it is entitled *Fight Back!—The Ungentle Art of Self Defense, as recommended by the Federal Trade Commission* and is available through the Commission's publications office in Washington, D.C. It is worth the reader's careful attention.

Not all of the States have yet established offices comparable to New York's Bureau of Consumer Frauds and Protection; those that have do not have the budget or the staff this one enjoys. Further, not all consumer complaints fall under the jurisdiction of an Attorney General's office; some, for example, should be brought to the attention of a District Attorney. Readers seeking relief and aid might well start by contacting their State Attorney General's office, their District Attorney, their Better Business Bureau, Chamber of Commerce, or Legal Aid Society. All are equipped to suggest courses of action. In a case involving a large sum of money (furniture that was never delivered, for example, but on which a deposit was paid), readers may wish to consult an attorney. Local and state Bar Associations can recommend qualified lawyers. Certainly no consumer should hesitate to take action; the experience of law enforcement agencies is that such action often leads to a satisfactory settlement of complaints, generally without litigation. A customer who has received no satisfaction after complaining to the store is often surprised how quickly he receives it after a governmental agency telephones or writes the management.

It is my belief that all complaints should also be registered with the Better Business Bureau. This organization is, of course, a private agency and has no law enforcement powers, but it carries enormous weight. It is supported by businessmen and merchants, the overwhelming majority of whom are honest and who are as anxious as is the consumer to rid the marketplace of those who defile it. In most cases, it is the honest merchant who actually does the best job of acting as the consumer's watchdog. An FTC attorney tells me that most complaints about misrepresentations in advertising come from the dishonest merchant's ethical competitors; of course they have a business reason in fighting the cheats, but in doing so they champion the consumer. The efforts of such ethical merchants and businessmen deserve the support of the public—and, in my opinion, it is these retailers who deserve the patronage of the public as well.

Cherry-Picking for Consumers

We've heard a lot about how some discount stores "cream" or "cherry-pick" only the most profitable items. We've seen how their slogan is "thick on the best, to hell with the rest." It's time the consumer used those slogans for the benefit of his own budget! Let's see how the American shopper himself can "buy the best" and say "to hell with the rest."

A certain percentage of the merchandise of discount stores is often sold at a loss, a near loss, or at a very small markup, often in order to "bait" you into the store. The smart shopper buys this merchandise and is careful about other items in the store.

Because most discounters have not told us what their markups are *per item*, we must refer back to the only authoritative and full study we have on the subject, *The Discount Merchandiser's* Marrud Study. If we assume that Marrud's margin pattern continues to be that reflected in The Marrud Study, then its pages will tell us which products carry low markups at its discount drug concessions. [Readers who would like to study the full list of gross margins per category are referred to pages M-22 through 29 of the December, 1963, issue of *The Discount Merchandiser.*]

At Marrud, the following product categories carried gross margins of over 50 percent (i.e., markups of over 100 percent): bath oils and salts, combs and brushes, hairnets and caps, mirrors, shoelaces, hair bows and bandeaus, and greeting cards. Clearly, these do not carry the 22 to 24 percent margins of which discount-house enthusiasts so proudly boast.

The following products carried gross margins of between 45 and 50 percent (i.e., markups of over 81.8 percent or more): zippers, lip salves, bobby pins and curlers, miscellaneous hair needs, shoeshine accessories, smoking accessories, gift-wrap accessories, loose-leaf binders, decorative trimmings, sponges and bulk candy. Clearly, these also are not much different from the preceding group.

The following products carried gross margins in excess of 40 percent (i.e., markups of over 66.6 percent): vitamins, sanitary belts and accessories, feminine hygiene aids, artificial sweeteners, gauze, first-aid kits, miscellaneous drugs, talcum and dusting powder, lipsticks and lip make-up, suntan lotions, manicure accessories, miscellaneous shave needs, deodorizers, rubber gloves, toilet-article kits, lighter fluids, pens, pencils, pen-pencil refills, stationery accessories, party decorations and favors, note and composition books, loose-leaf fillers, paper pads and tablets, metal and paper files, marking pens, inks and accessories, letter paper and envelope combinations, lunch kits and school bags, drawing implements, pencil kits, sewing implements, miscellaneous sewing needs, thread, braids, ribbons and bindings, buttons, and decorative trimmings. None of these qualify as carrying "low-low" margins either.

We know from the magazine study that Marrud's average gross margin was 33.4 percent and that there were 304 items on which Marrud maintained its lowest margins. These items carried margins of 24 percent or less. They also happened to fall into the often-quoted 22–24% "discount-type margin" range. Certainly they were marked up far lower than most items in conventional retail drugstores and, presumably, represented really substantial bargains.

Toothpaste, headache remedies, oral antiseptics, dietary preparations, and chewing gum were categories of products that fell into this group. The shopper at Marrud who looked for low markup bargains had reason to welcome these. He might, however, have decided to reserve his biggest welcome for the toothpaste, on which Marrud's margin was only 17.3 percent, and for the dietary preparations, on which the gross margin reported in *The Discount Merchandiser* was 12.5 percent. Of all the groups of products The Marrud Study listed, these two were marked up the least.

Markups are, of course, only one way for the consumer to know he's getting a good price. It does not always indicate whether a product is a discount or not. An item on which a discounter tags a 50 percent markup may still be a discount and a bargain, if the conventional retail store in his area sells it at a 75 percent markup. It should be noted, however, that aside from careful comparison shopping on each item, the consumer has no way of determining whether a product has truly been discounted.

I have been unable to find detailed gross-margin charts for other discount operations. Finding out which items represent a genuine bargain in this atmosphere of secrecy entails more work.

The way to go about it is the way my mother recently did. Deciding that she wanted a television set, she started by making up her mind which brand she wanted. Then she visited several stores to see the selection of sets available, to find out what models she could get in that brand name. She noted down the year, the model number, and the price of two or three she liked. Having finally decided she wanted a 19-inch portable and a stand to go with it, she compared the prices being charged for that *exact model.*

She visited two major Manhattan department stores, two big New York City discount houses, and a couple of neighborhood appliance dealers. The prices, she says, were all "pretty much the same," but she ended up buying the set from a radio-TV dealer around the corner from her home, because his price was about four dollars cheaper, he threw in the stand for nothing, provided free delivery, and guaranteed service for a year.

It seems like a lot of trouble and I, personally, might have cut my own comparison shopping in half. She, however, feels that any purchase involving $100 or more deserves the time and effort she put into it, and she is certain, at least, that she got her television set at a fair price. She would have been happy to get a discount on it, but she couldn't. Not that the item was "fair-traded" or anything like that; it just turned out that the price offered by the two discount houses she visited was substantially the same as the price charged by almost everybody in town. Without ever having read the Federal Trade Commission chairman's definition of a real discount, she understood that such a discount must carry a price considerably lower than that being charged by the discount store's competitors in the same area.

The one essential ingredient in her shopping expedition was this: she compared the retail price on a specific model, made in a specific year. Of course she was shown name-brand TV sets that had different model numbers, were of different technical specifications and design, and were several years old, but she was not interested. She knew:

1. What brand she wanted.
2. What model she wanted.
3. What year make she wanted.
4. How much others charged for it.

Armed with these four pieces of information, she did not get misled. The fact that the discount stores she visited tagged their TV sets with a high "list price" did not impress her. She knew the "list" was meaningless, because none of the stores at which she had done her comparison shopping charged this alleged "list price" for the same set.

If you know—by having checked it out personally and not by just assuming it—that 100 tablets of Anacin cost less at your discount store than they do at your neighborhood drugstore, then they may well be meant as "bait." That means, of course, that they are real discounts. Like the canes that the concessionaire at the World's Fair virtually gave away, those Anacins are the discounter's best advertisements. He knows that many Americans who get those Anacins at his cut price will become "sold on discounting," will assume that the rest of his merchandise is similarly discounted, and will tell their friends all about it.

The thing to remember, however, is this: others may be paying higher markups to make up for the bargain you get! If you recommend such buying to your friends, the chances are that they will be subsidizing your loss-leader buying.

You may know for certain that the discounter's price on a specific toaster, electric shaver, steam iron, or watch is lower than the price being charged by his neighboring competitors and is, therefore, a real discount. Are you prepared to buy that bargain if it means other shoppers may buy "profit-boosters" to make up for your loss leader?

This is a question each reader must face for himself.

Notes

CHAPTER 1

Reference Sources:

"Quality and Price Stabilization," Hearings before a Subcommittee of the Committee on Interstate and Foreign Commerce, House of Representatives, 87th Congress, 2d Session, on H.R. 636 *et al.* June 11-15, 1962. (U.S. Government Printing Office, Washington, D.C., 1962; No. 87600) Referred to herein as *1962 House hearings.*

"Quality Stabilization," Hearings before a Subcommittee of the Committee on Commerce, United States Senate, 87th Congress, 2d Session, on S.J. Res. 59. April 9, 19, 23; May 24 and 25, 1962. (U.S. Government Printing Office, Washington, D.C., 1962; No. 85238) Referred to herein as *1962 Senate hearings.*

"Quality Stabilization—1963," Hearings before a Subcommittee of the Committee on Interstate and Foreign Commerce, House of Representatives, 88th Congress, 1st Session, on H.R. 3669. April 23-26, May 14 and 15, 1963. (U.S. Government Printing Office, Washington, D.C., 1963; No. 99685) Referred to herein as *1963 House hearings.*

Also, *The Discount Merchandiser*, April, 1963; "The Decline of 'List-Price' Advertising," by Attorney Sidney A. Diamond, *Advertising Age*, October 21, 1963; interviews, August/September 1964, with New York City Commissioner of Markets Albert S. Pacetta, James Wright, Richard Ebbole; interviews, January, 1965, State of New York Assistant Attorneys General Barnett Levy and Stephen E. Mindell, both of the Bureau of Consumer Frauds and Protection, Department of Law, State of New York, and with Samuel Breidenstein, Better Business Bureau, Detroit, Michigan.

CHAPTER 2

[1] As quoted in 1962 Senate hearings, p. 471.

[2] 1958 Senate hearings, p. 151. ["Discount-House Operations," Hearings before a Subcommittee of the Select Committee on Small Business, United States Senate, 85th Congress, 2d Session, on Competitive Impact of Discount-House Operations on Small Business. June 23, 24, and 25, 1958. (U.S. Government Printing Office, Washington, D.C., 1958; No. 28043). Referred to herein as *1958 Senate hearings.*]

[3] E. B. Weiss, *Marketing's Stake in the Low-Margin Retailing Revolution* (New York: Doyle Dane Bernbach Inc., 1961), p. 18.

CHAPTER 3

[1] Testimony of Henry R. Peters, November 13, 1963, as provided in "Quality Stabilization," Hearings before a Subcommittee of the Committee on Commerce, United States Senate, 88th Congress, on S. 774. June 5, August 19, September 9, October 9, November 7, 13, December 9, 1963, January 22, 23, and February 19, 1964. (U.S. Government Printing Office, Washington, D.C., 1964; No. 21-305), pp. 292-293. Referred to herein as *1963-1964 Senate hearings.*

[2] McCandless quote from *The Discount Merchandiser*, January, 1964, p. 26; Rosenstein quote from 1962 House hearings, p. 395.

[3] *The Discount Merchandiser*, December, 1961, as quoted in 1963 House hearings, p. 39.

[4] As quoted in 1961 House hearings, p. 217.

[5] 1962 House hearings, p. 122.

[6] Louis D. Brandeis, "Cut-Throat Prices: The Competition That Kills," *Harper's Weekly*, November 15, 1913.

[7] 1963 Senate hearings, p. 232.

[8] *The Discount Merchandiser*, January, 1963, p. 30.

[9] 1958 Senate hearings, pp. 195, 211, 277-279; 1962 Senate hearings, p. 255; 1962 House hearings, pp. 280-286; 1963 House hearings, pp. 45, 255-256; 1963-1964 Senate hearings, pp. 187, 203, 346, 352, 378, 465, 489, 578 *et seq.* See Addendum A, Chapter 3, pp. 154 ff.

[10] Material from "The Marrud Study," in *The Discount Merchandiser*, December, 1963, and by Senator William Proxmire, *Congressional Record*, April 29, 1964.

CHAPTER 4

[1] Sears, Roebuck & Co., advertisement, *Look*, July 14, 1964.

[2] Testimony of Robert E. Carter of Hub Furniture Co., Baltimore, Md. (vice president and chairman, governmental affairs committee, National Retail Furniture Association), 1962 Senate hearings, pp. 228, 229.

[3] *Ibid.*

[4] *Guides Against Bait Advertising*, U.S. Federal Trade Commission; issued November 24, 1959. (Reprinted in Appendix, pp. 209-211.)

[5] 1963 House hearings, pp. 241 *et seq.;* also 1963-1964 Senate hearings, pp. 107 *et seq.*

[6] Interviews, January, 1965, Barnett Levy and Stephen E. Mindell, Assistant Attorneys General, Dept. of Law, State of New York.

[7] 1962 Senate hearings, p. 327.

CHAPTER 5

[1] *New York Herald Tribune*, January 9, 1964.

[2] Sears, Roebuck & Co. advertisement, *Look*, July 14, 1964.

[3] Interviews, Commissioner Albert S. Pacetta and others, N.Y.C. Dept. of Markets, 1964–1965.

[4] United States Court of Appeals for the District of Columbia, opinion quoted in "The Decline of 'List-Price' Advertising," by Sidney A. Diamond, attorney, *Advertising Age*, October 21, 1963.

[5] E. B. Weiss, *op. cit.*, p. 19.

[6] *Ibid.*, p. 27.

[7] 1962 Senate hearings, p. 220.

[8] David R. Buschman, "The Great Sewing Machine Racket," Better Business Bureau report BBB-15.

[9] David R. Buschman, "TV Without Tears," Better Business Bureau report BBB-9.

[10] Facts You Should Know About Schemes," Better Business Bureau—Educational Division. © by Boston Better Business Bureau.

CHAPTER 6

[1] 1962 House hearings, p. 392.

[2] David R. Buschman, "The Great Sewing Machine Racket,' Better Business Bureau report BBB-15.

[3] *American Stock Exchange Investor*, December–January, 1964.

[4] Isadore Barmash, *New York Herald Tribune*; also Weiss, *op. cit.*, p. 17.

[5] 1963–1964 Senate hearings, pp. 349 *et seq.*

[6] *The Wall Street Journal*, May 17, 1962.

[7] *Home Furnishings Daily*, November 5, 1963.

[8] Charles E. Silverman, "The Distribution Upheaval III: The Department Stores Are Waking Up," *Fortune*, July, 1962, p. 60.

[9] *The Discount Merchandiser*, January, 1963, p. 21.

[10] Weiss, *Marketing's Stake*, p. 60.

[11] *The Wall Street Journal*, October 26, 1964.

CHAPTER 7

[1] *The Discount Merchandiser*, January, 1963.

[2] *Survey of Consumer Expenditures 1960-61*, Bureau of Labor Statistics, U.S. Department of Labor (Supplement 3, Part A, to BLS Report 237-38, July, 1964). See Addendum A, p. 000.

[3] *The Discount Merchandiser*, October, 1963.

[4] *Ibid.*, December, 1963, p. M-18.

[5] *Home Furnishings Daily*, April 3, 1958, quoted in 1958 Senate hearings, p. 430.

[6] 1958 Senate hearings, pp. 144, 393–394.

[7] 1962 Senate hearings, p. 72.

[8] Silverman, *op. cit.*

CHAPTER 8

[1] Brandeis, *op. cit.*

[2] Testimony of Nessie Nides, Extension of Remarks, *Congressional Record*, September 17, 1963.

[3] Brandeis, *op. cit.*

[4] E. B. Weiss, speech before Minneapolis Advertising Club, January 24, 1963.

[5] *Business Week*, November 16, 1963.

[6] Representative Thomas M. Pelly of Washington, Extension of Remarks, *Congressional Record*, October 7, 1963, citing Department of Commerce figures.

[7] *Ibid.*

[8] *The New York Times*, August 19, 1962, cited by Senator William Proxmire of Wisconsin, 1963 House hearings, p. 19.

[9] Statement of Maurice Mermey before a special subcommittee of the Senate Committee on Commerce, U.S. Senate, August 19, 1963.

[10] 1962 House hearings, p. 84.

[11] Victor Lebow, statement, 1958 Senate hearings, p. 4.

[12] 1962 House hearings, p. 164.

[13] *The Discount Merchandiser*, January, 1964.

[14] Address, Minnesota Retail Hardware Association convention, Echo Lake, Minnesota, August 27, 1963.

[15] Pelly, *op. cit.*

[16] *Washington Post*, June 7, 1961.

[17] *American Stock Exchange Investor*, February, 1964.

[18] *Barron's*, April 22, 1963.

[19] 1958 Senate hearings, p. 35.

[20] *Ibid.*, p. 160.

[21] *Ibid.*, pp. 253–254.

[22] 1962 Senate hearings, pp. 432 *et seq.*

[23] *Ibid.*, pp. 230 *et seq.*

[24] *Ibid.*, p. 120.

[25] *Ibid.*, p. 264.

[26] Extension of Remarks, *Congressional Record*, April 17, 1964.

[27] Weiss, *Marketing's Stake*, pp. 82–87.

[28] 1963 House hearings, p. 63.

[29] 1962 Senate hearings, p. 469.

CHAPTER 9

[1] 1958 Senate hearings, pp. 426–427; also, 1962 Senate hearings, p. 428.

[2] 1962 Senate hearings, p. 461.

[3] Statement before Subcommittee on Commerce and Finance, House Interstate and Foreign Commerce Committee, April 23, 1963.

[4] Cited in *What's in a Name?* (Schering Corp., Bloomfield, N.J.).

[5] 1963 House hearings, p. 183.

[6] *Home Furnishings Daily*, September 14, 1960.

[7] United States Federal Trade Commission Complaint, Docket #8276, February 2, 1961.

[8] Interviews, Asst. District Attorney Joseph Stone, New York County, N.Y., January, 1965.

[9] 1962 Senate hearings, pp. 222–223.

[10] *The New York Times*, August 5, 1964.

[11] *Home Furnishings Daily*, February 11, 1964.

[12] *Ibid.*

[13] *Op. cit.*, January 11, 1964.

[14] *Business Week,* December 14, 1963.

[15] King Features release, February 15/16, 1964.

[16] *New York Herald Tribune,* December 15, 1963.

[17] *Michigan Business Review,* January, 1962.

[18] *Insider's Newsletter,* January 27, 1964; also *Home Furnishings Daily,* January 15, 1964.

[19] Interviews, Asst. District Attorney Joseph Stone, N.Y. County, January, 1965; also, Address by Joseph Stone entitled "The Prosecution of Trademark Counterfeiting and Mislabeling in New York County," given before the 80th Annual Meeting, U.S. Trademark Assoc., May 17, 1957, and reprinted in *The Trademark Reporter,* Vol. 48, No. 3, March, 1958.

[20] *Time,* January 15, 1964.

[21] *The Wall Street Journal,* March 23, 1960.

[22] H.M.C. to Author, August, 1964.

[23] *Home Furnishings Daily,* March 9, 1961.

[24] 1962 Senate hearings, p. 13.

[25] 1962 House hearings, p. 450.

[26] 1962 Senate hearings, pp. 218–219.

[27] *Printer's Ink,* August 5, 1960.

[28] *Home Furnishings Daily,* April 18, 1962.

[29] *Op. cit.,* April 17, 1961.

[30] *Ibid.*

[31] *Op. cit.,* March 9, 1961.

[32] *Op. cit.,* October 2, 1959.

[33] *Op. cit.,* January 11, 1961.

[34] *Op. cit.,* March 9, 1961.

[35] *Consumer Reports,* October, 1963.

[36] 1962 Senate hearings, p. 99.

[37] 1963 House hearings, p. 376.

[38] *Printer's Ink,* January 22, 1960.

[39] 1962 House hearings, pp. 22–23.

[40] *Home Furnishings Daily,* April 4, 1961.

[41] *Op. cit.,* March 9, 1961.

[42] 1962 House hearings, p. 183.

[43] *Printer's Ink,* June 2, 1962.

[44] 1958 Senate hearings, p. 424.

[45] 1962 Senate hearings, p. 72.

CHAPTER 10

[1] From *Selected Letters of Robert Frost,* edited by Lawrance Roger Thompson (New York: Holt, Rinehart and Winston, 1964).

[2] Address before the 1963 Fourth Annual Promotion Conference, International Council of Shopping Centers, October 14, 1963, Detroit, Michigan.

[3] Marion M. Brown, "Furniture at Retail," *Home Furnishings Daily,* January 3, 1964.

[4] 1958 Senate hearings, pp. 401–402.

[5] *Fortune,* May, 1962.

[6] Sam Stern, real estate manager, Neisner Bros., as quoted in *The Discount Merchandiser,* January, 1964, p. 24.

[7] Nathaniel Schwartz, editor-in-chief, *The Discount Merchandiser,* editorials, January and April, 1963.

[8] Weiss, *op. cit.,* p. 27.

[9] *New York Herald Tribune,* January 7, 1964.

[10] 1962 House hearings, p. 400.

[11] Speech before New York Security Analysts, November 6, 1961.

[12] Extension of Remarks of Hon. Catherine May of Washington, *Congressional Record,* April 20, 1964.

[13] Statement before the House Interstate and Foreign Commerce Committee, January 19, 1915.

[14] Extension of Remarks of Hon. John Dent of Pennsylvania, *Congressional Record,* September 17, 1963.

[15] *Business Week,* February 3, 1962, as cited in 1963 House hearings, pp. 385–386.

Addenda

CHAPTER 1

A. The true number of discount stores in the U.S.A. is hard to arrive at. As far back as 1958, Professor Joseph Klamon of Washington University, St. Louis, Missouri, said the total came to about 10,000, a fivefold increase from 1952's 2,000. Even earlier, in 1954, columnist Sylvia Porter said there were 10,000 discount houses in the country, with about 1,000 of them in New York City. (Cited on page 119, 1958 Senate hearings.) One top authority, columnist Earl Lifshey, more recently counted the number of what he calls "rigidly defined, true, full-line discount department stores" and arrived at 2,169 *in this category alone*. (*Home Furnishings Daily*, December 4, 1963) "Full-line discount department stores" of course are the biggest in size and the smallest in number.

CHAPTER 3

A. So astounding is the omission of significant data on the part of the "modern mass merchandisers" that it is worth noting some of the figures which they did offer.

In 1958, Joseph L. Nellis, speaking for the National Association of Consumer Organizations Inc. (NACO), stated that their average gross margin ranged from 15 to 25 percent. He did not at the time disclose any figures for individual items to show how this 15 to 25 percent figure was arrived at. (1958 Senate hearings, p. 195.)

Also in 1958, an affidavit filed in 1953 by William P. Stansbury, manager of Pay-Less Drug Store, Tampa, Florida, which listed about 40 items on which his price was lower than that suggested by the manufacturer, was made an appendix to a statement by Alex Akerman of the National Anti-Price Fixing Assoc. This did not disclose any figures for other items in the Pay-Less store. (1958 Senate hearings, p. 211.)

Still again in 1958, Robert A. Bicks of the U.S. Department of Justice, produced a "nationwide survey" of 132 selected items on which "savings opportunities" were offered. These items came to an average total of 119 available in each city in the survey, a statistically meaningless segment of the items sold. Bicks also did not offer any figures to show the gross margins or markups maintained in the stores surveyed. (1958 Senate hearings, pp. 277-279.)

In 1952, Representative Emanuel Celler, defending price-cutting despite his exemplary record as a liberal Congressman, offered a private survey on which he seems to have based virtually his entire argument for over more than a decade. This survey amounted to 10 items! (1962 Senate hearings, p. 255.) In 1962, he enlarged upon it by adding 24 more products throughout the country. The only thing his figures showed me was that cut-price operators sold certain items for less in nine cities. In Miami, these consisted of 7 items; in Indianapolis, 7; in Louisville, 7; in Columbia, S.C., 6; in Seattle, 5; in Spokane, 2; in Huntington, W. Va., 3; in Minneapolis, 7; and in Cleveland, 8. (1962 Senate hearings, pp. 268, 269.)

In 1962, Charles Fort of Food Town Ethical Pharmacies, Inc., Baton Rouge, La., at the request of the committee submitted a list of about 70 items he sold for less than the price charged in so-called "fair trade" states. The list, he admits "reflects a small part of more than an estimated 50,000 [patented prescription drugs]."

Markup or comparative price figures for the rest of his store, which accounts for sales of $20,000 a day, were not part of his testimony. (1962 House hearings, pp. 280-286.) On Monday, August 19, 1963, Charles Fort appeared before a subcommittee of the Senate Committee on Commerce and, under questioning by Senator Vance Hartke of Indiana, the chairman, discussed how some discounters operate. He said, "I will tell you what we have found as a small businessman that brings us the greatest volume, and that is to price everything as low as we can and make a profit. Not to jack them up, not to get Japanese goods and make 100 percent. I don't even do that. *Now a lot of discount houses do that, so they make 100 percent on one item and sell below cost on another.* They think that is good, but that is not the way to do it. If you are going to live year after year with those consumers, they are going to find out and they are smart . . . *There are places making 1,000 percent on some merchandise and selling some below cost; that is going on today, right now . . .*" [Author's italics.] (1963-1964 Senate hearings, p. 144.)

In 1963, Representative Celler again trotted out his 1952 survey and added to it seven more items he'd bought in Maryland and in Washington, D.C., in September, 1962. He did not provide markup figures on any of these, but based virtually his entire defense of the discounter on the fact that he'd saved some money on these seven items! (1963 House hearings, p. 45.)

Also in 1963, George J. Nevole, manager of the G-E-X store in Hampton, Virginia, arguing for the discounters, provided the House of Representatives with "evidence" of the low markups in the G-E-X chain. This "evidence" consisted of prices on *six* items which he sells below the manufacturer's suggested retail price. (1963 House hearings, pp. 255, 256.)

The *1963-1964 Senate hearings* contain some further figures. Howard Waller, president of The Corondolet Corp., Oakville Branch, Memphis, Tenn., listed 19 products on which he showed both his stores' original prices and higher prices resulting from a Tennessee "fair trade" act. The list also showed the percentage of profit under both pricing situations. His stores had sold these 19 products at a profit ranging from 23.7 to 30.0 percent; after "fair trade," the range was from 40 to 50.

Jack C. Holley of Webb's City, Inc., St. Petersburg, Fla., offered a statement in which he included a list of 24 products, contrasting the manufacturer's suggested retail price and Webb's City's own price. He provided no information about margins or markups in Webb's City.

Stanley H. Feldberg, president of Zayre Corp., Natick, Mass., provided a list of 24 products sold in Zayre stores in the Washington, D.C., area, also contrasting the manufacturer's recommended price and Zayre's own, lower, price. Mr. Feldberg emphasized in his testimony that Zayre stores sell at low markups and do not "fool the public by offering some goods at a low markup, and then employ a high markup on other so-called less competitive goods." He did not, however, tell the Senators what Zayre's markup was, either average or on all products in the stores.

Joseph Marcus, president of GEM International, Inc., St. Louis, Mo., provided a much more extensive list of products and prices, all of them items now sold under fair trade and merely indicating that, on these products, GEM'S former price had been lower than its fair trade price.

William H. Orrick, Jr., of the Department of Justice compared liquor prices in Washington, D.C., where they are low, to liquor prices in New York State, where they are higher. He also provided a number of price comparisons in actions brought under "fair trade" laws. The same two lists were again submitted by Representative John D. Dingell of Michigan.

A list of 25 products, with the "suggested retail price" and "Webb's price" contrasted, was submitted by J. E. "Doc" Webb, president of Webb's City, Inc., St. Petersburg, Fla. The list did not contain figures showing either average margins or markups throughout the store, or margins or markups on all items in the store.

Finally, a statement submitted on behalf of National Bellas Hess, Inc., a nationwide retail organization, makes the point that markups at its stores range from 20 to 30 percent across the board, on all merchandise. Figures to substantiate this, however, were not supplied. Instead, the company provided figures showing that, on six different items ranging from Old Spice after-shave lotion to Whitman's Sampler chocolates, it offered markups ranging from 18.8 to 25.9 percent. These figures are, of course, precisely the kind that Senator Proxmire had been looking for, but the sample seems too small to be meaningful. National Bellas Hess specializes in mail-order retailing and also owns and operates large retail centers known as the G-E-X stores in the East, Midwest, and South. It is questionable whether the six items listed constitute a fair sample of, for example, all merchandise in any one G-E-X store. (1963-1964 Senate hearings, pp. 187, 203, 346, 352, 378, 465, 489, 578 *et seq.*)

There may, elsewhere or on other occasions, have been other figures offered by discount-store enthusiasts but, like Senator William Proxmire, I have not come across them. They were not apparent to me in my study of Senate and House subcommittee hearings over almost six years. In this connection, it seems significant that *The Discount Merchandiser* apparently regards The Marrud Study as the first significant disclosure of this kind. Hailing the decision of Marrud's president to cooperate in the study, the editors expressed the hope that it "would do much to ameliorate the image of discounting and that his cooperation might get others in the industry to lift the so-called 'veil of secrecy.'" The president of Marrud himself referred to the existence of this industry secrecy. Introducing the Study, he writes, "It is my own hope that this represents the beginning of a healthy exchange of information of benefit to us all. In other retailing fields such as super markets and department stores, the motto seems to be: 'There are no secrets.' As a result, volumes of information are published as guideposts for those industries. We need to do the same. It will make better merchants of us all."

B. The following statements elaborate on the use of the loss leader:

(1) Philip Cortney, James Lloyd Fri, and Richard N. Sears, in a joint statement, said:

"There is no mystery in regard to the technique of discount selling. In order to stay in business, this type of store must realize a minimum gross margin on its total sales just the same as any other retailer. Thus, for every dollar he sells below his required percentage markup, he must sell an equal volume above his markup. In brief, the formula for operating under a discounting policy is simply to surround every deeply discounted item (loss leader) with three or four 'profit-boosters.' " (1963 House hearings, pp. 429-431.)

(2) Maurice Mermey, director of the Bureau for the Advancement of Independent Retailing, New York City, said in 1959:

"If some products are sold at profitless prices, other products bringing a high profit must be sold to make up the deficit. Therefore the retailer who practices loss-leader merchandising must have a storewide pricing policy that involves higher-than-average-profit prices; in this way he makes the profitless bait bargains pay off. When a price-cutter claims that his 'bait' prices are due to his efficiency which he alleges permits him to operate on a 15- or 20-percent gross margin, we must ask ourselves what prices go into this gross margin. For the price-cutter can and does make up a 'mix' of storewide prices which will yield him an average 15- or 20-percent gross margin annually. Some of these pricings will yield the price-cutter no profit, or 5, 10, or 20 percent. Other pricings will yield him 40, 60, 100 percent, and in one case reported by the Federal Trade Commission, the markup went as high as 1,100 percent.

"There is no magic secret of efficiency and no philanthropy for the consumer involved here. It is simply price juggling. No price juggler who bleeds so profusely for the

American consumer has dared open his complete set of audited books to show what prices and margins go into his 15- or 20-percent gross margin. . . . One thing is certain—the price-cutter is not selling everything in his store at a profit-less price, nor is he selling everything at a 15-percent markup. Even to attempt this would be to commit business suicide." (1959 Senate hearings, p. 370.)

(3) Justice Louis D. Brandeis wrote: "The more success-ful the individual producer of a trade-marked article has been in creating for it a recognized value as well as a wide sale, the greater is the temptation to the unscrupulous to cut the price. Indeed a cut-price article can ordinarily be effec-tive as a 'mis-leader' only when both the merits and the established selling price are widely known." (Brandeis, *op. cit.*)

(4) The "bait" aspects of loss-leader selling are described in a statement by John A. McCandless, vice president of Neisner Brothers. "What better loss-leader is there than a toy every kid in the country has seen on television?" (*The Discount Merchandiser,* January 1964, page 26.) His com-ment helps to explain why nearly 50 percent of the toys in the country were already in 1961 moving through discount stores. (Weiss, *op. cit.,* p. 13.)

(5) "Those who cut prices on branded merchandise do not do so from purely altruistic reasons," writes Herbert Koshetz of *The New York Times.* "Admittedly, they are seeking to create store traffic, and know that the customer who came in to buy the cut-price item will stay to buy others that are sold at regular profits. . . . It stands to reason, therefore, that if he sells one-tenth of his goods at severely cut prices, then some part of the other nine-tenths must be marked above his average to meet his earnings requirements. The consumer buying that portion of his goods may not be getting anything resembling a bargain." (*The New York Times,* July 21, 1963)

(6) Attorney Sidney Waller of Chicago says "no [anti-loss-leader] legislation of any kind would be necessary" if merchants indeed did offer loss-leader-type bargains throughout their stores. "The laws of arithmetic would soon take care of such a merchant." (1958 Senate hearings, p. 90.)

C. The fact that the lure to the public almost invariably consists of nationally branded merchandise is explored by three writers for *Home Furnishings Daily*. "Brands are nearly as important as customers for discounters.... For the discounter, the ability to advertise national brands at a discount price has long been the most important part of his hard goods operation. The big brand at a low price conveys value and establishes a true 'discount' identity.... National brands, even the stanchest supporters of private brands agree, are essential in the first few years of a discount store's operation to create images of reliability, quality, and value." (Alvin M. Winters, *Home Furnishings Daily*, April 11, 1963.)

"Remove the identifying trademark from any well-known product and the retailer who was ready to buy it before won't do so now. He has good reason. For the trademark of such a product provides immediate public recognition and acceptance for it; without it, all that remains is just so much material of unknown quality and reliability." (Earl Lifshey, *H.F.D.*)

"Let's quit shadowboxing on the discount facts of life. Which brand name lines are the discounters most hellbent to get...? Isn't it those lines whose birthright and market right have been most scrupulously protected through clean, administered distribution.... We don't have to name names. If you've been around in the home-goods business for a few years, you should know by now...." (Raymond S. Reed, *H.F.D.*, February 14, 1962.)

Daily News Record, another retailing trade paper, says "Brands are the backbone of thousands of stores in the United States. Remove the backbone and you have crippled the store." (*Daily*

News Record, May 18, 1962, quoted in 1962 House hearings, p. 173.)

D. Defining bait advertising, Representative Chet Holifield says he means by it practices "where a discount house, for example, obtains a dozen or two dozen Arrow shirts and puts a big two-page ad in the paper and says $5 Arrow shirts will be sold next Monday at $4.19 or $3.69. The public knows that the Arrow shirt is a real value at $5. It is established in the marketplace. They see this ad. The women come in to buy the Arrow shirts."

Holifield says that in some such cases they will find the store does indeed have a few dozen Arrow shirts, but that these often will be offsizes, many of them in shopworn condition. Also, there are very few of them and they sell quickly. "But hundreds of women who come in to buy that Arrow shirt, to get that bargain . . . find that they do not have any more, that they have run out. There is a big table there, maybe 50 feet long, stacked four feet high with white shirts that look just like Arrow shirts, and these are on sale for $4.19 or maybe even $3.99. The woman customer who comes in to get her husband a shirt does the natural thing. She goes over. Not being a real good judge of merchandise—and she cannot be a good judge of every type of merchandise—she takes one of those no-name-brand shirts." The shirt she buys, says Holifield, who has experience in the retail men's wear business, may have five buttons on the front, instead of seven. It may be a single-stitch shirt instead of a double-stitch. It may have a count of 30 percent fewer threads to the square inch, with the balance being made up of starch that vanishes in the first wash. "The result," says Holifield, "is that that woman gets an unsatisfactory article and she wastes her money because she does not get 100 percent value on the dollar." (1962 House hearings, pp. 62-63.)

E. Loss leaders also go under other names, but their effect is the same. They are sometimes called bait merchandise, promotionals, promotional merchandise, or traffic items. Their effect, as stated, is to take customers away from conventional retailers by insinuating, in substance, that "This guy has been sticking you for 40-some-odd years. Why don't you come and buy from us?" (1962 House hearings, p. 400.)

F. The discounter who referred to a policy of handling "only basic merchandise" (*See Chapter 6*), is also quoted in *The Discount Merchandiser* on the subject of loss leaders in his operation. His operation, he says, tries to avoid this "as much as possible." He says that only one out of every 20 items his stores advertise is a loss leader, the remainder being sold "at a legitimate profit." (*The Discount Merchandiser*, October, 1963.) This is, of course, merely increasing the confusion, for the effect can be that the one item out of the 20 that is offered as a loss leader can lead shoppers to believe that the other 19 are similarly priced.

G. "The nationally advertised quality brand-name products become profitless pawn for the exclusive advantage of those sellers who pursue a consistent policy of loss-leader and discount-selling schemes," says R. J. Wilkinson, executive manager of the Master Photo Dealers' and Finishers' Association. He points out also that no one makes a profit on the sale of such products, neither the price-cutter, nor the conventional retailer who finds he cannot sell these products any more. "Thousands of the conventional service-type retailers eventually abandon the product," Wilkinson says, "and when that happens, the discounters can't and won't try to sell it either." (1962 Senate hearings, p. 463.)

H. Is loss-leader selling on the ascendancy? Herbert Koshetz, of *The New York Times*, flatly predicts that unless remedies are applied "loss-leader merchandising will again be on the ascendancy, much to the consternation of small merchants whose business rests heavily on the nationally advertised brands. At the same time, consumers attracted by cut prices on branded merchandise will find themselves faced with large assortments of unbranded goods which, if purchased, will more than offset any savings they may achieve on the cut-price items ..." (*The New York Times*, January 26, 1964.)

Years ago, says E. B. Weiss, discounters were "whispering" their prices in the marketplace and not "screaming" them as they do today. (Weiss, *op. cit.*, pp. 5, 7.) In those early days, many discounters dealt almost exclusively in appliances and TV sets, and their merchandise was genuinely discounted, with few soft goods being carried to be marked up high enough to counter the losses. Today, however, many discounters put 70 to 80 percent of their stock in soft goods, home furnishings, food, drugs, etc. (*ibid.*, p. 14.) These allow for high hidden margins of profit and permit the store to "scream" their loss leaders at the public.

I. There is no Federal statute against loss-leader selling as such. Section 3 of the Robinson-Patman Act prohibits the sale of merchandise at "unreasonably low prices" under certain conditions, for example, if it can be proved that the practice is followed in order to destroy competition or to eliminate a competitor. The maximum penalty is $5,000 in fines, imprisonment for one year, or both. Under certain circumstances, this offense can also constitute a violation of the Federal Trade Commission Act, although selling below cost *per se* is not prohibited by the FTC Act. Still, while bait advertising and predatory price-cutting may in some situations be illegal under Federal law, the remedy is not available to private persons. Furthermore, as Chairman Dixon of the FTC points out, time is the real killer here. A very good attorney, Dixon says, "within the framework of due process can keep one of those cases alive a pretty good time ... from four to five years." During that period, Dixon adds, "very often the party that complained disappears from the American scene. He is gone...." (1958 Senate hearings, pp. 259–260, and 1962 House hearings, pp. 112, 122–123, and 323.) One can easily imagine where he has gone: to the retailing graveyard. As for loss leaders that are misrepresented in advertisements, not much can be done about them either. Attorney Ira Millstein points out that "few states even prosecute false advertising to any significant degree." (Ira Millstein, "The Federal Trade Commission and False Advertising," *Columbia Law Review*, March, 1964.)

The FTC is hopeful that Congress will give it temporary restraining or cease-and-desist powers pending final disposition of a case. As an FTC attorney explained to me, the violation all too often has been completed before the FTC can issue its cease-and-desist order, or get a consent decree agreed to.

In the *1963 Annual Report of the Federal Trade Commission*, the FTC called for three types of new legislation. The first dealt with corporate mergers, but the second and third are pertinent to this book. The FTC urged the enactment of laws that would:

"2. Amend section 5 of the FTC Act so as to empower the Commission to issue a temporary restraining or cease and desist order, pending completion of proceedings by the Commission in all cases in which the Commission is authorized to issue a complaint and final order to cease and desist thereunder, when the Commission has reason to believe that its action would be in the public interest and would prevent irreparable harm.

"3. Amend the FTC Act so as to make it clear that the Commission has jurisdiction to prevent the continuance of sales over which it has jurisdiction, where such sales are below cost and have an adverse competitive effect regardless of the intent of the sellers in making the sales."

In the opinion of this author, such laws are indeed badly needed.

J. The final comment on loss leaders came from a Senate committee report:

"Gains realized from loss-leader selling are short-lived. The practice is a vicious one and defeats itself. No merchant, however large, can afford to continue loss-leader selling indefinitely. He must engage in other practices in order to recoup his losses. And such other practices of necessity require that he sell other merchandise at high profits. The consumer must sooner or later discover the fallacy of the loss-leader selling technique, and then the retailer loses the goodwill of his customers and their patronage." (1962 Report of the Senate Select Small Business Committee, to the Senate Interstate and Foreign Commerce Committee.)

K. The margin requirements of independent neighborhood stores are often vastly exaggerated and are often considerably lower than might be expected by consumers. The Merchants Service of National Cash Register Company, Dayton, Ohio, reports the following in its *Expenses in Retail Businesses:*

Appliance and radio-TV dealers who offer service as well as merchandise maintain a national average gross margin of 27.25 percent; auto parts dealers, 34.92 percent; bookstores, 37.5 percent; neighborhood children's and infants' wear stores, 30.3 percent; department stores doing under $1 million in sales volume, 33.65 percent; neighborhood dry goods and general merchandise stores, 29.4 percent; furniture stores with sales below $250,000, 38.48 percent; neighborhood gift, novelty, and souvenir stores, 39.6 percent; grocery stores, 16.59 percent versus supermarkets, 18.83 percent (grocery stores doing under $50,000 average 16.19 percent); hardware stores in counties with populations ranging from 350,000 to two million and doing $100,000 to $200,000 in sales volume, 33.80 percent; hardware stores in counties with over two million population and doing the same sales volume, 32.80 percent; hardware stores in semirural areas, same volume, 32.15 percent; hardware stores in rural counties, same volume, 33 percent; hardware stores in all other counties, same volume, 28 percent; meat markets, 20.11 percent; men's wear stores, 35.1 percent; men's wear stores handling women's wear also, 36.6 percent; office supply and equipment dealers, 15.15 percent; paint and wallpaper dealer-distributors, 33.48 percent; retail pharmacies: average, all stores, 36 percent, sales between $100,000 and $120,000, 35.4 percent; shoe stores with sales volume under $50,000, 33.8 percent; specialty stores with sales volume under $1 million, 36.55 percent; sporting goods stores with sales volume under $75,000, 29.0 percent (national average, all stores, 29.9 percent); toy stores, 34.1 percent (neighborhood toy stores, 32.7 percent); and variety stores, 35.97 percent.

The words *margin* and *markup* need clarification. There are two ways of figuring markup: one based on cost (what the retailer paid for the item), the other based on selling price (what he charged the consumer). Markup based on selling price means the same as *margin* and to avoid confusion I have used only the word "margin" for this concept. When I refer to markup, I refer to what consumers are more interested in: the difference between what the consumer pays for the product and what the store paid for it.

If a retailer buys an item for one dollar and sells it for $1.40, his *markup* is 40 cents or 40 percent. His *margin*, of course, remains 40 *cents*, but the percentage figures go down, because margins are calculated on selling price. His margin is 40 cents on $1.40 selling price, or 28.56 percent.

The following table converts margins (or gross margins, as they are sometimes called) into markup figures.

10%	margin equals	11⅑%	markup
15%	"	"	17⅔%	"
20%	"	"	25%	"
25%	"	"	33⅓%	"
26%	"	"	35%	"
27¼%	"	"	37½%	"
28⁴⁄₇%	"	"	40%	"
30%	"	"	42⁶⁄₇%	"
31%	"	"	45%	"
33⅓%	"	"	50%	"
35½%	"	"	55%	"
37½%	"	"	60%	"
40%	"	"	66⅔%	"
42⁶⁄₇%	"	"	75%	"
50%	"	"	100%	"

(*continued on next page*)

	margin	equals		markup
60%	"	"	150%	"
66⅔%	"	"	200%	"
70%	"	"	233⅓%	"
75%	"	"	300%	"
80%	"	"	400%	"
83⅓%	"	"	500%	"
90%	"	"	900%	"

CHAPTER 4

A. Bait-and-switch practices, says Senator A. S. Mike Monroney of Oklahoma, "are trade practices which are well established and which are recognized in the trade, to use and hitchhike only on the national advertising value and the quality imprint on the merchandise with no thought of ever selling the advertised merchandise. Some irate customer may be able to take it away from the salesman, but the salesman can put up an awful resistance, if he knows he is getting no commission at all, or a reprimand for selling the loss-leader advertised. But if he sells the switched product that he is supposed to sell, then he would not only be complimented on pushing that, but would receive an additional bonus for the sale. That goes all through various lines, clothing, appliances, and things of that kind." (1962 Senate hearings, p. 17.)

B. Bait merchandise that has been "nailed down" is also referred to as a "kicker" and the practice of switching is also called "slotting." Use of special incentives ("spiffs") for salesmen is a clear indication of bait-and-switch policies, says the Federal Trade Commission. When such policies exist, says the FTC, the store "makes use of a sales plan or method of compensation for salesmen or penalizing salesmen, designed to prevent or discourage them from selling the advertised product." (*Guides Against Bait Advertising, op. cit.*)

C. Several further examples of baiting-and-switching:

(1) Representative Chet Holifield tells of a bait-and-switch operator who maintained four or five sizes of a brand-name suit in his store while prominently advertising the brand for sale. They would, says Holifield, fit about one man in a thousand. (1962 Senate hearings, p. 33.)

(2) Representative Ray Madden reports: "In my office last week, I got a letter from a retired retailer in Virginia who used to be in the clothing business. He was astonished to find a quality brand suit advertised [in] a great big ad in the local paper at $38 ... the price ordinarily was $72. He said, 'Out of curiosity I will get there early and see what this is all about.' When he got down there he discovered there were five off-sized suits which had been in the store a long time, which they couldn't sell, but they used the brand name to get the people in the store." (1962 House hearings, p. 21.)

(3) John W. Hubbell, vice president of Simmons Company, makers of Beautyrest mattresses: "A case in point is a large discount store in New York which advertised the fact that it had Beautyrest mattresses at cut prices, despite the fact that it was not an authorized sales outlet for the Simmons Co. Many customers told us our merchandise was maligned in this discount house. This was no surprise, because the store found it necessary to degrade our merchandise to avoid selling it. (It was difficult for the store to get a supply on the one hand, and they had to sell it at a loss on the other hand.) One of our employees and his wife went to this discount house as shoppers and were exposed to a tirade of untruths about the Beautyrest mattress. This discount house advertised the Beautyrest because it wanted to attract trade. It felt that it would be able to cope with the situation by sales manipulation (polite word for misrepresentation). The store switched consumers to an inferior product which it could buy at a cheaper wholesale price.

A fictitious price label on the cheaper mattress led the public to think that the mattress was worth $20 more than its real value. This inflated price label was a device to aid the discounter." (1962 House hearings, p. 412.)

(4) Leonard B. Sadow, assistant to the chairman of the board of Longines-Wittnauer Watch Company, New York City, says it is "common for cut price outlets to sell old watches that have passed through several dealers' hands as presently new and perfect." Many discount stores, he says, sell mostly watches in "so-called promotional lines which bear exaggerated retail prices and which permit, therefore, substantial discounts. The discount or cut price operator rarely concentrates on the good or fine watch which has been offered at a reasonable retail price. However, he does not leave these brands alone. Generally he manages to obtain indirectly a few of the preferred trademark watches and exhibits these with the multitude of promotional watches to give the impression of broad stock. Yet, because of the lower profits involved and the difficulty of obtaining some of these brands, he instructs his sales people to sell completely away from these lines and frequently talk them down. Many times he stocks a private brand of his own against which he can give a large discount. To promote the sale of his own brand watch as against the fine watch lines that he is slowly devitalizing, he offers his sales people special money incentives called spiffs. Many times an enterprising sales clerk in a cut price outlet can make substantial additional money selling the special promotional watches and getting the so-called spiffs." (1962 Senate hearings, p. 232.)

D.   Regarding off-brand merchandise, to which customers are switched, and regarding quality and value in such merchandise:

(1) Kermit C. Krum, president of Krum's Photographic, a store in Battle Creek, Mich., tells of a factory salesman for low-quality merchandise who wanted to set the Krum store

up as an outlet for his factory. He told Krum, "You can sell our merchandise for 25 per cent off and still maintain your usual mark-up." Krum showed the salesman the door, but says "our discounting competitors welcome him." (Letter to former Representative Peter Mack, dated June 12, 1962, 1962 House hearings, pp. 433-434.) When such merchandise is sold to the public, it is of course often vastly overpriced. The suggestion that it is "discounted" can, therefore, often be dismissed.

(2) Regarding quality and value, Quality Brands Associates of America, Inc., says, "There is likely to be a great difference between the quality requirements of a national brand name product and those in an 'off-brand' product. The 'off-brand' merchandise is pushed in 'one-shot deals,' and targets of opportunity where a quantity of cheaply made goods can be dumped on the market at a quick profit. The manufacturer of off-brand products, having no great investment in advertising, and no established brand name reputation to maintain, can then easily change the name on the product and come back for more. A customer, disappointed in the short erratic life of the first product, may buy it again under a different name, never realizing both are made by the same manufacturer." (*The Case for Quality Stabilization*, published by Quality Brands Associates of America, Inc., Gary, Ind.)

(3) Vice President Hubert H. Humphrey's comment regarding bait-and-switch techniques (while a U.S. Senator):

"It might be that Munsingwear sells down the street for $2 and a block away it sells for $1.19. When they get you at the $1.19 store, you don't come out with Munsingwear; you come out with a gunny-sack." (1962 Senate hearings, p. 122.)

(4) Senator A. S. Mike Monroney reports that he has seen the same mattress with price tags varying from $29.95 to $79.95. Often the high price is fictitious. The salesman,

he reports, then says to his customer, "Gosh, you know, this is only $5 or $10 off, but I can give you $40 off on this other mattress." "Nobody," says Monroney, "knows what is under the cover of that mattress, except the man who bought it and maybe he did not know how many springs it had, what kind of cotton, long or short staple, or felt or hair." (1962 Senate hearings, p. 226.)

(5) The president of a St. Louis-based domestic linens firm that sells in about 40 discount houses, says that "smokescreen advertising" often lures the public into buying second-rate merchandise. In his own field, for example, an inch here and there is often trimmed off sheets; 63-by-99-inch sheets are sold at low prices while the rest of the prices in the linen department remain high and pillows are often stuffed with chicken feathers instead of goose feathers. (*The Discount Merchandiser*, January, 1964, p. 35.)

(6) E. B. Weiss points out that discounters, once their "discounting images" are established, "put in their own controlled brands" particularly in such lines as women's ready-to-wear. It is in such lines, Weiss says, that "powerful brand names are few and where the public is totally unable to determine values." (Weiss, *op cit.*, p. 28.)

E. In a year-end report on the appliance business, Manning Greenberg, columnist for *Home Furnishings Daily*, interviewed three appliance dealers about the "biggest challenge" they would face next year. These men (who preferred to remain nameless) were, says Greenberg, "three of the best known appliance dealers in the country." The one answer he received from all was, "I have to find a way to increase gross margin." Two of them proposed to do this by adopting the following techniques. The first said, "There's only one thing we can do and that's get the customers to buy the most profitable items. To do that we're going to push our sales training to a fare-thee-well. Our salesmen aren't going to ask what the customer wants to spend. They're going to ask what they need. They're going to talk benefits and features and point out that the few extra dollars won't make any difference in the long pull. And then they're going to ask for the order." In other words, they're going to switch the customer up to a higher-priced item, or "put him on the elevator," as the trade calls it.

The third man interviewed was even more frank. "My drive in 1964 will be toward boldness. I'm going to do things I've never done before. I'll have nail-downs on the floor; our ad layouts will be punchier; we'll employ the same tactics as our big store competition.... While we're going to push low-end goods [i.e., low-price, low-quality goods] in our ads we're going to trade the customer to higher-priced merchandise.... Our prices will be competitive, but we're going to push profitable goods and consumer benefits. If the customer balks on a price, we're going to let her walk, if making the sale means an inadequate profit...." (*Home Furnishings Daily*, December 31, 1963.) [This apparently means he will bait the customer in with low-priced goods, but will let her walk out empty-handed rather than sell her those goods—presumably the "nail-downs."]

F. Martin Mayer writes: "As the discounter moves into new areas and meets rising costs, he is tempted to advertise a brand name at a big saving, and then to 'switch' the customer in the store from the brand to something that carries the store's own name, on which the markup may be quite high. There's no doubt that such things happen...." ("Fair Trade or Foul, The Battle Rages Again!" *The Saturday Evening Post*, April 11, 1964.) The fact that "the markup may be quite high" on items the consumer regards as a low discount is precisely what misleads many an American shopper.

CHAPTER 5

A. Raymond S. Reed, widely-read *Home Furnishings Daily* columnist:

"Who is suggesting today's 'suggested list price'? Who is

comparing today's 'Comparable Value'? From some of the lulus we've seen in recent newspaper ads, we might guess the Grimm brothers, if those famous collectors of fairy tales hadn't departed this vale of tears over 100 years ago. Furthermore, the professors Grimm published their folk and fairy tales to *delight* their readers. In sorry contrast, many modern merchants publish phony list prices to *delude* them.

"What is the purpose of a list price? Does a manufacturer establish a 'suggested list price' for the benefit of his loyal, franchised, stocking account who will protect it... or [for a] ruthless price-cutter who wants to riddle and wreck it? Sometimes we can't help but wonder. The manufacturer who sets up a list price which he knows nobody will ever observe, obviously doesn't care what happens to his product or prestige, once it has left his shipping platform. Realistically, he hasn't issued a list price, only a license to murder it in the marketplace. What about his goodwill? Don't be silly. After all, that's only listed at one buck on his balance sheet. . . ."

Reed goes on to explain that many discounters are "ardent supporters" of "suggested list prices." Such supporters, he says, "adore and encourage the *inflation* of all 'list prices,' " presumably because such high list prices make their alleged discounts ever more attractive. He also notes that they will fight the "stabilization" of resale prices, i.e., laws that fight price-cutting and support the trademark's owner's right to maintain his resale price. Such laws aim at extending to independent manufacturers the same "built-in" protection enjoyed by manufacturers who sell direct to consumers, either through their own stores, through franchised dealers, or through sales personnel calling directly at the home.

Reed then refers to another tactic which is well-known in the trade but which is misunderstood by the general buying public. He says there are discounters who claim they show a higher price on the tag "for identification only." This is often sheer gobbledygook, meant to bamboozle the authorities along with the consumer. It is a favorite tactic of those "whose aim [in the words of the FTC] is to walk as closely as possible to the line between legal and illegal conduct." (As quoted in *Advertising Age*, January 13, 1964.)

"The discounters wish to maintain the 'suggested list price' only to provide consumers with a 'means of identification,' so help them," Raymond Reed writes with irony. "For example, the discounter who advertises a 36-piece electric train set at '72 percent OFF the open-stock, mfr. sugg. list' isn't really quoting you a comparative. He's merely making it easy for you to identify the right set. All you have to do is decide which train set you'd be nutty enough to buy piecemeal, at open stock prices. If a 72 percent deduction from the total amounts to the discounter's advertised price, you've got it. Otherwise, you'll just have to keep on trying.

"An FTC examiner once observed, 'The general populace knows that a list price is only a means of identification and a starting point for value to be fixed, ultimately, by forces of competition. The list price method of doing business, however it may be abused or subverted to harmful practices, has become a way of life'! In a somewhat contradictory finding, the FTC has also ruled, 'Manufacturers may lawfully apply 'reasonable' suggested list prices to retailers, so long as they warn the retailers, in print, against using them as deceptive comparatives.' Who is kidding whom?

"An evasive by-product of the 'suggested list price' taboo is the 'Comparative Value.' This nifty little gimmick can contrive a $94 comparative on a $39 promotional mattress. How can anyone justify such a wild and wooly claim? It's easy. If the $39 mattress had been made, one at a time, by Tiffany, and was button tufted with cultured pearls, it probably *would* have to retail at 94 bucks."

As Reed points out in his column, "There are manufacturers who establish suggested list prices and firm resale prices . . . who manage to make them stick, who make sure they are strictly observed by the retailer and hence, respected by the consumer. These manufacturers set a realistic, competitive price that will provide a decent markon for the merchant, as well as a topflight value for his customer. After which, they run a tight shop, keep a vigilant watch on their distribution, never stand for any dirty work or monkey business at the retail crossroads. How do they do it? Mostly, with a simple, four-letter synonym of 'intestinal fortitude.' " (Raymond S. Reed, *Home Furnishings Daily*, November 8, 1963.)*

B. In the matter of inflated list prices, artificial "discounts" and other fraudulent ticketing policies, the reader is urged to refer again to prior examples in Chapter 1, viz., the phony $99.50 tags on suits allegedly discounted to $63; the switching of manufacturer's price-tags on watches; the inflation of "list" prices on off-brand mattresses; the Sunbeam Mixmaster and Regina Floor Waxer case history.

C. The president of the discount-store linens supply company cited earlier admits that "there is no shortage of merchandise at $13 to $13.75 per dozen wholesale." He deplores the fact that many discounters "pounce on these goods to retail at $1.77, while trying to convey to the customer that this is a bona fide $1.98 value." (*The Discount Merchandiser*, January 1964, p. 34.) Such practices are easiest in soft goods (such as clothing, etc.) where, as we noted, E. B. Weiss says the public is unable to assess value. Earl Lifshey of *Home Furnishings Daily* points out why such practices are increasing. "The real reason [why discounters are] moving deeper into the soft goods area stems primarily from the fact that it is potentially more profitable. One can always manipulate the markup much more effectively on 'blind' items like soft goods than one can on easily identifiable, branded products bearing a manufacturer's model number, if not list price." (*Home Furnishings Daily*, December 4, 1963.)

* Reprinted by permission of HOME FURNISHINGS DAILY (November 8, 1963). Copyright (1963), Fairchild Publications, Inc.

D. Justice Brandeis, addressing the House Interstate and Foreign Commerce Committee, January 19, 1915, said: "Value consists of five things. First, in the making of a good article ... not only in the sense of its being good in quality, but an article which meets a need, a desire of the people. That is one thing. The next thing is that the article should be known, because it may be ever so good but if it is not widely known it will not do the producer or the world any good. And the third is that the article should not only be known, but should be known as being worth the price at which it can be had in the community. There is a fourth requirement: the article to become very valuable should not only be known and known to be worth the price but it should be easily accessible to possible purchasers, for the public will not make a sacrifice of time and effort in order to get it. And I might add a fifth requirement: *that a man buying it may buy it lightly; that is, without having to go through any agony in making up his mind whether, when he takes the article at the price at which it is offered, he is going to get his money's worth.*" [Author's italics.]

Defined in Justice Brandeis' enlightened terms, many products today offer very little true value indeed. After being subjected to the "modern mass merchandising" techniques so widely used in discounting, a product may be (1) questionable as to quality; (2) no longer easily accessible as their distribution network is destroyed; (3) questionable as to price; and (4) filled with agony and doubt for those consumers who, with good reason, suspect they've been tricked by phony price tags.

E. Questionable "discounts" may be arrived at in sundry ways. One technique is to offer a big trade-in allowance. Despite it, the actual retail price paid by the consumer may prove to be no saving. One chain, for example, entered into an agreement with the Bureau of Consumer Frauds and Protection of the Attorney General of the State of New York in such a matter. It had published a newspaper advertisement offering $200 trade-ins "on your old TV set regardless of age, make or condition" towards the purchase of a color TV. The agreement said it would desist from using this ad and from "offering to the general public by means of newspaper advertisement or otherwise a trade-in allowance for the purpose of disguising the true retail price or creating a false impression that a reduced price or special price is obtainable only by such trade-in."

F. The practices described in this chapter are particularly interesting when put alongside the big profits reaped by many discounters who claim to the public that they are satisfied with big volume. Discounters, says Weiss, get "an extremely high return on investment—the true guide to store performance." He adds that no other mass retailer comes close. Some discounters, he says, show a return on investment 100 to 1,000 percent higher than other chains. (Weiss, *op. cit.*, pp. 17-19.) "The discount firm realizes a return on investment that is above average," is the more conservative language employed by two New York University School of Retailing researchers, who analyzed 133 retail firms. (David J. Rachman and Linda J. Kemp, in *Journal of Retailing*, quoted in *The Discount Merchandiser*, April, 1963, p. 10.) Return on investment, however, is only one measure of the profitability of discount houses. Another is net profit after taxes. "Our whole operation is predicated on developing sales from which we can realize a net profit of between four and six percent after taxes," says Keystone's Harry Miller. It should be noted that average retail net profits after taxes are often below two percent for independent merchants so often charged with making too much money on their merchandise. The Retail Jewelers of America believe their members make about *one* percent and the Retail Hardware Association says that the profits of the country's 22,000 independent hardware stores dropped to 0.75 percent by 1960. (1962 Senate hearings, pp. 241, 453.) There are discounters whose profits may actually be far higher than the figures show. Weiss claims that "many discount outlets keep their figures confidential." (Weiss, *op. cit.*, p. 12.) This, of course, is supported by the editors of *The Discount Merchandiser* and by the president of Marrud, who hail The Marrud Study's disclosures as so unprecedented.

G. One unorthodox way in which an individual discounter could finance some of his growth and his operations might be by using his customers' money. The files of New York's Bureau of Consumer Frauds and Protection contain a number of instances where relatively large sums of money are held as deposits by discounters, only to be returned without interest some time later, with the explanation that the purchased material was not available after all. A few hundred dollars held for two or three months might not finance much of an operating expense, but if a merchant were to make a regular practice of this, it could be meaningful. In a tightly run operation, where cash flow is a top concern, such retention of interest-free deposits could prove to be significant financing. (I am not, of course, referring to legitimate deposits against merchandise that is actually available and actually delivered at a later date.)

CHAPTER 6

A. Hilliard J. Coan, president of Hills Supermarkets, Inc., addressing the New York Society of Security Analysts on November 6, 1961, made this comment, pertinent to this discussion of discount food departments: "You just can't sell dollar bills for 79 cents and make money," he said. "If you can, there must be another gimmick somewhere. I suspect the gimmick is that existing margins are just too high in other lines that are subsidizing and supporting this type of operation." One way of making money by doing this, of course, may be to sell *some* dollar bills for 79 cents, and others for $1.50.

B. *Fortune,* underscoring the use of discount food as bait, quotes one executive as saying that food is used so frequently as a loss leader that the lessee cannot survive. "A good many [food] chains are trying to expand the sales of nonfood items, which carry a higher markup than foods," says *Fortune*. "Supermarkets have already become the largest single outlet for health and beauty preparations (shampoos, toothpaste, hair sprays, deodorants) and for nylon stockings..." (*Fortune*, May, 1962.) The statement is in line with what we had to say about food outlets going into the discounting of general merchandise, because this often carries a substantially higher markup.

C. In 1962, *Dun's Review & Modern Industry* magazine warned that "general reports from the retail trade indicate that many more discounters will be turning to food as a traffic item [i.e., as bait] in the future." Already in 1962 almost 15 percent of discount stores surveyed by Dun & Bradstreet had grocery departments, 51.7 percent of which were operated by concessionaires. (*Dun's Review & Modern Industry*, October, 1962, p. 101.)

D. Concerning the argument of whether food discount departments are more profitably run by lessees or by discount-store management, *The Discount Merchandiser* quotes one discounter as saying that they may be best used for bait purposes when owned by the discounter himself. He was asked if "in the long run the pro-rated margin will rule?" (The pro-rated margin is the device whereby high-markup merchandise subsidizes loss-leader merchandise.) "In other words," asked *The Discount Merchandiser*, "the store makes a profit, and that's it, regardless of what goes on in any particular department at any one time?" Marcus replied that this would work so long as the discounter had "a mix" that would give him a profit—that is, if he marked other goods up sufficiently. "This goes back basically to the concession-versus-the-owner-operation philosophy of doing business," he said. "If you concession out a food operation and then expect it to lose money, it won't work because the food operator doesn't want any part of that. He's willing to be fair [presumably is willing to run *some* foods as bait at loss-leader prices] but he can't afford to lose money. By controlling all the facets of the business as we do, we have a better chance on balance to work out the store profit picture." (*The Discount Merchandiser*, April, 1963, pp. 25-27.)

E. The A. C. Nielson Co., a Chicago market research firm, revealed in 1961–1962 that 983 discounters with over 10,000 square feet already handled food products, doing $1,200,000 worth of business. (*The Discount Merchandiser*, October, 1963, p. 20.)

F. Mike Goldgar, chairman of United Star Companies, Atlanta, Georgia, predicts that, by 1972, the discount field will consist of 500 stores averaging 200,000 square feet, that groceries "run as a subsidy department" will account for almost a third of the total volume, and that 45 percent of all soft goods, "including fashion merchandise," will be produced abroad. (*Home Furnishings Daily*, February 13, 1962, quoted by Representative Richard L. Roudebush of Indiana, 1963 House hearings, p. 39.) The Goldgar figures indicate that half of the high-markup soft goods will be of cheap foreign make and that these, together with the remainder of the soft goods sold, will subsidize one-third of the discount store's sales. Under such a plan, two-thirds of the merchandise must be marked up high enough to compensate for the large amount sold at a loss or at a near loss.

CHAPTER 7

A. The latest available Bureau of Labor Statistics survey gives consumer expenditures by family-income categories. The category selected for use was that of $5,000-$6,000 a year, since the average national family income after taxes is $5,906.

B. Some merchants claim not to cherry-pick. One such is Barney Goldberg, president of Gateway Sporting Goods, who told *Barron's* magazine that his store stocks $75,000–$100,000 worth of merchandise, as against competitors' $25,000. The magazine says that he carries "every conceivable leisure-time device or garment." *Barron's* then quotes Goldberg as stating, "Of course our mark-ups on such [slow-moving] items are a bit higher." *Barron's* reports that the business done on slow-moving merchandise "is what keeps Gateway's ratio of net profit to sales at a handsome 3.3 percent..." (*Barron's*, June 17, 1963.)

C. Proctor Paint & Varnish Co., Inc., of Yonkers, N.Y., advertises its 10-point program for discounters in *The Discount Merchandiser*, underscoring the advantages of buying Proctor products, while at the same time revealing the profits to be made via such reduced-inventory policies. Proctor features: "Small inventory and high turnover rate with proven 35% to 40% profits." (*The Discount Merchandiser*, April, 1963.)

D. An article on book merchandising in discount stores, which appeared in *The Discount Merchandiser* (January, 1964), says that books are items "that can be taken on promotionally to beef up traffic flow as an in-and-outer." However a discounter arranges his book department, the magazine urges "he should stay with the basics. That means, no outdated texts, poetry or 'way out' titles." It advises self-help and do-it-yourself bestsellers for Midwestern discounters and suggests that New York discount stores should stock bestsellers and mysteries. It urges discounters to "maintain an image of book bargains before the public eye" and says this is best done by stocking 75-100 titles "mostly of the romantic-sex type."

Louis Davis of Davis Book Wholesalers Inc., N.Y., a subsidiary of Cosmo Book Distributors, suppliers to many major discounters, specializes in selling publishers' overstocks and remainders and in "setting up special sales promotions for the retailer who doesn't usually sell books," the magazine says. The public, however, may erroneously be under the impression the books have been *discounted;* they may not be aware of the fact that these titles may not be selling anywhere at the list price. A full-page Davis ad, on the inside front cover of the October, 1963, issue of

The Discount Merchandiser, features these points: that the books "represent excess inventory from prime publishers"; that they provide "instant bargain appeal"; that each book carries the original price imprint of from $3.00 to $5.95 and that these book promotions spell "profit and good-will" for the discounter. Interestingly, the article on book merchandising noted above begins with the statement that "To the discounter, the book represents a low-priced item (a $4.95 bargain table special for 50 cents, for example) enjoying a wide mass appeal that he can sell at a comfortable markup of 40 percent, or so." Davis suggests in the article that the bargains should be labelled as "Publishers' overstock" and that the signs should note "original $3 to $5 editions, 59 cents, two for 99 cents" instead of merely "special, books 59¢." Such correct labeling would, of course, be highly commendable, for it would make it difficult for shoppers to regard the books as "discounts," i.e., as books selling for less than they are currently selling for elsewhere.

E. Maurice Mermey points out that the United States Government ironically maintains a very rigid resale price maintenance policy for its own publications. The Superintendent of Documents insists that resellers of government documents adhere to the price marked on the book. They are offered to retailers at a 25 percent margin (25 percent off list price), and a one-dollar book can be bought for 75 cents. But the reseller is required by agreement with the Superintendent of Documents to sell that book for $1.00. (1962 Senate hearings, pp. 198-199.) This is "price-fixing," pure and simple, apparently unobjectionable to the Government when the Government does it.

CHAPTER 8

A. The explosive growth of discounting began shortly before 1950. A little more than ten years later, the industry suffered a major convulsion. Infighting and cut-throat competition *among discounters themselves* led to what the trade calls The Big Shakeout in Discounting. In 1961, E. B. Weiss predicted the upheaval. There would be, he said, a shakeout of the "weak sisters of discounting; continued mergers and amalgamations within the discount field; the emergence of really powerful national discount chains." (Weiss, *op. cit.*, p. 7.) "When the squeeze comes, as it inevitably must," said management consultant Helen Webb, a discounting expert, "at least 60 percent" of U.S. discounters would be closed, sold, or merged into powerful chains. (*Barron's*, February 5, 1962.)

The shakeout occurred partly because of the explosive growth of discounting. As *Fortune* points out, "it sometimes seemed that discounters had to do little more than put up a sign and install shopping carts." (*Fortune*, May, 1962.) Stores were established at a fantastic rate and profits plowed back into more stores. As competitors entered the field, many discounters found themselves overextended and under-capitalized. The "squeeze" of which Helen Webb spoke had come. The result, said *Discount Store News* on October 7, 1963, was an "ordeal by fire." By the end of 1962, according to Dun & Bradstreet, 146 discount house companies were either in receivership or "financially embarrassed." Creditors found themselves holding $75 million in bills.

By January, 1963, things had worsened and more discounters went under. "Some of the crackups," says *Barron's*, "were spectacular." One leased-department operator went under in August, 1962, to the tune of $10 million. By 1964, many of those which remained picked up the pieces and put them into increasingly strong combinations. (*Barron's*, April 22, 1963.) An interesting phase of the growth of discounting occurred as many small merchants went out of business. There were distributors who observed this and decided to go into discounting themselves. Many of them, however, also failed because they specialized in one line of merchandise. This failed to give them the pricing flexibility of a discount operation that sold more than one line. Such a discounter could always undersell them in their specialty, for he could make up his losses elsewhere in the store. They quickly found that selling one line of merchandise at a "low discount-type margin" was impossible; success apparently demanded that there be other merchandise in the store that could carry high markups, to serve as "profit-boosters."

B. Additional predictions regarding the increasing consolidation of discount stores:

(1) Mike Goldgar, chairman of United Star Companies, Atlanta, Ga., is quoted as predicting that discounting will consist of 500 stores in 1972. E. B. Weiss, who predicts 6,000-8,000 discount stores in shopping centers alone may turn out to be more accurate. (*Home Furnishings Daily,* February 13, 1962, and 1963 House hearings, p. 39.) In reading much of the trade press, one sometimes can get the impression that the ideal in terms of the discounter would be *one immense store,* centrally located, with the rest of the country forming a huge parking lot adjacent to it.

(2) Isadore Barmash, formerly retailing writer for the *New York Herald Tribune* now with *The New York Times,* seems more realistic when he predicted that the future lies with six or ten national discount chains which in themselves will be consolidations of many regional chains. Each, he said, will probably have sales of $500,000 a year up. (*New York Herald Tribune,* October 14, 1963.)

(3) Weiss predicts that discount stores will open up adjacent to or in just about every single shopping center in the U.S.A. Eventually, he says, these shopping center discount stores, numbering between 6,000 and 8,000, will really be "discount cities," for the trend is towards enormous, one-stop shopping facilities. These may get up to 300,000 square feet in size, making them "giants." Weiss says that not more than 200 traditional department stores in the U.S. exceed 235,000 square feet. (Weiss, *op. cit.,* pp. 67, 68.)

(4) The extent of discounting's growth in just one

American city is described by columnist Isadore Barmash in the *New York Herald Tribune*. Between 1958 and the end of 1963, Barmash says, more than 100 discount stores have opened in Chicago. (*New York Herald Tribune*, December 16, 1963.)

(5) Ray Brewster points out the disparity between the rate of growth of smaller independent stores and that of big well-financed chains. During a 10 year period of "enormous growth in national product, population and purchasing power," the larger units increased their volume by 1,000 percent, while independents rose only 150 percent. (1958 Senate hearings, pp. 61, 62.)

(6) E. J. Korvette, Inc. is, says Weiss, the fastest-growing of them all. In fact, it shows "the fastest growth of any retailers in the modern history of retailing." (E. B. Weiss, *Advertising Age*, January 20, 1964.) Two years earlier, Eugene Ferkauf, Korvette's founder, was quoted as saying, "All we hope for this company is that it should do all the merchandising business in the United States." (*Time*, July 6, 1962.)

(7) "The discounters won't withdraw from the scene" says Nathaniel Schwartz in *The Discount Merchandiser*. "They continue to press their advantage ... It is quite possible that the discounters this year [1963] will add another $2 billion to their sales, bringing the industry total up to the $9 billion mark." (*The Discount Merchandiser*, editorial, October, 1963.)

C. The early growth of discount stores was described in the following words by John W. Anderson, president, The Anderson Company, Gary, Indiana:

"Certain general observations may be made safely about discounters, such as that they after all are businessmen, in business to make or take a profit, but not necessarily by the same methods used by other businessmen. It is interesting to note that discounters often would deny others the pricing methods they employ. We have in our files letters from some of the long-time prominent discounters seeking our advice as to methods of dealing with price-cutting competitors. Examples include department stores long accustomed to baiting customers by noisily cutting prices on honored trademarked products that produce less than 10 percent of their store volume, but who cry for help when a discounter pops up and uses them as demonstrators of popular home appliances which the customer then buys from the discounter.

"Another facet of discount operations which seems to distinguish the breed is that they are adept at posing as the champions of the consumer's interest. Any discounter worthy of the name can pluck a halo from thin air at a moment's notice and parade demurely across the public stage as a benefactor of humanity.

"There is nothing novel about the practice of discounting—it has been with us always . . . Modern price cutters, who are now called discounters, assume a more ominous aspect than discounters of the past, for reasons which will be mentioned.

"Discounters, as we know them today, are of comparatively recent origin. Many of them started on a small investment immediately after World War II." Anderson says some evolved into discounting after black-market and gray-market operations during the war. "Most of us can remember the period of shortages and rationing," he says. "Then came the release of the huge reservoir of pent-up demand for all consumer items. This torrent of demand swept many discounters into prominence." Anderson says that the transition from operators "who could get goods, for a price, when goods were scarce, to a discounter who could offer a special price when goods became plentiful, was a short step up the ladder of business respectability. . . ."

"One had to 'know someone,' or mention the right name, or have a club membership card in order to enter the sanctum. . . . These operations often were conducted from darkened basements and lofts, where the consumer was permitted to peer dimly at his purchase through the slats of a shipping crate. Naturally, everything was sold 'as is' and all sales were for cash and were 'final.' Prices included nothing for service, often soon needed sorely ..." (1958 Senate hearings, pp. 315-316.)

D. As chains become superchains, the result is predictable. "In the long run, the bigger the big get, the greater the need for government control," says Attorney Stanley A. Weigel of San Francisco, California. "This is not because bigness is bad. It is because bigness is powerful. Big power, economic or other, simply has to be controlled to protect the public welfare. And the more government control, the more the American free enterprise system must yield, in one form or another, to the techniques of a controlled economy and of economic regimentation—always the forerunner of other aspects of statism." (1958 Senate hearings, p. 352.)

E. The effect of retail store attrition *upon communities* is cited by Maurice Mermey. "Main Street U.S.A. is beginning to look more and more like the child who is losing her baby teeth—lots of vacant spaces, each with a 'for rent' sign. More and more the absentee owner is taking over the retail purchasing power of the communities of America—returning to these communities goods and services, to be sure, but contributing virtually nothing to the life of the community." (1962 Senate hearings, p. 194.)

F. The fact that governmental supervision of the distributive process is the rule—except at the retail sales stage—has been described by Representative Chet Holifield of California, as follows:

"Let me describe the chain of production and distribution of a national branded item of merchandise. I use an Arrow shirt, for example, as I am now, and have been a retailer of Arrow shirts and other national brand items of union-made men's wear for more than 25 years.

"Link No. 1: Production of cotton: Competition modified by legislation (crop control and price support). The Congress has enacted price support bills for 30 years in the field of agriculture. Each of these acts has modified competition—for the purpose of the beneficial, all-over impact on society as a whole.

"Link No. 2: Tranportation costs from raw cotton to the retailer's store. Here competition again has been modified by legislation of Congress. For example—legislative authority to set interstate commerce rates based on the cost incurred by the transportation companies, including the component union-wage level of all employees.

"Link No. 3: The production of textile cloth and manufacture of the same into final garment; this is indeed two links. Every link of production is based on fixed costs, including union wages.

"Link No. 4: Distribution of the final garment to the consumer. Now, it is in this field that no legislative protection exists for the independent businessman, who serves in this final link in the chain of production and distribution. Here we have complete competition; unmodified by any type of legislative protection. As a result, 'scab' practices run wild.

"The decent merchant who wishes to retail good merchandise made in union-wage factories finds himself at the mercy of the 'price gimmick,' 'deceptive advertiser,' the mass-handler of nonunion-made merchandise.

"These practices are threatening the last link in the distributive chain. The independent operator cannot last if he is forced to operate in a cost-of-operation area where his costs are rigid until it reaches the point of delivery to the consumer. There it is suddenly faced with ruthless competition ...

"The independent retailer's cost area contains many noncompetitive areas. I cite a few:

"(a) Wages, in most areas unionized. They are fixed.

"(b) Rents: Percentage of sales based on a retail scale related to different kinds of businesses plus traffic count of people who would pass in front of his door.

"(c) Insurance: All old line insurance companies charge almost identical rates.

"(d) Interest rates on commercial loans. Usually the smaller merchant pays an identical rate to all banks in a trade area.

"(e) Transportation costs on goods; as noted before, these costs are noncompetitive, fixed by interstate commerce rates.

"(f) All fixed noncompetitive rates set up by public utilities commissions which, incidentally, include a floor of guaranteed profits to the utilities above their investment and costs. And in most instances, a guaranteed wage to their employees. A fixed wage to their employees, fixed by negotiation.

"(g) Last, but not least, the manufacturer must supply the retailer any specific item at a nondiscriminatory price. I refer, of course, to the provisions of the Robinson-Patman Act. The nondiscriminatory price for an identical item gives the retailer some protection as between himself and a competitor retailer, but it also establishes a fixed noncompetitive price for the wholesale cost of the item.

"As a result of all these areas of fixed or semifixed costs, the retailer does not have the benefit of competition in the components of his cost of doing business. His investment in inventory is a cost which deserves a fair profit return. His time and skill deserve a fair recompense. If we demand that he face unmodified competition at the point of distribution, we deny him the right to a fair profit and say that the law of the jungle must control and apply to this area only in our distributive system . . ." (Extension of Remarks of Hon. John Dent, *Congressional Record*, August 20, 1963.)

G. How some conventional retailers have faced up to the problems of discount store competition is illustrated by recent developments at Interstate Department Stores, Inc., a vast retail chain. As reported by the *New York Herald Tribune*, sales for the fiscal year ending January 31, 1965 were predicted at $375 million, compared to the previous year's $311 million. The chain has *tripled* sales in the past five years. Today, the paper says, Interstate makes 75 percent of its money from its 51 discount operations and 25 percent from its 34 "conventional" stores.

(*New York Herald Tribune*, May 25, 1964.) This seems to me an example of "if you can't lick 'em, join 'em" and an avenue not open to the small retailer who lacks the funds of Interstate.

H. *Home Furnishings Daily* interviewed several Philadelphia manufacturers, retailers, and distributors about what happens on the retail level when manufacturers care too little about the protection of their products at the end of the distributive pipeline. "We have a very sick industry on our hands," one distributor said, referring to the fact that "once the merchandise passes through the shipping doors, the manufacturer couldn't care less where it winds up, how it is sold or for how much it is peddled." He adds that distributors are often traded off against each other "until somebody cracks." Then nationally advertised loss-leaders are available. (*Home Furnishings Daily*, December 26, 1963.) This situation does indeed prevail in much of the market, though more responsible manufacturers, who are in a more highly competitive position, care deeply about what happens to their products after they leave the shipping room.

I. Henry R. Peters, the pharmacist whose experience was given in Chapter 3, refers in the following words to his life as a small, independent retail druggist: "... Let me tell you a little more about our operation. While we have been able to survive, in addition to working 16 hours a day we have to deliver in the entire metropolitan area. We have to render that service because there are still a lot of people who are just plain lazy to get out and do their own shopping. They like to pick up the telephone and shop. These operators [the discounters] will not do that. They cannot afford that, especially on these items that they advertise.

"Second, I have to join every professional organization, church groups, and other organizations, such as the civic organizations, and being on the Board of Pharmacy, a former instructor of pharmacy at Howard University, I have had to project my personality to these people and convince them that price alone should not be the only determining factor in the prescription field or where you purchase the health needs for yourself and your family."

J. In addition to the retail chains like Sears, Roebuck and Montgomery Ward which have their own retail outlets and, because of them, are often largely immune to discounting competition, particularly on their own private brands, there are yet other retail areas which are protected against the erosion of price-cutting.

(a) House-to-house salesmen account for some $2 billion of sales a year. Each brand is sold to consumers at prices that are set by manufacturers. Avon cosmetics is a good example; in-home sales personnel have made Avon the biggest cosmetics manufacturer in the nation.

(b) Brand owners who sell on consignment set the retail price which dealers must charge for their branded products.

(c) Lastly, private brands sold exclusively in manufacturer-owned retail outlets and in retail stores of the Sears type are immune to discounting.

K. Louis Rothschild, executive director of the National Association of Retail Clothiers and Furnishers, tells what may happen to a small retailer if and when he protests about loss leaders. If, for example, a discount store cuts the price of a nationally advertised brand shirt and, if there are four stores in town which have been selling this shirt for years and are now hurt, they may individually and without concert protest to the manufacturer. But if they do it together, they may be charged by the Government with acting "in restraint of trade." These four little retailers are then regarded as forming "a combination in restraint of trade"! This is so, says Rothchild, "even if they happen to play golf foursome and talk about it at the country club." (1962 House hearings, p. 174.)

L. The situation of the small, independent retailer has been further described in the following terms. "Small business," says Representative Ancher Nelsen of Minnesota, "is suffering from no want of sympathy, but what seems to be lacking is understanding." (1963 House hearings, p. 33.) The small retailer's situation, says Marketing Consultant Victor Lebow, "remains precarious and his prospects even dimmer." Lebow calls him "expendable" and says that he seems to serve one function only, "to exhaust his capital and his borrowings to pay for inventory which eventually chokes him to death." As an entrepreneur, Lebow adds, "he has to accept the risks, but as a small businessman in an age of giants he is faced by forces which perhaps only the interposition of Government can regulate." (1958 Senate hearings, pp. 6-7.)

M. Concerning the discounter's much-vaunted "efficiency," Professor Alfred E. Oxenfeldt of Columbia University's Graduate School of Business points out that it is because of the discounter's "very large sales volume . . . rather than because of economics of operation" that he achieves low costs. The "salient point," Oxenfeldt adds, is "that the discount house is outstanding because of its ability to attract a large number of customers, relative to its facilities." (1958 Senate hearings, p. 400.)

N. Can we consumers stand by indifferently as one independent retailer after another is forced out of business and as near-monopolistic chains proliferate? An answer to this question was offered by the United States Supreme Court in 1959, when it referred in the following terms to the exclusion of small business from competition:

"It interferes with the natural flow of interstate commerce. It clearly has, by its 'nature' and 'character,' a 'monopolistic tendency.' As such it is not to be tolerated merely because the victim is just one merchant whose business is so small that his destruction makes little difference to the economy. Monopoly can as surely thrive by the elimination of such small businessmen,

one at a time, as it can by driving them out in large groups."
(Klors, Inc., *v.* Broadway-Hale Stores, Inc., 1959 Trade Cases,
paragraph 69, 316; 359 U.S. 207; 79 S. Ct. 705.)

O. Decision of Judge Perry, U.S. District Court for Northern
Illinois, in the case of *United States v. Arnold, Schwinn & Co.*,
Dec. 29, 1964: "To put it bluntly, if Schwinn were Sears, Roe-
buck & Co., its largest bicycle competitor, or if it were General
Motors Corporation, it would be able to do exactly what it has
done in franchising retail dealers with no penalty attached either
through its own retail stores and salesmen as Sears, Roebuck &
Co., does or through direct franchising on a nation-wide scale as
General Motors and other giant corporations do.

"And penalized for what? Being a pygmy, compared to its
giant bicycle competitors, Sears, Roebuck & Co., and Montgomery Ward & Co.? Yes, if the plaintiffs' theory of the law
applicable should be adopted by this court. Here, however, we
do not even have the case of David and Goliath, where a well-
directed stone from a slingshot might equalize the contestants.
We do not even have the case of a pygmy pitted against a Cy-
clops, where a poison arrow might make competition a reality.
What we do have is a microscopic Lilliputian whose extension
ladders would not be able to mount the little toe of its Brob-
dingnagian foes.

"Now it appears to this court that if General Motors, Sears,
Roebuck & Co., Montgomery Ward & Co., Ford Motors Co.,
and other international corporations can rely upon a sound and
long-established principle of common law and safely choose its
customers, deal, and refuse to deal, with whomsoever it will,
and wherever it will, so can a small business firm such as is
Schwinn. There is another rule of law laid down and established
at common law just as firmly as the aforesaid principle, and
corollary to it: That is the rule of common law that generally
what one may do himself he may likewise do by or through an
agent. As a matter of fact and law that is how General Motors
acts—by an officer.

"Now that is also what Schwinn has done. In place of acting through a vice president, it has acted through a distributor. It has made agents of its distributors, in the same manner that it could make an agent of a corporate official, say its president or vice president, or other officer. True it may be that in some of its relationships with its distributors, it has dealt with them in another capacity. In some instances some of its distributors have bought merchandise outright from Schwinn and have become owners in their own right. In some instances they hold the merchandise on consignment. In those cases where a distributor has bought bicycles outright and taken title to them, certainly Schwinn could not prevent it from selling to any franchised dealer, no matter whether the dealer was in the territory assigned to the distributor or not. But in a case where Schwinn still had title to bicycles and the distributor is a mere agent—or salesman —Schwinn has the right to dispose of its own goods in the same manner as if the goods were in its own warehouse here in Chicago.

"Neither is there any question but what Schwinn may lawfully contract with its distributors upon the condition that all of their sales shall be made to duly franchised retailers for the reason that its relationship with its distributors is that of agency and the sale is not made to the distributors for use but as an intermediate step to the retailer who sells to the public. Only the retailer buys outright and owns title and may sell to whom he chooses, but he may not use his retail franchise as a guise to become in fact an agent for a discount store or for wholesaling purposes.

"The retailer buys to sell to the public and not to resell to another retailer who may not have adequate service or may not otherwise meet the approval of Schwinn. When a retailer enters into such activities he forfeits his rights under his franchise wherein he represents Schwinn in selling to the public."

CHAPTER 9

A. One manufacturer whom the discounters have apparently so far failed to affect is Magnavox. Although two major discount chains have reportedly been franchised by Magnavox, both apparently continue to sell it for "list." Magnavox it appears only recently let down the bars to discounters. The company had always picked its dealers carefully and dealt directly with them. This eliminated much of the 16 percent distributors' markup and allowed Magnavox to pass more profits on to its dealers. As a result, Magnavox was a popular item in the trade, which put it in a strong position to resist discounting. It believed, says *Fortune*, "that poor service and, ultimately, lower-quality products would inevitably result" from discount pricing. (*Fortune*, February, 1964, pp. 133-134.)

B. The fact that American manufacturers have often sought cheaper labor abroad was underlined in a statement by Representative Thomas M. Pelly of Washington, made before a special subcommittee of the U.S. Senate. He said, *inter alia:* ". . . we are in overproduction right now here at home, because an ever-increasing percentage of our factories are moving branch plants to foreign countries, there to use the same tools and dies, the same know-how and creative ingenuity, but with native labor at a fraction of the hourly cost . . . those products are being sent back to the prostituted bargain marts of America for cheap, cheap pricing . . . the workers of America are the largest group of consumers of foreign, nonunion, falsely advertised, cheap products . . ." (*Congressional Record*, October 7, 1963, Extension of Remarks.)

C. The issue of *value*, as distinct from mere price, was the subject of the following observations by John W. Anderson, president of The Anderson Company, Gary, Indiana: "Except in relation to what you get for what you pay—price means nothing.

The shrewd housewife—guardian of the family budget—must relate value to price." Anderson points out that a product that has been made "captive" by a discounter who uses it as store traffic bait "soon has the quality squeezed out of it" under the price-cutter's demand for ever lower cost to him. "He must have those lower and lower costs," Anderson says, "so he can make further cuts in the retail price of the product." These, he says, are often needed because discounters compete with each other and often attempt to provide ever greater bargains as bait for the "uninformed consumer." (Address before 5th annual convention, The Automotive Wholesalers of Illinois, October 26, 1963.)

D. The proliferation of private brands is the subject of endless discussion in the trade and business press and no attempt is made here to list articles on the subject. The following views are, however, given because they seem particularly to the point:

1. Willard Campbell, director of retail research for Ralph Shockey & Associates, retail marketing specialists, told a workshop session of the National Retail Merchants Association that private brands had grown for the following reasons: ability to buy more for the same money; price controlled by the store, not the resource, allowing flexibility in reducing the price for special promotions; greater initial mark-on; production of merchandise to meet the store's specifications; a greater average initial mark-on (Campbell repeats this point here in his compilation; one assumes the stress here is on the "average"); necessity of customers coming to your store to get private label merchandise (some private brands, such as Sears' Kenmore, have established a reputation for themselves and are virtually in the class of nationally advertised brand names). [Parenthetical remarks are author's.] (*Home Furnishings Daily,* June 19, 1964.)
2. Charles W. Wood, vice president and general merchandise manager of Montgomery Ward & Co., speaking

before the National Housewares Manufacturers Association, stated that Montgomery Ward hoped that by 1965, 80 percent of its volume would be in its own brand merchandise. One reason given is the rise of discounting. "Basically, these stores [the discount stores] merchandise on the principle of showing the customer 'islands' of identifiable loss leaders in a sea of profitable items," Wood says. (*The Discount Merchandiser*, January 1963, p. 14.)

3. Representative Chet Holifield of California states: "The only reason for private brands is that the national brand has been made profitless by loss-leader tactics. The average retailer, if there is such, has no objection to private brands. Personally I hope all my competition [Holifield owns a retail store] resorts to private brands. I prefer to sell the Arrow or Manhattan or the Van Heusen shirt any day rather than a private brand . . . only the powerful retailer has the resources to move into the private brand area . . ." (*Congressional Record*, June 18, 1963, Extension of Remarks.) Holifield makes a crucial point: that the private brand, whose price is *fixed* by the retailer-manufacturer, is immune to the predatory price-cutting inflicted on national brands.

E. Among other sources of merchandise for discount stores are bankrupt shops. "Mostly we take advantage of buying bankrupt stocks or other special deals in low-end furniture and women's and children's apparel, and shoes," says Wendell E. Ray, president, Discountland of Dade, Inc., Miami, Florida. *Home Furnishings Daily* adds, "In apparel, as well as in furniture, buying of special deals allows the store to maintain high markup, since, 'We don't give anything away.'" (*Home Furnishings Daily*, December 26, 1963.)

F. Reduction of quality as an inevitable outcome of some discount store tactics was stressed by Philip Cortney, president of Coty and an economist of reputation: "The so-called discount houses are the worst enemies of trademarked goods. The material recently filed with the Securities and Exchange Commission by a Kansas City drug chain which operates, under leases, drug departments in so-called discount houses shows that the original concept of 'true discounting'—selling everything at a lower price or markup—is being slowly laid away in favor of the old-fashioned system of loss-leader price-cutting. If the policies of the so-called discount houses were to become generally prevalent, the result would be that the manufacturer would have to try to reduce his costs by reducing the quality of his goods. Mass production, mass consumption, and employment would suffer, because it is most probable that under such circumstances the manufacturer of trademark goods would dispose of less money to spend on advertising, thus reducing the demand for his goods. The short-term results of the price policies of the discount houses may have a deceptive attractiveness. However, there is no doubt that the long-term result would be to harm competition, to the detriment of the consumer and of our economy." (Statement inserted into Extension of Remarks by Representative Thor C. Tollefson of Washington, *Congressional Record*, July 12, 1962.)

G. The effect of discounting on the distributive system in American manufacture is the subject of the following statement by Senator Hugh Scott of Pennsylvania, made April 23, 1963, before the Subcommittee on Commerce and Finance, House Interstate and Foreign Commerce Committee:

"... Most manufacturers of consumer products must devote considerable effort and money to establishing and maintaining a stable system of distribution through which may flow the manufacturer's production. In many industries, the great bulk of consumer goods are sold most effectively and economically through a network of relatively small retail outlets, served by wholesalers of one type or another.

"The only known method by which a manufacturer can enlist the essential cooperation of wholesalers and retailers, in the process of creating a stable system of distribution, is to make it potentially profitable for his retailers to deal in his product. Only the anticipation of a profit causes retailers to perform those services necessary to bring the product to the favorable attention and convenient reach of the public. It is the firm conviction of many manufacturers that their further growth cannot be achieved without the confident cooperation of great numbers of small independent wholesalers and retailers.

"Predatory price-cutting by so-called discounters on certain categories of products inexorably tends to tear down a manufacturer's painfully acquired distribution system. The promotional efforts of the resellers dwindle and wane, for the sale of the product has been made no longer profitable to them. Reaction to destructive discounter competition at the retail level is varied. Some retailers drop the line; others give it less display space and less sales effort; others put the price-cut item under a counter and concentrate on the sale of not-yet price-raided substitute items.

"Even retailers who merely attempt to maintain a retail price that covers their cost of the product come to be regarded unfairly by their customers as profiteers. The consumer often comes to feel that the manufacturer has been greedily overpricing his product, while the incentive of independent resellers to continue merchandising the product has been destroyed.

"In both cases clearly the goodwill of the public for the product is destroyed. In any event at sharply varying retail prices, confidence in and demand for the product will not long prevail. A retailer will not continue to function as a mere displayer of the unfairly discredited product, as a mere showcase, a convenient backdrop, against which the price-baiting discounter can perform. . . . his deceptive magic.

"In the mind of the consumer, a standard price is presumed to set a standard of value for the product. It is in effect a promise by the manufacturer to the consumer that the particular product offers good competitive value at its price. Predatory price-cutting gives unfairly the lie to this promise. It shouts to the consuming public that the product is not worthy of its confidence—that the true measure of its value is the discounter's store-traffic baiting price.

"Thus the price-cut product is . . . downgraded and debased; the good product thus loses consumer acceptance; it loses sales volume. All segments of the distributive economy—the consumer, the reseller, and the manufacturer—are hurt by trespassers that force an honored brand name to compete with itself in price . . ."

H. The value of the brand name is the subject of the following observations:

1. By Senator Hugh Scott (April 23, 1963, statement): "The brand name identifies the product of one person or corporation and distinguishes it from the products of others. The brand is a symbol by which the consumer identifies and buys products that have given him satisfaction in the past— and by which he avoids unsatisfactory products. The brand becomes a symbol, or measure, of public goodwill for the product it identifies. A manufacturer who has built up a valuable trade name, and who believes that his ability to serve the public efficiently can best be promoted by choosing a particular apparatus for distribution, should be able to take the necessary steps to protect it . . ."

2. Attorney Daphne Leeds of Washington, D.C., a consultant in the field of trademark law and unfair competition, answers the question of what a trademark is by saying:

"It is not anything technical or complex or monopolistic. It is a brand name or a symbol which identifies the goods of one person and distinguishes them from another. It is a word or a symbol by which the consumer identifies and buys that which has satisfied him in the past and by which he avoids that which is unsatisfactory. It is a tool of competition which supports freedom of choice in the marketplace, and it is the symbol of the goodwill of the producer of the goods identified by it. As branded merchandise moves through the channels of trade from producer to retailer to consumer, title to the physical property changes hands but title to the trademark and the goodwill which it symbolizes remains in the producer." (1962 House hearings, p. 156.)

I. The effect of a large national network of independent retailers upon the price paid for a product by the consumer is illustrated by the Pyrex nine-inch pie plate introduced by Corning Glass in 1916 at one dollar each and selling today for 39 cents. This item, says the company, is basically unchanged since 1916 except for glass quality. If its market were destroyed by price-cutting, it would of course be naive to think that the manufacturer could be able to hold the price down. A market for an item like this is eroded by "cherry-picking." President Waterman of Corning Glass Works says the company's 45,000 retailers have to stock a minimum assortment of 26 different sizes and shapes. In addition, they must stock replacement covers, handles, percolator pumps, etc. "Such an assortment," says Waterman, "necessarily includes some items which would be rather slow turnover items, but the neighborhood retailer carries them because he is responsive to the needs of his customers and has built his business on rendering a complete service." Many discounters, as has already been noted, will sell only those items in the line which are most popular and generally refuse to carry a complete selection or replacement parts; in addition, they may drop even the popular items once they have served their bait purpose. (1962 Senate hearings, p. 77.)

J. Leon Hartman points out that in the retail camera field, so many merchants have gone out of business that a new business has sprung up: camera repair shops, which no longer even try to sell, but mainly service. They make money, he says, "on the consumer's hard luck." Hartman goes on to say, "Our industry has an interest . . . related to national defense, when it comes to providing the armed services with the optics they need and the mechanics they need for this reconnaissance work that is so important. I recall President Eisenhower was so proud to show how they had a camera which could take a picture from eight miles up and show the wagon wheels, the spokes on a car. Well, that was not an American-made lens that took that picture; nor was it an American-made unit that actually held the lens in that camera." (1962 Senate hearings, p. 222.) Further on the matter of quality in more earthbound products, *Home Furnishings Daily* (March 9, 1961) says "Steam irons were cited as the most troublesome items [in electric housewares]. Many are equipped with cheap gaskets, and soon start leaking. Others clog easily, while many get cord shorts because of short rubber or spring guards and cheaply-made cords." *Printer's Ink* (August 5, 1960) in a major survey of deteriorating quality says that "Some appliances that were once considered almost foolproof—such as refrigerators—are now sprouting crops of troubles, and seriously shaking customers' confidence." Economist Snyder speaks of this quality decline as follows: "The long history of production and consumption shows that deterioration of product quality standards is a natural and direct reflex of distressed conditions under which price fighting has become the order of the day. Inevitably the consumer finds himself victimized by the anarchistic conditions in the marketplace and, of course, he—in turn—adds his voice to the hue and cry." (1962 Senate hearings, p. 99.)

Glossary

BAIT MERCHANDISE: Famous-brand merchandise priced to bait customers into the store. The Federal Trade Commission defines "bait advertising" as an alluring but insincere offer to sell a product or service that the advertiser in truth does not intend to sell. It says its purpose is to switch customers. As the terms "bait" and "bait advertising" are used in this book, however, they refer to the "bait" or "lure" aspect of an offer. These "bait" offers may be quite genuine, and a customer may emerge from the store with the item advertised; as used here, such merchandise is often "loss-leader" merchandise (*q.v.*) and is used to create store traffic and a discounting image. As the FTC uses the term "bait advertising," the stress is on "baiting-and-switching." For a discussion of that, see next term; for the FTC's definition, see page 209.

BAITING-AND-SWITCHING: Luring customers with merchandise the store actually does not intend to sell. The U.S. Federal Trade Commission defines it as "an alluring but insincere offer to sell a product or service which the advertiser in truth does not intend to sell" in order "to switch customers from buying the advertised merchandise and to sell something else, usually at a higher price or on a basis more advantageous to the advertiser."

BARGAIN: FTC Chairman Paul Rand Dixon says that "to be a genuine bargain, the offering price must be a reduction from the price being charged by the advertiser's principal competitors, those who sell in competition with him in his own trade area."

BORAX: Name frequently given to cheap furniture and other goods.

BRANDED MERCHANDISE / BRAND-NAME MERCHANDISE: Merchandise carrying a manufacturer's trade name, trademark, or brand name. As used in this book, these terms signify identifiable branded merchandise, or nationally advertised famous brands. They designate merchandise behind which a manufacturer will stand, expecting to sell it under its brand name for many years and having committed large sums of money to its perfection, advertising, and promotion. See also *Off-Brands* and *Private-Label Merchandise*.

CHERRY-PICKING: The policy of "thick on the best, to hell with the rest" or of handling only "basic merchandise" and not providing a full selection. The emphasis is solely on high turnover merchandise. See also *Creaming*.

CLOSED-DOOR DISCOUNT STORE: Membership-card discount store. Some of these restrict membership to government employees, school teachers, etc., while others offer membership to almost anyone. Annual dues are generally collected.

CREAMING: Another term for *cherry-picking* (*q.v.*), descriptive of many discount stores' wish to stock only the "cream" off the top of any product line.

FAIR-TRADED ITEMS: Merchandise that is priced by the manufacturer in accordance with so-called Fair Trade laws.

IN-AND-OUTERS: Merchandise meant to be bought on impulse, often on the way in or on the way out of the store.

KICKER: Merchandise used for bait and loss-leader (*q.v.*) purposes.

KICKING AROUND: The treatment a lot of merchandise gets from retailers when used as bait or as a loss leader. Such merchandise, after a while, is said to have been "kicked around," often to the point where no retailer will sell it any longer. See also *Kicker*.

LEASED DEPARTMENT, LEASED-DEPARTMENT OPERATOR: A concessionaire who contracts for space and services within a discount store is said to operate a leased department. Frequently such a department is part of a huge nationwide leased-department chain, selling through individual leased departments in discount stores from coast to coast.

List / List Price: Used interchangeably with "manufacturer's recommended price," "manufacturer's suggested retail price," and often even "value" and "comparable value." The reader is referred to pp. 46-47 of this book for an evaluation of these terms.

Loss Leader: Merchandise sold for bait purposes at deeply discounted prices. Loss-leader merchandise is not necessarily sold at an actual loss (i.e., below cost), but often carries only a small markup, on which the store makes little or no profit once overhead and the cost of selling are added to the wholesale price of the item. See also *Bait Merchandise*.

Low-End Merchandise: Inexpensive merchandise of lower quality, the kind that had been sold, prior to the rise of discounting, primarily in stores in poorer neighborhoods and in store basements. Today it forms the basic stock of many discount houses, with a few quality brand names thrown in "to spice" the selection.

Margin: As used in this book, margin represents the difference between the retailer's delivered cost and selling price, expressed as a percentage of selling price. See page 167 for full discussion.

Markup: As used in this book, the term is the same except that it is expressed as a percentage of delivered cost. See page 167 for full discussion.

Nail-Downs: Merchandise that is "nailed to the floor," "nailed to the shelf," or just "nailed down" is merchandise that salesmen are encouraged *not* to sell. This is often loss-leader or bait merchandise (*q.v.*) carrying a national brand name, with which the store is unwilling or reluctant to part. Salesmen are urged to switch customers to substitute off-brand merchandise on which the store realizes a high profit. See also *Baiting-and-Switching*.

Off-Brands / Off-Brand Merchandise: As used in this book, these terms signify merchandise carrying brand names that are not readily identifiable, nor nationally advertised famous trademarks.

Manufacturers of off-brand merchandise may be fly-by-nighters, or they may be nationally famous, in the latter case producing a special line of off-brand merchandise, frequently for discount houses. In either case, the advertising and promotion investment is usually lower than it is for a famous nationally advertised brand. Many an off-brand manufacturer has no need to stand behind his product, for he generally remains unknown to the public and can simply change the brand name on his merchandise whenever he wishes. Much off-brand merchandise is also produced abroad, often in the Far East.

PRE-TICKETING: Tagging an item with a retail price tag by the manufacturer is called pre-ticketing. Some manufacturers supply discounters with artificially high price tags, so as to allow for a high markup and a spurious "discount." In other cases, manufacturers may pre-ticket their product to protect the public, only to have the tickets themselves switched at the retail level.

PRIVATE-LABEL MERCHANDISE: Merchandise that bears the store's own name or bears the name of a line of goods identified with the store. Manufactured to the store's own specifications.

PROFIT-BOOSTERS: Merchandise in a store that offsets the losses sustained in that store's loss-leader department. Usually off-brand and private-label merchandise, often soft goods (*q.v.*) carrying high markups despite their low prices. This is the merchandise that may be overpriced to make up for losses sustained on the store's few real discounts.

PROMOTIONAL ITEMS: Merchandise that has great price appeal to the consumer because it appears to be a big bargain. Thus a "promotional mattress," for example, is one that may be advertised as a comparable value to a much more expensive mattress. In actual fact, of course, such promotional items may be priced very low because they are often off-brand, low-quality merchandise.

PUTTING THEM ON THE ELEVATOR: Switching customers to high-price and high-profit merchandise after having baited them into the store with advertised and often discounted brand-name items. Similar to baiting-and-switching in some cases, except that the switch is toward higher-priced goods.

SCHLOCK / SCHLOCK MERCHANDISE: Low-quality merchandise.

SLOTTING: Another term for switching the customer after he has been baited by a brand-name item. See also *Baiting-and-Switching*.

SOFT GOODS: Virtually anything in a store that is not hard goods. Thus the term includes clothing, drugs and drug products, books, and pre-packaged merchandise. (Appliances, furniture and the like, are hard goods—or white goods.)

SPIFFS: Special bonuses that salesmen are paid for switching customers, usually to higher-profit off-brand products.

SWITCH / SWITCHING: See *Baiting-and-Switching*.

TRAFFIC APPLIANCES / TRAFFIC-APPLIANCE DEPARTMENT: Appliances that are used to bring in store "traffic."

Appendix 1—FTC Guides

Guides Against Bait Advertising[1]
[Adopted November 24, 1959]

*   *   *

BAIT ADVERTISING DEFINED.

Bait advertising is an alluring but insincere offer to sell a product or service which the advertiser in truth does not intend or want to sell. Its purpose is to switch consumers from buying the advertised merchandise, in order to sell something else, usually at a higher price or on a basis more advantageous to the advertiser. The primary aim of a bait advertisement is to obtain leads as to persons interested in buying merchandise of the type so advertised.

1. BAIT ADVERTISEMENT.

No advertisement containing an offer to sell a product should be published when the offer is not a bona fide effort to sell the advertised product.

2. INITIAL OFFER.

No statement or illustration should be used in any advertisement which creates a false impression of the grade, quality, make, value,

---

[1] For the purpose of these Guides "advertising" includes any form of public notice however disseminated or utilized.

currency of model, size, color, usability, or origin of the product offered, or which may otherwise misrepresent the product in such a manner that later, on disclosure of the true facts, the purchaser may be switched from the advertised product to another.

Even though the true facts are subsequently made known to the buyer, the law is violated if the first contact or interview is secured by deception.

3. DISCOURAGEMENT OF PURCHASE OF ADVERTISED MERCHANDISE.

No act or practice should be engaged in by an advertiser to discourage the purchase of the advertised merchandise as part of a bait scheme to sell other merchandise.

Among acts or practices which will be considered in determining if an advertisement is a bona fide offer are:

(a) the refusal to show, demonstrate, or sell the product offered in accordance with the terms of the offer,

(b) the disparagement by acts or words of the advertised product or the disparagement of the guarantee, credit terms, availability of service, repairs or parts, or in any other respect, in connection with it,

(c) the failure to have available at all outlets listed in the advertisement a sufficient quantity of the advertised product to meet reasonably anticipated demands, unless the advertisement clearly and adequately discloses that supply is limited and/or the merchandise is available only at designated outlets,

(d) the refusal to take orders for the advertised merchandise to be delivered within a reasonable period of time.

(e) the showing or demonstrating of a product which is defective, unusable or impractical for the purpose represented or implied in the advertisement,

(f) use of a sales plan or method of compensation for salesmen or penalizing salesmen, designed to prevent or discourage them from selling the advertised product.

4. SWITCH AFTER SALE

No practice should be pursued by an advertiser, in the event of sale of the advertised product, of "unselling" with the intent and purpose of selling other merchandise in its stead.

Among acts or practices which will be considered in determining if the initial sale was in good faith, and not a stratagem to sell other merchandise, are:

(a) accepting a deposit for the advertised product, then switching the purchaser to a higher-priced product,

(b) failure to make delivery of the advertised product within a reasonable time or to make a refund,

(c) disparagement by acts or words of the advertised product, or the disparagement of the guarantee, credit terms, availability of service, repairs, or in any other respect, in connection with it,

(d) the delivery of the advertised product which is defective, unusable or impractical for the purpose represented or implied in the advertisement.

(NOTE:

SALES OF ADVERTISED MERCHANDISE.

Sales of the advertised merchandise do not preclude the existence of a bait and switch scheme. It has been determined that, on occasions, this is a mere incidental by-product of the fundamental plan and is intended to provide an aura of legitimacy to the over-all operation.)

Guides Against Deceptive Advertising of Guarantees.

[Adopted April 26, 1960]

* * *

The following Guides have been adopted by the Federal Trade Commission for use of its staff in evaluation of the advertising of guarantees. They have been released to the public in the interest of education of the businessman and the consumer and to obtain voluntary, simultaneous and prompt cooperation by those whose practices are subject to the jurisdiction of the Federal Trade Commission.

The Guides enumerate the major principles applicable to the advertising of guarantees although they do not purport to be all-inclusive and do not attempt to define the exact border lines between compliance with and violation of the law.

The Federal Trade Commission Decisions, upon which these Guides are based, indicate that the major difficulty with this type of advertising has been the failure to state adequately what the guarantee is. Concerning this, an appellate court stated: "Ordinarily the word, guarantee, or warrantee,* is incomplete unless it is used in connection with other explanatory words. To say a ... [product] or other subject is guaranteed is meaningless. What is the guarantee? The answer to this question gives meaning to the word 'guaranteed.' "

The Guides have application not only to "guarantees" but also to "warranties," to purported "guarantees" and "warranties," and to any promise or representation in the nature of a "guarantee" or "warranty."

Adversary actions against those who engage in deceptive advertising of guarantees and whose practices are subject to Commission jurisdiction are brought under the Federal Trade Commission Act (15 U.S.C., Secs. 41-58). Section 5 of the Act declares unlawful "unfair methods of competition in commerce and unfair or deceptive acts or practices in commerce."

THE GUIDES

In determining whether terminology and direct or implied representations concerning guarantees, however made, i.e., in advertising or otherwise, in connection with the sale or offering for sale of a product, may be in violation of the Federal Trade Commission Act, the following general principles will be used:

* Author's note: "warrantee" is presumably a clerical error for "warranty."

I–GUARANTEES IN GENERAL.

In general, any guarantee in advertising shall *clearly and conspicuously disclose—*

(a) *The nature and extent of the guarantee.*
This includes disclosure of—
  (1) What product or part of the product is guaranteed,
  (2) What characteristics or properties of the designated product or part thereof are covered by, or excluded from, the guarantee,
  (3) What is the duration of the guarantee,
  (4) What, if anything, any one claiming under the guarantee must do before the guarantor will fulfill his obligation under the guarantee, such as return of the product and payment of service or labor charges;

and

(b) *The manner in which the guarantor will perform.*
This consists primarily of a statement of exactly what the guarantor undertakes to do under the guarantee. Examples of this would be repair, replacement, refund. If the guarantor or the person receiving the guarantee has an option as to what may satisfy the guarantee this should be set out;

and

(c) *The identity of the guarantor.*
The identity of the guarantor should be clearly revealed in all advertising, as well as in any documents evidencing the guarantee. Confusion of purchasers often occurs when it is not clear whether the manufacturer or the retailer is the guarantor.

II–PRORATA ADJUSTMENT OF GUARANTEES.

Many guarantees are adjusted by the guarantor on a prorata basis. The advertising of these guarantees should clearly disclose this fact, the basis on which they will be prorated, e.g., the time for which the guaranteed product has been used, and the manner in which the guarantor will perform.

If these guarantees are to be adjusted on the basis of a price other than that paid by the purchaser, this price should be clearly and conspicuously disclosed.*

Example: "A" sells a tire with list price of $48 to "B" for $24, with a 12 months guarantee. After 6 months use the tire proves defective. If "A" adjusts on the basis of the price "B" paid, $24, "B" will only have to pay ½ of $24, or $12, for a new tire. If "A" instead adjusts on the basis of list price, "B" will owe ½ of $48, or $24, for a new tire. The guarantor would be required to disclose here the following: that this was a 12 months guarantee, that a list price of $48 would be used in the adjustment, that there would be an adjustment on the basis of the time that the tire was used, and that he would not pay the adjusted amount in cash, but would make an adjustment on a new tire.

(Note: Guarantees which provide for an adjustment based on a fictitious list price should not be used even where adequate disclosure of the price used is made.)

III—"SATISFACTION OR YOUR MONEY BACK" REPRESENTATIONS.

"Satisfaction or Your Money Back," "10 Day Free Trial," or similar representations will be construed as a guarantee that the full purchase price will be refunded at the option of the purchaser.

If this guarantee is subject to any conditions or limitations whatsoever, they shall be set forth as provided for in Guide I.

Example: A rose bush is advertised under the representation "Satisfaction or Your Money Back." The guarantor requires return of the product within one year of purchase date before he will make refund. These limitations, i.e., "return" and "time" shall be clearly and conspicuously disclosed in the ad.

IV—LIFETIME GUARANTEES.

If the words "Life," "Lifetime," or the like, are used in advertising to show the duration of a guarantee, and they relate to any life other than that of the purchaser or original user, the life referred to shall be clearly and conspicuously disclosed.

Example: "A" advertised that his carburetor was guaranteed for life, whereas his guarantee ran for the life of the car in which the carburetor was originally installed. The advertisement is ambiguous and deceptive and should be modified to disclose the "life" referred to.

V—SAVINGS GUARANTEES.*

Advertisements frequently contain representations of guarantees that assure prospective purchasers that savings may be realized in the purchase of the advertiser's products.

Some typical advertisements of this type are "Guaranteed to save you 50%," "Guaranteed never to be undersold," "Guaranteed lowest price in town."

These advertisements should include a clear and conspicuous disclosure of what the guarantor will do if the savings are not realized, together with any time or other limitations that he may impose.

Example: "Guaranteed lowest price in town" might be accompanied by the following disclosure:

"If within 30 days from the date that you buy a sewing machine from me, you purchase the identical machine in town for less and present a receipt therefor to me, I will refund your money."

(Note: The above guarantees may constitute affirmative representations of fact and, in this respect, are governed by Guide VII.)

VI—GUARANTEES UNDER WHICH THE GUARANTOR DOES NOT OR CANNOT PERFORM.

A seller or manufacturer should not advertise or represent that a product is guaranteed when he cannot or does not promptly and scrupulously fulfill his obligations under the guarantee.

A specific example of refusal to perform obligations under the guarantee is use of "Satisfaction or your money back" when the guarantor cannot or does not intend promptly to make full refund upon request.

VII—GUARANTEE AS A MISREPRESENTATION.

Guarantees are often employed in such a manner as to constitute representations of material facts. If such is the case, the guarantor not only undertakes to perform under the terms of the guarantee, but also assumes responsibility under the law for the truth of the representations made.

Example 1: "Guaranteed for 36 months" applied to a battery is a representation that the battery can normally be expected to last for 36 months and should not be used in connection with a battery which can normally be expected to last for only 18 months.

Example 2: "Guaranteed to grow hair or money back" is a representation that the product will grow hair and should not be used when in fact such product is incapable of growing hair.

Example 3: "Guaranteed lowest price in town" is a representation that the advertiser's prices are lower than the prices charged by all others for the same products in the same town and should not be used when such is not the fact.

Example 4: "We guarantee you will earn $500 a month" is a representation that prospective employees will earn a minimum of $500 each month and should not be used unless such is the fact.

Guides Against Deceptive Pricing

[Effective January 8, 1964]

*   *   *

GUIDE I—FORMER PRICE COMPARISONS.

One of the most commonly used forms of bargain advertising is to offer a reduction from the advertiser's own former price for an article. If the former price is the actual, *bona fide* price at which the article was offered to the public on a regular basis for a reasonably substantial period of time, it provides a legitimate basis for the advertising of a price comparison. Where the former price is genuine, the bargain being advertised is a true one. If, on the other hand, the former price being advertised is not *bona fide* but fictitious—for example, where an artificial, inflated price was established for the purpose of enabling the subsequent offer of a large reduction—the "bargain" being advertised is a false one; the purchaser is not receiving the unusual value he expects. In such a case, the "reduced" price is, in reality, probably just the seller's regular price.

A former price is not necessarily fictitious merely because no sales at the advertised price were made. The advertiser should be especially careful, however, in such a case, that the price is one at which the product was openly and actively offered for sale, for a reasonably substantial period of time, in the recent, regular course of his business, honestly and in good faith—and, of course, not for the purpose of establishing a fictitious higher price on which a deceptive comparison might be based. And the advertiser should scrupulously avoid any implication that a former price is a selling, not an asking price (for example, by use of such language as, "Formerly sold at $_____"), unless substantial sales at that price were actually made.

The following is an example of a price comparison based on a fictitious former price. John Doe is a retailer of Brand X fountain pens, which cost him $5 each. His usual markup is 50% over cost; that is, his regular retail price is $7.50. In order subsequently to offer an unusual "bargain," Doe begins offering Brand X at $10 per pen. He realizes that he will be able to sell no, or very few, pens at this inflated price. But he doesn't care, for he maintains that price for only a few days. Then he "cuts" the price to its usual level—$7.50—and advertises: "Terrific Bargain: X Pens, Were $10, Now Only $7.50!" This is obviously a false claim. The advertised "bargain" is not genuine.

Other illustrations of fictitious price comparisons could be given. An advertiser might use a price at which he never offered the article at all; he might feature a price which was not used in the regular course of business, or which was not used in the recent past but at some remote period in the past, without making disclosure of that fact; he might use a price that was not openly offered to the public, or that was not maintained for a reasonable length of time, but was immediately reduced.

If the former price is set forth in the advertisement, whether accompanied or not by descriptive terminology such as "Regularly," "Usually," "Formerly," etc., the advertiser should make certain that the former price is not a fictitious one. If the former price, or the amount or percentage of reduction, is not stated in the advertisement, as when the ad merely states, "Sale," the advertiser must take care that the amount of reduction is not so insignificant as to be meaningless. It should be sufficiently large that the consumer, if he knew what it was, would believe that a genuine bargain or saving was being offered. An advertiser who claims that an item has been "Reduced to $9.99," when the former price was $10.00, is misleading the consumer, who will understand the claim to mean that a much greater, and not merely nominal, reduction was being offered.

GUIDE II–RETAIL PRICE COMPARISONS; COMPARABLE VALUE COMPARISONS.

Another commonly used form of bargain advertising is to offer goods at prices lower than those being charged by others for the same merchandise in the advertiser's trade area (the area in which he does business). This may be done either on a temporary or a permanent basis, but in either case the advertised higher price must be based upon fact, and not be fictitious or misleading. Whenever an advertiser represents that he is selling below the prices being charged in his area for a particular article, he should be reasonably certain that the higher price he advertises does not appreciably exceed the price at which substantial sales of the article are being made in the area—that is, a sufficient number of sales so that a consumer would consider a reduction from the price to represent a genuine bargain or saving. Expressed another way, if a number of the principal retail outlets in the area are regularly selling Brand X fountain pens at $10, it is not dishonest for retailer Doe to advertise: "Brand X Pens, Price Elsewhere $10, Our Price $7.50."

The following example, however, illustrates a misleading use of this advertising technique. Retailer Doe advertises Brand X Pens as having a "Retail Value $15.00, My Price $7.50," when the fact is that only a few small suburban outlets in the area charge $15. All of the larger outlets located in and around the main shopping areas charge $7.50, or slightly more or less. The advertisement here would be deceptive, since the price charged by the small suburban outlets would have no real significance to Doe's customers, to whom the advertisement of "Retail Value $15.00" would suggest a prevailing, and not merely an isolated and unrepresentative, price in the area in which they shop.

A closely related form of bargain advertising is to offer a reduction from the prices being charged either by the advertiser or by others in the advertiser's trade area for other merchandise of like grade and quality—in other words, comparable or competing merchandise—to that being advertised. Such advertising can serve a useful and legitimate purpose when it is made clear to the consumer that a comparison is being made with other merchandise and the other merchandise is, in fact, of essentially similar quality and obtainable in the area. The advertiser should, however, be reasonably certain, just as in the case of comparisons involving the same merchandise, that the price advertised as being the price of comparable merchandise does not exceed the price at which such merchandise is being offered by representative retail outlets in the area. For example, retailer Doe advertises Brand X pen as having "Comparable Value $15.00." Unless a reasonable number of the principal outlets in the area are offering Brand Y, an essentially similar pen, for that price, this advertisement would be deceptive.

GUIDE III—ADVERTISING RETAIL PRICES WHICH
HAVE BEEN ESTABLISHED OR SUGGESTED
BY MANUFACTURERS (OR OTHER NON-
RETAIL DISTRIBUTORS).

Many members of the purchasing public believe that a manufacturer's list price, or suggested retail price, is the price at which an article is generally sold. Therefore, if a reduction from this price is advertised, many people will believe that they are being offered a genuine bargain. To the extent that list or suggested retail prices do not in fact correspond to prices at which a substantial number of sales of the article in question are made, the advertisement of a reduction may mislead the consumer.

There are many methods by which manufacturers' suggested retail or list prices are advertised: large scale (often nation-wide) mass-media advertising by the manufacturer himself; pre-ticketing by the manufacturer; direct mail advertising; distribution of promotional material or price lists designed for display to the public. The mechanics used are not of the essence. These Guides are concerned with *any* means employed for placing such prices before the consuming public.

There would be little problem of deception in this area if all products were invariably sold at the retail price set by the manufacturer. However, the widespread failure to observe manufacturers' suggested or list prices, and the advent of retail discounting on a wide scale, have seriously undermined the dependability of list prices as indicators of the exact prices at which articles are in fact generally sold at retail. Changing competitive conditions have created a more acute problem of deception than may have existed previously. Today, only in the rare case are *all* sales of an article at the manufacturer's suggested retail or list price.

But this does not mean that all list prices are fictitious and all offers of reductions from list, therefore, deceptive. Typically, a list price is a price at which articles are sold, if not everywhere, then at least in the principal retail outlets which do not conduct their business on a discount basis. It will not be deemed fictitious if it is the price at which substantial (that is, not isolated or insignificant) sales are made in the advertiser's trade area (the area in which he does business). Conversely, if the list price is significantly in excess of the highest price at which substantial sales in the trade area are made, there is a clear and serious danger of the consumer being misled by an advertised reduction from this price.

This general principle applies whether the advertiser is a national or regional manufacturer (or other non-retail distributor), a mail-order or catalog distributor who deals directly with the consuming public, or a local retailer. But certain differences in the responsibility of these various types of businessmen should be noted. A retailer competing in a local area has at least a general knowledge of the prices being charged in his area. Therefore, before advertising a manufacturer's list price as a basis for comparison with his own lower price, the retailer should ascertain whether the list price is in fact the price regularly charged by principal outlets in his area.

In other words, a retailer who advertises a manufacturer's or distributor's suggested retail price should be careful to avoid creating a false impression that he is offering a reduction from the price at which the product is generally sold in his trade area. If a number of the principal retail outlets in the area are regularly engaged in making sales at the manufacturer's suggested price, that price may be used in advertising by one who is selling at a lower price. If, however, the list price is being followed only by, for example, small suburban stores, house-to-house canvassers, and credit houses, accounting for only an insubstantial volume of sales in the area, advertising of the list price would be deceptive.

On the other hand, a manufacturer or other distributor who does business on a large regional or national scale cannot be required to police or investigate in detail the prevailing prices of his articles throughout so large a trade area. If he advertises or disseminates a list or pre-ticketed price in good faith (i.e., as an honest estimate of the actual retail price) which does not appreciably exceed the highest price at which substantial sales are made in his trade area, he will not be chargeable with having engaged in a deceptive practice. Consider the following example:

Manufacturer Roe, who makes Brand X pens and sells them throughout the United States, advertises his pen in a national magazine as having a "Suggested Retail Price $10," a price determined on the basis of a market survey. In a substantial number of representative communities, the principal retail outlets are selling the product at this price in the regular course of business and in substantial volume. Roe would not be considered to have advertised a fictitious "suggested retail price." If retailer Doe does business in one of these communities, he would not be guilty of a deceptive practice by advertising, "Brand X Pens, Manufacturer's Suggested Retail Price, $10.00, Our Price, $7.50."

It bears repeating that the manufacturer, distributor or retailer must in every case act honestly and in good faith in advertising a list price, and not with the intention of establishing a basis, or creating an instrumentality, for a deceptive comparison in any local or other trade area. For instance, a manufacturer may not affix price tickets containing inflated prices as an accommodation to particular retailers who intend to use such prices as the basis for advertising fictitious price reductions.

GUIDE IV—BARGAIN OFFERS BASED UPON THE PURCHASE OF OTHER MERCHANDISE.

Frequently, advertisers choose to offer bargains in the form of additional merchandise to be given a customer on the condition that he purchase a particular article at the price usually offered by the advertiser. The forms which such offers may take are numerous and varied, yet all have essentially the same purpose and effect. Representative of the language frequently employed in such offers are "Free," "Buy One—Get One Free," "2-For-1 Sale," "Half Price Sale," "1¢ Sale," "50% Off," etc. Literally, of course, the seller is not offering anything "free" (i.e., an unconditional gift), or ½ free, or for only 1¢, when he makes such an offer, since the purchaser is required to purchase an article in order to receive the "free" or "1¢"

item. It is important, therefore, that where such a form of offer is used, care be taken not to mislead the consumer.

Where the seller, in making such an offer, increases his regular price of the article required to be bought, or decreases the quantity and quality of that article, or otherwise attaches strings (other than the basic condition that the article be purchased in order for the purchaser to be entitled to the "free" or "1¢" additional merchandise) to the offer, the consumer may be deceived.

Accordingly, whenever a "free," "2-for-1," "half price sale," "1¢ sale," "50% off" or similar type of offer is made, all the terms and conditions of the offer should be made clear at the outset.

GUIDE V—MISCELLANEOUS PRICE COMPARISONS.

The practices covered in the provisions set forth above represent the most frequently employed forms of bargain advertising. However, there are many variations which appear from time to time and which are, in the main, controlled by the same general principles. For example, retailers should not advertise a retail price as a "wholesale" price. They should not represent that they are selling at "factory" prices when they are not selling at the prices paid by those purchasing directly from the manufacturer. They should not offer second or imperfect or irregular merchandise at a reduced price without disclosing that the higher comparative price refers to the price of the merchandise if perfect. They should not offer an advance sale under circumstances where they do not in good faith expect to increase the price at a later date, or make a "limited" offer which, in fact, is not limited. In all of these situations, as well as in others too numerous to mention, advertisers should make certain that the bargain offer is genuine and truthful. Doing so will serve their own interest as well as that of the public.

These Guides supersede the Guides Against Deceptive Pricing adopted October 2, 1958.

Appendix 2—Ten-Point Buying Guide for Consumers

The following is reprinted from *Your ABC's of Careful Buying: A Guide for the Consumer*, published by the New York State Department of Law:

1. DON'T be misled by the dealer who lures you to his establishment with an attractive advertisement of a standard brand item and then tries to talk you into a higher priced off-brand article. Be wary of the story that he is all out of the advertised item, or that there will be a long wait for delivery, or that what he now is trying to sell you is better than the advertised article.

2. DON'T be blinded by "bargains" offered at prices which are hard to believe. Check prices of the same quality merchandise or service offered by other dealers and make sure that the advertised article is what it is claimed to be. Such phrases as "reduced from," "made to sell for" and the like should act as a warning signal for you to check further.

3. DON'T be rushed into buying anything by talk of a "golden opportunity" or persuasion that it is a "last chance" to get in on a "good thing." Take your time, investigate, and make up your mind carefully.

4. DON'T allow a door-to-door salesman to leave merchandise with you on an "approval receipt," until he returns. He may not come back and you will find yourself receiving a bill for an article which you do not want. Always ask for the salesman's credentials.

5. DON'T permit a household appliance or television or radio set to be taken from your home for repairs without first receiving in writing an estimate of the probable repair cost. Obtain written assurance that no additional charges will be made without your consent, and that if you do not want the "extra" repairs the article will be returned to you immediately.

6. DON'T use the article delivered to you if you find that it is not the same as you ordered, but immediately notify the seller. If a finance company is involved, and your complaint is not satisfied, inform the finance company in writing of your complaint within 10 days after you receive the notice the finance company is required by law to give you. This is important because if you fail to do so, you may lose valuable rights and find yourself obliged to pay for something you do not want.

7. DON'T accept an oral guarantee. Get it in writing. Make sure you understand what it says and that it protects you fully. Be sure that installations of appliances and such furnishings as carpeting are guaranteed by a dealer, because a manufacturer can claim that a product's warranty has been voided if it has not been installed properly.

8. DON'T sign a contract without reading it carefully ... especially the fine print. Insist that all details of the sale be in writing. NEVER SIGN A BLANK CONTRACT OR A CONTRACT WITH BLANK SPACES IN IT. Demand and get a copy of the contract. Check with a lawyer if you don't understand it. Never sign a statement which states that work is finished until it actually is.

9. DON'T make financial commitments which you cannot possibly meet. When buying on the installment plan, remember that if you fall behind in your payments, the seller usually has a legal right to repossess the merchandise and sell it for whatever it will bring to meet part or all of your remaining indebtedness.

10. DON'T hesitate to investigate before buying. If you have any doubt about a dealer, check with the Attorney General's Office, Better Business Bureau in your area, your local Chamber of Commerce, or some other community organization which works to protect the consumer and the legitimate business man.

Appendix 3—Text of FTC brochure, *Fight Back!—The Ungentle Art of Self Defense as recommended by the Federal Trade Commission*

HOW CAN YOU AVOID BEING GYPPED?

And, if you have been, what can you do about it?

Here are some answers to both questions. The advice is based on the experience of attorneys for the Federal Trade Commission who have been tracking down business cheats for more than 50 years. Assisted by the vast majority of merchants who are honest, the FTC's gyp hunters have become experts on how fly-by-night and overly eager sellers bilk consumers.

The bait is presented in countless disguises, but always its purpose is the same: to trick you, the buyer, into thinking you are getting much more for your money than you had dared to hope—a bargain too "amazing" to be offered by reputable stores. Thus, you end up paying too much for what you get or not getting what you pay for. And your companion in sorrow is the honest merchant who has had your business siphoned away from him by the cheat.

The first line of defense against the gyp artists should be manned by you, the consumer. No governmental policing is as effective as the chin-pinching purchaser who is willing to shop for what he wants and who is intelligent enough to judge what quantity and what quality he should receive for the price he pays. Just plain old coldblooded shopping makes it tough on the gypsters. And reputable businesses welcome the buyer who gives honest merchandising the favorable consideration it deserves.

The second line of defense is manned by consumers with enough courage to make themselves heard after they have been gypped in their purchases, or even when they have succeeded in avoiding a trap set for the less sophisticated. Certainly it is not enough to silently "chalk up to experience" a purchase about which you were misled, or simply to congratulate yourself on not having been duped the way others might be. In these United States you can make your indignation heard, and gyp artists do not thrive on such attention. It might surprise you to find out how much good can be accomplished by a citizen with a legitimate complaint who will take the trouble to invite attention to it.

A good starting point is to protest directly to the seller (if you can find him!). Possibly the misrepresentation was done without his knowledge, in which case, he can take steps to assure against its repetition. There is even a chance he might square himself with you.

If, however, the fast-buck operator shrugs you off, you can carry your indignation further by registering your complaint with the organizations in your community devoted to maintaining proper conduct for business. A good example is the Better Business Bureau. And certainly your cause would be served if your complaint, backed by hard facts, went to the newspaper or radio or TV station that carries advertising for the product. It wouldn't take many such letters to deprive the huckster of his innocent readers and listeners. Truth in advertising is too important to these media to risk gaining a reputation for carrying phony ads.

A third line of defense is your local government. This is particularly important because most of the things you buy are marketed only locally, and the seller is not engaged in interstate commerce. The result is that you have to depend not on the federal government but on your city or state for protection. Nearly all of the states have statutes aimed at misrepresentation of products and services. And in some states these laws are enforced with vigor.

Certainly it behooves you to find out what kind of state (or city) protection is available to you. And if none is, you might want to help improve the situation.

Your fourth line of defense is the Federal Trade Commission. Congress gave it the broad responsibility to halt "unfair methods of competition in commerce and unfair or deceptive acts or practices in commerce." Thus, not only were all the known deceptive practices outlawed but any new ones that might be invented. Other responsibilities of the FTC include policing the labeling of furs, woolens and other textile products, and guarding against the sale of dangerously flammable wearing apparel.

With this much authority for the FTC, you might wonder why the federal government could not handle the entire job of protecting consumers from being cheated. There are good reasons why it cannot, the principal one being that Congress never intended to establish the huge Gestapo that would be needed to police every store and salesman in the country. Not only would the cost be prohibitive but businessmen have demonstrated that, with very few exceptions, they are quite capable of policing themselves. Indeed, the FTC provides valuable guidance to them in this self-policing effort.

The FTC's fight against consumer deception is directed at gyp schemes that have an actual or potential impact on the public, as distinguished from actions to settle private controversies. In short, it has neither the staff nor the money to tackle cases that do not have sufficient *public* interest. Also, the FTC has concentrated its force on halting law violators who do at least some of their selling across state lines.

Thus, while the FTC can not undertake to settle your private or purely local difficulties, it does stand ready to halt important instances of deception—and at no cost to the one who brings the complaint. The reason for this is that the FTC never brings an action on behalf of an individual; instead, it must itself investigate the matter and then act only if there appears to be sufficient public interest in stopping it. Nevertheless, alert consumers perform a valuable service to FTC by inviting its attention to deceptive practices that should be investigated.

The way to do this is simple: just write a letter to the Federal Trade Commission, Washington 25, D.C. The letter should give as many facts as you have available, including any evidence of the chicanery, such as a copy of misleading advertising used to sell the product or the service. (Too many applications for complaint are long on indignation and short on facts that would help the FTC to determine whether the matter warranted investigation.) In writing this letter you have FTC's assurance that your identity will be completely protected. If the deception has sufficient public interest and the FTC is the appropriate authority to tackle the job, your obligation is ended. The FTC will take over the matter from that point on. You will, of course, be advised of what disposition is made of your application for FTC action.

What kinds of action might the FTC take? Depending on the gravity of the law violation, it could be settled by the violator giving FTC assurance and evidence that the improper act would be immediately discontinued. (And this would be no empty assurance because the violator would be in no doubt that a second offense would bring quick formal action.) The FTC, however, might well decide the violation was too serious to be settled by such an assurance of discontinuance, in which case it would issue a formal complaint looking to the issuance of a cease-and-desist order forever prohibiting the respondent from engaging in the illegal act. Should the order be violated thereafter, the FTC would bring action in court seeking a fine of up to $5,000 per day for each violation of the order.

Thus, the FTC provides you, the consumer, with a final defense against many instances of deception in the marketplace. But it is important to remember that you can do a great deal for yourself by following this advice:

1. Shop more before you buy.
2. Bring your complaint first to the seller.
3. Report false advertising to the media carrying it.
4. Report deception to local organizations concerned with better business standards.
5. Write the facts to the Federal Trade Commission.

Index

Index

232